MODERN HUMANITIES RESEARCH ASSOCIATION

CRITICAL TEXTS

VOLUME 25

Editor
Catherine Maxwell
(English)

CASIMIR BRITANNICUS

CASIMIR BRITANNICUS

ENGLISH TRANSLATIONS, PARAPHRASES, AND EMULATIONS OF THE POETRY OF MACIEJ KAZIMIERZ SARBIEWSKI

Revised and Expanded Edition

Edited by

Krzysztof Fordoński

Piotr Urbański

MODERN HUMANITIES RESEARCH ASSOCIATION
2010

Published by

The Modern Humanities Research Association,
1 Carlton House Terrace
London SW1Y 5AF

© The Modern Humanities Research Association, 2010

Krzysztof Fordoński and Piotr Urbański have asserted their right under the Copyright, Designs and Patents Act 1988 to be identified as the authors of this work.

Parts of this work may be reproduced as permitted under legal provisions for fair dealing (or fair use) for the purposes of research, private study, criticism, or review, or when a relevant collective licensing agreement is in place. All other reproduction requires the written permission of the copyright holder who may be contacted at rights@mhra.org.uk.

The completion of this work was made possible thanks to a financial grant awarded by the Ministry of Science and Higher Education of the Republic of Poland.

First published 2010

ISBN 978-1-907322-12-9

ISSN 1746-1642

Copies may be ordered from www.criticaltexts.mhra.org.uk

Table of Contents

Introduction	17
Maciej Kazimierz Sarbiewski	17
Sarbiewski in England	20
On Editing Casimir	27
Acknowledgments	30
List of Abbreviations	31
Poems	33
Translation of a Latin Epigram on Casimire by George Jeffreys	33
1. George Hils (publ. 1646)	35
To the Censuring Reader	35
When the hateful forces of the Thracians departed out of Pannonia. Ode 1. Lib. 1.	36
To Aurelius Lycas. That he would not complain too much of adverse fortune. Ode 2. Lib. 1.	38
To Tarquinius Lavinus. Ode 13. Lib. 1.	39
To Publius Memmius. That the shortness of man's life is to be lengthened by good deeds. Ode 2. Lib. 2.	39
A Departure from things human. Ode 5. Lib. 2.	40
To Publius Memmius. Ode 7. Lib. 2.	42
To Asterius. Ode 8. Lib. 2.	43
Out of Solomon's Sacred Marriage Song. Ode 19. Lib. 2.	44
Dirae in Herodem. Ode 24. Lib. 2.	44
Out of Solomon's Sacred Marriage Song. Cant. 2. *Stay me with flagons etc.* [...] Ode 25. Lib. 2.	47
To Egnatius Nollius. That we ought to be of an even and upright mind against the inconstancy of fortune. Ode 4. Lib. 3.	48

To Marcus Silicernius. That those are the true riches which are fetch'd from the goods of the mind. Ode 6. Lib. 3.	49
To Aurelius Fuscus. That all human things are frail and uncertain. Ode 12. Lib. 3.	49
To Caesar Pausilipius. The kingdom of a wise man. Ode 3. Lib. 4.	50
To Q. Dellius. That our life ought not to be instituted so much by popular example, as by the guiding of reason. Ode 10. Lib. 4.	52
To Sigismundus Laetus. He commends the despising of vain-glory, and silence. Ode 11. Lib. 4.	53
To Ianus Libinius. He excuses his retiredness. Ode 12. Lib. 4.	54
To Caesar Pausilippius. That adversity is to be endured with a constant mind. Ode 13. Lib. 4.	55
To Crispus Laevinius. Being asked why he sung so often as he travelled, he answers. Ode 14. Lib. 4.	55
To Munatius. That nothing in human affairs is not full of tediousness. Ode 15. Lib. 4.	56
Out of Solomon's Sacred Marriage Song. Chap. 1.7. *Tell me, o thou whom my soul loveth [...] etc.* Ode 19. Lib. 4.	57
Out of Salomon's sacred marriage song. *My beloved spake [...] etc.* Ode 21. Lib. 4.	58
To Ianusius Skuminus. When he performed the Funeral obsequies of his most dear Wife. Ode 30. Lib. 4.	59
To Albertus Turscius. Of his Dreams, and Lyricks. Ode 32. Lib. 4.	61
To Quintus Tiberinus. Ode 34. Lib. 4.	62
To Paulus Coslovius. Ode 35. Lib. 4.	63
To Paulus Iordanus Ursinus, Duke of Bracciano. He commends the pleasantness of the Country, where, in the feasts of September, he retired from Rome. Ode 1. Lib. Epod.	65
To the Fountain Sona, When he returned. Ode 2. Lib. Epod.	69

A Palinode. To the second Ode of the book of Epodes of Q. H. Flaccus. The praise of a Religious Recreation. Ode 3. Lib. Epod.	69
Epig. 4. *Let my beloved come into his Garden*. Cant. 5.	72
Who is thy Beloved? Out of Cant. 5. Lib. Epig. 37.	73
Epig. 40	73
Epig. 48. To— bearing Lilies in her hand.	73
Ex Lib. Epigr. 51. To Iohan de Lugo, when after a long sickness, he returned to his intermitted Lecture of Repentance.	73
The voice of Christ upon the Cross: I Thirst.	74
2. Sir Philip Wodehouse (1608–1681)	**75**
[Epig. 54]	75
[Epig. 34]	76
[Epig. 33]	76
Epig. 8. Canz. Through Towns and Streets M. Magdalen.	76
Epig. 14	76
Epig. 10	77
Epig. 15	77
Epig. 5	78
Epig. 6	78
Epig. 11	78
Epig. 74. To Caecilian.	79
Epig. 16	79
Epig. 64	79
3. Sir John Denham (1615–1669)	**81**
An Elegie Upon the Death of Lord Hastings.	82
4. Richard Lovelace (1618–1657)	**83**
To his Dear Brother Colonel F. L. immoderately mourning my Brother's untimely Death at Carmarthen.	83

5. Abraham Cowley (1618–1667)	85
The Extasie.	86
6. Edward Sherburne (1618–1702)	89
On Captain Ansa, a bragging Run-away. *Casimire*.	89
Amphion, or a City well ordered. *Casimer*.	90
To the Eternal Wisdom: Upon the Distraction of the Times.	91
Draw Me, and I will follow Thee.	92
If a Man should give all the substance of his House for Love, he would value it as nothing. Cant. 8.	92
Mary Magdalen weeping under the Cross.	92
The Message.	93
7. Lucy Hutchinson (1620–1681)	**94**
Casimiri Epig. Lib. Unus. Ep. XXXIV. Love is strong as Death. Can. 8.6.	94
8. Henry Vaughan (1621–1695)	95
Casimirus, Lib. 4. Ode 28.	96
Casimirus, Lib. 2. Ode 8.	96
Casimirus, Lib. 3. Ode 22.	97
Casimirus Lyric. Lib. 3. Ode 23.	97
Casimirus, Lib. 4. Ode 15.	98
Casimirus, Lib. 4. Ode 13.	99
The Praise of a Religious Life by Mathias Casimirus. In Answer to that Ode of Horace, *Beatus Ille qui procul negotiis*, etc.	100
9. John Hall of Durham (1627–1656)	104
To the Earl of Huntingdon, On the death of his Son.	104
10. Lady Mary Chudleigh (1656–1710)	105
The Elevation.	106
The Happy Man.	106
The Song of the Three Children. Paraphras'd Casimir II 5.	107

Table of Contents

11. John Norris (1657–1711)	**109**
The Elevation.	109
12. Thomas Brown (1662–1704)	**112**
Casimire, Ode 23. Book 4. To the Grasshopper.	112
13. John Chatwin (c. 1667 – after 1685)	**114**
Ad Rosam. The eighteenth Ode of the Last Book of the Lyricks of Casimirus. On the Virgin Mary's Annual Coronation.	114
In Imitation of the 23rd Ode of the 4th Book of Casimirus. Ad Cicadam.	115
14. "Oxford Hands" (1685)	**116**
Ode the 18th Book the 4th of Casimire Pariphrastically Translated. The Rose with which he vow'd to Crown the Virgin Mary with every June.	116
Out of Casimire. To Quintus Tiberinus. Ode the 34th Book the 4th.	117
Casimire Ode the 25th Book the fourth. A Dialogue between the Child Jesus and the Virgin-Mother, taken partly out of the First, Fourth, Fifth, Sixth and Seventh Chapters of the Canticles.	118
Ode the 15th of the First Book of Casimire imitated, encouraging the Polish Knights after their last Conquest to proceed in their Victory.	121
15. Isaac Watts (1674–1748)	**125**
The Preface to *Horae Lyricae*	126
Seeking a Divine Calm in a Restless World. Casimire, Book IV. Ode 28.	126
Breathing Towards the Heavenly Country. Casimire. Book I. Ode 19. Imitated.	127
On Saint Ardalio, who from a Stage-Player became a Christian, and suffered Martyrdom.	128
Strict Religion Very Rare.	128
To William Blackbourn, Esq. Casimir. Lib. II. Ode 2. Imitated.	130

To Mrs. B. Bendish. Against Tears.	131
The celebrated Victory of the Poles, over Osman the Turkish Emperor, in the Dacian battle. Translated from Casimire. Book IV. Ode 4 with large Additions.	132
To the Discontented and Unquiet. Imitated partly from Casimire, Book IV. Ode 15.	138
To John Hartopp, Esq; now Sir John Hartopp, Bart. Casimire, Book I. Ode 4. Imitated. July 1700.	140
To Thomas Gunston, Esq. Happy Solitude. Casimire, Book IV. Ode 12. Imitated.	142
Salvation in the Cross. Hymn Book II, 4.	144
Imitation of an Ode of Casimir.	145
The Hebrew Poet.	145
16. Thomas Yalden (1670–1736)	**151**
Against Immoderate Grief: An Ode in Imitation of Casimire. To a Young Lady Weeping.	151
17. Samuel Say (1676–1743)	**153**
To his Harp: In Imitation of the Ode of Casimire.	153
Occasion'd by the Tenth Ode of the Second Book of Casimire.	154
An Emblem of the Shortness of Human Pleasure. To the Grasshopper.	155
18. John Hughes (1678–1720)	**157**
Advertisement	158
The Ecstasy. An Ode.	158
An Image of Pleasure. In Imitation of an Ode in Casimire.	164
19. Samuel Philips (b. 1684)	**165**
Casimire, Ode 13 Book 4. Against Immoderate Grief Paraphrastically Translated.	165
20. Aaron Hill (1685–1750)	**167**
The Transport.	167

21. William Duncombe (1690–1769)	169
Casimire, Book II. Ode 2. Imitated.	169
22. Anonymous Translations from Various Magazines (1738–1822)	171
The Ascension. Imitated from Casim. Ode 6th of his second Book.	171
An Ode of Casimire, Ad Cicadam.	175
Casimire, Ode 26. Ad Auram.	175
Ode to the Air. Imitated from Mat. Casimir.	176
Casimir, Epigram XIII. *Lampades eius lampades ignis* Cant. VIII. 6.	177
Casimir, Lib. II. Ode VII. To Publius Memmius.	178
Ode from Casimir.	179
Casimir, Lib. I. Ode XIII. To Tarquinius Lavinus.	180
Casimir, Book IV. Ode XXIII. To The Cicada.	180
To Aurelius Lycus. Against immoderate Complaint in Adversity.	181
Casimir, Book III. Ode 22. To Caesar Pausilipius.	182
Casimir, Book II. Ode 26. To The Virgin Mother, when Poland was afflicted with War, Famine, and unseasonable Weather.	183
To Philidius Marabotinus. Translated from Casimir. Lib. IV. Ode 31.	184
Casimir, Epigram XIV. *Draw me, we will run after thee.* Cant. I 4.	185
Casimir's Address to the Dormant Rose. (From the Latin.)	186
Ad Memmium. Ode 7, Lib. II.	186
Ad Pausilippium. Ode 22 Lib. III.	187
Casimir, Lib. I. Ode 1. On the Departure of the hostile Thracians from Pannonia.	188
Ode of Casimir. To His Lyre.	190

23. Joshua Dinsdale († c. 1750)	191
An Imitation of the Second Ode of the First Book of Casimire.	191
The Remedy. In Imitation of Casimire.	192
The Ecstasy.	193
24. Mary Masters (c. 1694–1771)	196
On a Fountain. Casimir, Lib. Epod. Ode 2.	196
Casimir, Lib. I. Ode 2.	197
25. Henry Price (c. 1702 – after 1741)	200
To William Okeden Esq. Imitated from Casimir.	200
The First Ode of The First Book of Casimir. Written to Pope Urban VIIIth when the Thracian Forces Departed out of Pannonia. Inscribed to William Milner Esq. by Mr Price.	201
26. James Hervey (1714–1758)	204
Ode from Casimire.	204
27. Anne Steele alias Theodosia (1717–1778)	205
The Elevation.	205
28. Thomas Gibbons (1720–1785)	209
To Mr Roffey. Commencing a Poet. A Pindarick Ode Imitated from Casimire Book II. Ode XV.	210
Vicissitude, or the Mutability of Human Things. Casimir, B. I. Ode 2. To a Friend.	212
The Nocturnal Elevation. Casimire, B. I. Ode 19. Imitated.	214
The Ecstasy; or an Adieu to Earth and an Ascent to Heaven. Casimir, B. II Ode 5.	215
Fortitude. Casimir. B. 3. Ode 4. Imitated and Enlarged. To a Friend.	218
To a Young Gentleman. Partly imitated from Casimir. B. 3. Ode 22.	220
29. William Mason (1725–1797)	222
Ode of Casimire Translated.	223

30. John Glasse (c. 1730 – after 1765) — 225
Epigram XVI of Casimire. — 225

31. *Μέλη Εφημέρια* (publ. 1783) — 226
Taken for the Most Part from Casimire's Ode In Auram. — 226
From Casimir's Ode In Rosam. — 227

32. Talbot Keene (c. 1737-1824) — 228
The Ode of Casimire, To the Grass-Hopper. Translated. — 228

33. John Pinkerton alias Robert Heron (1758-1826) — 229
To his Harp. — 229

34. Robert Burns (1759-1796) — 231
I dream'd I lay. — 232

35. William Margetson Heald (1767-1837) — 233
Casimir, Book II Ode 3. — 233
To the Grasshopper. B. 4. O. 23. — 234
To the Rose. B. 4. O. 18. — 234
To Publius Memmius. B. 2. O. 2. — 235

36. Joseph Hucks (1772-1800) — 237
To a Stream. — 237

37. Samuel Taylor Coleridge (1772-1834) — 238
Ad Lyram. — 239
Lines: To a Friend in Answer to a Melancholy Letter. — 239

38. William Herbert (1778-1847) — 241
From Casimir Sarbievius. Book 2. Ode 2. — 242

39. John Bowring (1792-1872) — 243
Sapphics. To a Rose. Intended to be used in the garlands for decorating the head of the Virgin Mary. Lib. IV ode 18. — 244
Sapphics. To the Polish and Lithuanian knights. Lib. IV ode 36. — 244
Sapphics. To Publius. Lib. 2 ode 2. — 246
Choriambics. To the Cicada. Lib. IV ode 23. — 247

Alcaic. To his lyre. Lib. II ode 3.	247
To Liberty. Free translation. Lib. IV ode 38.	248
40. Jesse Kitchener († 1829)	**252**
Book 1 Ode 2. To Aurelius Lycus. Admonishing him not to complain of Adversity.	252
Book 1 Ode 6. To the Sovereigns of Europe, on the Recovery of the Eastern Empire.	253
Book 1 Ode 7. To Telephus Lycus. On the instability of human Affairs.	256
Book 1 Ode 8. An invective against Slothfulness and Effeminacy of the Age.	258
Book 1 Ode 13. To Tarquinius Lavinius.	260
Book 1 Ode 17. On Royal Lenity.	261
Book 2 Ode 3. To his Harp.	263
41. Caroline de Crespigny (1795–1864)	**264**
To My Lyre. From the Latin of Casimir Sobieski.	264
To a Rose. From the Latin of Casimir Sobieski.	265
42. John Docwra Parry (c. 1800 – c. 1845)	**266**
Silviludium III. Supposed to be spoken during a hunting expedition of Vladislaus King of Poland	266
43. Richard Coxe (1800–1865)	**268**
Wood-Notes; the Silviludia Poetica	268
Preface [fragments]	268
Silviludium I. When Ladislaus IV King of Poland, came to hunt in the woods at Bersti	269
Silviludium II. To the Dew. Dance of shepherds when Ladislaus went out in the morning to hunt at Soleczniki	270
Silviludium III. Dialogue between a Poet and Courtier sitting together in the shade, while Ladislaus is hunting at Kotra	271

Silviludium IV. To the Breeze – that it would assuage the toil and heat for Ladislaus while hunting in the Merecian plains of noontide 272

Silviludium V. Song. The poet wanders through the meads and woods, while the court employs its leisure in hunting, or the sweetnes of celestial love 274

Silviludium VI. To the Moon, when Ladislaus was hunting on a Monday 276

Silviludium VII. To the Shadows, that, while Ladislaus was hunting at Merecina, they would protect the sportsmen from the heat 278

Silviludium VIII. To the lake Motela. Dance and songs of Fishermen 279

Silviludium IX. Dance and Song of Harvestmen, when Ladislaus was hunting shortly before his marriage 282

Silviludium X. Song of the Zephyr. To Ladislaus arriving at Leypuni at Eventide 283

44. Francis Sylvester Mahony (1804–1866) as Father Prout 285

Odarum Lib. 3 Ode XV. To the Bees (armorial bearings of the Barberini family), on Urban the Eight's elevation to the Pontificate. 286

Ode IV Book 4. Ode on the signal Defeat of the Sultan Osman, by the Army of Poland and her Allies. September 1621. 287

45. John Sheehan (1809–1882) 293

Floral Gems 293

To the Violet, With which the Poet is about to crown the Head of the Infant Saviour, On the Feast of Corpus Christi. 293

To The Rose, With which the Poet is about to crown the Head of the Madonna, On Lady Day in Spring. 294

46. William Crosse (publ. c. 1850) 296

Ode VII. Book I. 296

Ode XV. Book I. When Ladislaus, king of Poland, led his army into winter-quarters, after defeating Osman, the Turkish emperor. 298

Ode I. Book I. When the hostile forces of the Thracians had quitted the country. 300

Ode XIX. Book I. He aspires to the celestial abodes. 302

Ode III. Book II. To His Lyre. 304

Bibliography 305

Index of Original Poems by Maciej Kazimierz Sarbiewski 313

Introduction

Maciej Kazimierz Sarbiewski

The name of Maciej Kazimierz Sarbiewski, in Latin Matthias Casimir Sarbievius, once so famous that the poet was recognisable throughout Europe by his middle name alone (i.e. Casimir or Casimire), means very little to contemporary readers either in Poland or abroad. Even university students of Polish literature may not be familiar with it unless they show an extraordinary interest in Baroque poetry and poetics. And yet among Polish writers Sarbiewski was one of the first to enjoy a truly international fame which did last for over two centuries. His popularity abroad cannot be compared to that of any other Polish author before the twentieth century. He was justly considered one of the greatest Latin poets of his time.

This single adjective 'Latin' explains his disappearance from contemporary histories of Polish literature. Sarbiewski wrote no poems in Polish that we know of, only a single sermon has survived from his Polish works, and it is doubtful that he wrote any poetry in his native language at all. He belonged to the European movement which started at the beginning of the Renaissance – Neo-Latin poetry. Humanists all over the continent attempted to revive the language of the ancient Romans, not only as a means of scholarly and scientific communication, but also as the language of literary creation. In the sixteenth and the seventeenth as well as the early eighteenth century Latin was a medium of expression used not only for such works as More's *Utopia* or Copernicus' *De revolutionibus,* but also for the composition of original works of poetry and drama.

Although it did not take long for literatures in national languages to develop, Neo-Latin literature remained quite lively until the beginning of the eighteenth century when French became the language of the educated European elites.

Poland alone could boast a number of internationally recognized Neo-Latin poets such as Klemens Janicki (Clementius Ianicius), Szymon Szymonowic (Simon Simonides), and Jan Kochanowski (Ioannes Cochanovius). Sarbiewski, however, was by far the most famous.

This outstanding Neo-Latin poet and theorist of literature was born in 1595 in Sarbiewo, a village in the central Mazowsze province. The Jesuits from the college in nearby Pułtusk, where he was sent as a twelve year old boy, soon recognised his extraordinary talents; at the age of seventeen he became a novice. He was sent first to continue his education in Vilnius and later to Braniewo in Pomerania where he studied philosophy at the Collegium Hosianum. When he completed his course of studies, Sarbiewski taught poetics and rhetoric at Jesuit colleges, starting in Kroża (now Krażiai in Lithuania), in Samogitia, then going on to Polotsk (now in Belarus). This was also the period of his first literary attempts; his debut, a Latin laudatory poem dedicated to Jan Karol Chodkiewicz, was published in 1619. In 1620 he began further studies in philosophy at the Vilnius Academy which he continued at the Collegium Germanicum in Rome from 1622 to 1624.

The time spent in Rome was extremely important for Sarbiewski's literary career. Although his fellow Jesuits had recognized his literary talents, they found him most useful as a teacher, not a poet. Their order's main task at the time was to combat the Reformation and their tool in the fight was education. Away from his teaching duties Sarbiewski had an opportunity not only to study and write, but also to get to know personally scientists, scholars, and men of letters who gathered at the court of Pope Urban VIII. Many such contacts survived long after his return to Poland. It was also in Rome that he met the Polish Crown Prince Vladislas Vasa. Sarbiewski's talents were recognized by the literary Pope Urban VIII himself who awarded the young Polish poet a poetic laurel and gold medal in 1625. In the same year a large collection of his poems was published in Cologne, Germany.

The awards came in the last months of Sarbiewski's stay in Rome. It is not known why he was forced to return to

Poland. Some sources claim that he had enemies at the papal court who hastened his departure. It is much more probable, however, that the Jesuits needed him back in Poland to continue his educational work. Sarbiewski returned from Rome in 1625 and he was almost immediately sent again to teach in Polotsk where he worked for three more years. In 1628 he was transferred to the Vilnius Academy where he lectured in rhetoric, philosophy, and theology. In this academy, he acquired his doctor's degrees in philosophy in 1632 and theology in 1636.

It was during his stay in Vilnius that an enlarged collection of lyrics composed in Rome was published, first locally, under his supervision (1628), and then in Antwerp (1630) and Leiden (1631). In 1632 a new edition of *Lyricorum libri IV* was published once again in Antwerp, this time with the title-page designed by Peter Paul Rubens. The volume soon sold out and was reissued in 1634 in an impressive print-run of five thousand copies. Sarbiewski lived in Vilnius until 1635; in 1633 he was made the Dean of the Philosophy and Theology Department at the Jesuit Academy there.

He was ordained a priest in 1623, and took his last holy orders in 1629 in Vilnius. In 1635, the former Crown Prince Vladislas, now King Vladislas IV Vasa, who apparently had not forgotten their meeting in Rome, summoned Sarbiewski to Warsaw to appoint him court preacher, the post once held by a fellow Jesuit Piotr Skarga (1536–1612). The new job turned out even more arduous than teaching duties, not only because it required preaching daily. As the king was a keen huntsman, Sarbiewski was forced to spend weeks on end with him on hunting expeditions. In March 1640 Sarbiewski resigned from his post. He died suddenly in April 1640 in Warsaw.

Author of over 130 odes (collected in four books like the odes of Horace) and 145 epigrams, Sarbiewski also wrote an epic poem *Lechias*, an imitation of *Jerusalem Delivered* by Torquato Tasso. It was never published and only a fragment of the eleventh book has survived. For over a century he was credited with writing *Silviludia*, a court masque for the King, but the text was ultimately discovered to be merely a free adaptation of a Neo-Latin work of Mario Bettini.

The odes of Sarbiewski, characterised by erudition and a deep understanding of poetry, especially ancient poetry, bear the mark and influence of Horace. Many are paraphrases or parodies, as they were called then, of Horace's poems. Some of his contemporaries claimed that Sarbiewski not only equalled but surpassed Horace in his poetry and he was known in his lifetime as the Christian or Sarmatian Horace, as the famous Dutch humanist Hugo Grotius called him in 1625. In his epigrams Sarbiewski follows Martial in his art of conciseness, concepts, and punch-lines.

Sarbiewski was also the author of several works in literary theory, such as *Praecepta poetica* and *De perfecta poesi sive Vergilius et Homerus*, none of which, however, was published before the middle of the twentieth century. A treatise which deals with basic concepts of Baroque poetics was entitled *De acuto et arguto [...] sive Seneca et Martialis*. Originally written in Polotsk, it was first presented in Rome in 1623 as a lecture and later corrected by the author. Another treatise, *De perfecta poesi sive Vergilius et Homerus*, addresses the issues of the epic. Sarbiewski also left an unpublished mythographical treatise *Dii gentium*.

Sarbiewski in England

It may seem strange when we bear in mind the popularity that Sarbiewski enjoyed throughout Europe (we know of at least sixty Latin editions of his lyrics, of which fifteen were prepared in Poland) that the number of available translations into modern languages is far from impressive. In his native Poland Sarbiewski was only occasionally translated by such of his contemporaries as Jan Andrzej Morsztyn or Samuel Twardowski. His fellow Jesuit Franciszek Bohomolec edited in 1767 a small collection of existing Polish translations by over ten different poets. The first complete edition of Sarbiewski's lyrics in rather inaccurate Polish renderings by Władysław Syrokomla appeared in 1852. A more critically acclaimed edition prepared by Tadeusz Karyłowski in the late 1920s was published as late as 1980. A selection of the most recent Polish translations by Elwira Buszewicz appeared in 2003, a more complete edition is still in progress. Many poems were also translated into numerous European languages such as Italian, Flemish, Lithuanian, French, Czech, and German.

The mystery is not difficult to solve. As long as his fame lasted, Sarbiewski was popular among the educated elite who knew Latin and did not need translations to access his works. Furthermore, the conciseness of his poetry makes it rather difficult to render both its form and content in translation. The gradual disappearance of Latin as the common European language coincided with a change of literary tastes as new generations of readers were not interested in Baroque poetry or Neo-Stoicism any more. What made Sarbiewski a poet known and recognized by the European cultural community of the seventeenth and eighteenth century – the choice of Latin, the universal language – brought him lack of recognition in later times.

The country where Sarbiewski enjoyed the greatest popularity outside his native Poland, as measured by the number of known translations, was, rather surprisingly, England. Sarbiewski, a Jesuit priest, might have seemed there a much more appropriate candidate for an arch-enemy than for a revered master of poetics. Nevertheless, he enjoyed a long-lasting popularity there for three reasons. The first was his fascination with Horace's poetry which was quickly taken over from him by the English poets of the early seventeenth century, replacing an earlier interest in poetry fashioned after Pindar. The second was that his poetry became widely known through being introduced into the grammar school curriculum, where it was read and translated. Last but not least, Sarbiewski's poetry was for the English a means of getting acquainted with contemporary intellectual fashions of the Continent. It was attractive because it was saturated with influences from a variety of different circles of cultural traditions (Stoicism, Ignatian spirituality, Platonism, Hermeticism, etc.). Some of these traditions could have been used to contest the official culture as happened, for example, in the case of the Dissenters and Nonconformists.

Quite obviously, these influences could at least to some degree be accepted without the existence of translations. Although the Church of England was separated from Rome during the reign of King Henry VIII and no longer used Latin as its language of liturgy, fascination with antiquity and interest in the Latin language and literature did not entirely disappear in Great Britain. Quite the contrary, Latin remained an important part of school curricula until the second half of the nineteenth century. There seemed, consequently, little actual necessity for preparing and publishing translations. There was, however, a longstanding tradition of using translation of Latin poetry as a means of teaching the language. Some of the surviving English translations of Sarbiewski's poems were probably the result of such exercises. We must not, however, suppose that all the translations that we know are merely student linguistic exercises.

It was not always the case that a fascination with Sarbiewski's lyrics resulted in translations or imitations, especially in Latin. In many instances poets such as the Neo-Latin author Anthony Alsop 'knew Sarbievius but did not choose to follow him closely' (Money 1998: 12). The list of poets in whose works influences of the Polish Jesuit can be traced is quite impressive and includes such authors as Joseph Addison and Dr. Samuel Johnson. We can find references to Sarbiewski in the poems or studies of George Daniel of Berwick, Isaac Watts, Samuel Taylor Coleridge or the last major English Neo-Latin poet, Walter Savage Landor.

Although lasting for over two hundred years, the interest of the English in Sarbiewski's poetry was by no means a fixed part of the literary landscape. It was more likely a recurrent theme. Sarbiewski would become fashionable again and again whenever his poetry responded to some needs of English poets and readers or when it could be used for some purpose of theirs. We can indicate six such waves of popularity.

The first wave of interest appeared almost immediately after Sarbiewski's death when his poetry became fashionable among the Royalists. On the one hand numerous of his odes are saturated with the spirit of Neo-Stoicism, very fashionable at that time. On the other hand his works in translation could be used to express Royalists sentiments in disguise, the translators felt free to choose original poems which suited their intentions and alter the original content. The first to employ Sarbiewski for the purpose was most probably Richard Lovelace who translated one of his odes as an expression of grief after his brother's death in a battle. Two poems by Sir John Denham and John Hall from the volume *Lachrymae Musarum* (1649), allegedly intended as mourning the late Lord Hastings but actually commemorating the execution of Charles I, also belong to this group. The most impressive testimony of the fashion is the first edition of Sarbiewski's poems in English translation which appeared in 1646. It was also the first published collection of translations of his works in the world. The edition of thirty-five poems was signed simply 'G.H.', but the dedication gives a more complete name of George Hils.

The second wave of interest in Sarbiewski's poetry appeared a quarter of a century later in the Restoration period and ended before the 17th century was over, leaving behind approximately eleven translations. John Norris was probably the most famous of the translators acting in the period although their number is large and includes Lucy Hutchinson, Lady Mary Chatwin, Thomas Brown and the anonymous group of translators of the volume *Poems by Oxford Hands* (1685).

The third wave of interest originated among the Dissenters in the early years of the 18th century. The most numerous and interesting translations in the period are those of the dissenting minister and hymn writer Isaac Watts for whom Sarbiewski was 'the noblest Latin Poet of modern ages'. It is truly striking that Watts, famous as the author of religious hymns and spiritual songs, used Sarbiewski's poems as material for his works. Nonconformists who translated or imitated Sarbiewski included other preachers such as Samuel Say and Watts' disciple and biographer Thomas Gibbons together with Anne Steele, a religious poet of some stature known under her pseudonym Theodosia, and Robert Proud, an American Quaker. However,

Nonconformists by no means had a monopoly on translations of his works. Successful clergymen in the Church of England such as William Mason, James Hervey, and Thomas Yalden, also translated his poems in the period.

The fourth group which overlaps the former chronologically are (mostly minor) Augustan poets whose interest in Sarbiewski starts in the second quarter of the 18th century. We do not find here any memorable names although opera lovers may recognize that of Aaron Hill. This period was characterized by the increasing popularity of magazines and several translations appeared in the magazines of the period such as *The Gentleman's Magazine* and *The London Magazine*.

The fifth wave of Sarbiewski's popularity seems to have been prompted by a reprint of the Barbou edition (the first in 1759 and the second in 1791, both in Paris) of his poems, copies of which arrived in Great Britain with the French émigrés in the early 1790s. We witness the sudden appearance of seventeen translations between 1794 and 1796 alone, approximately one in ten of all we know. Coleridge explicitly presents the Barbou edition as his source. This wave seems to foretell the arrival of Romanticism, as could be guessed from the participation of Coleridge, but actually ends before the beginning of the new literary period and inasmuch as we can talk of translations of Sarbiewski produced in the Romantic period, only two or three poems can be described as Romantic translations.

The sixth wave spans the first half of the 19th century and includes mostly late Romantic and early Victorian curiosity seekers. Their interest in Sarbiewski has little to do with fascination with his poetry or sharing his views. For most of the representatives of this group Sarbiewski is no longer an important presence, a poet speaking on current topics. He is treated rather as an interesting but quite ancient exhibit, his works worthy of inclusion e.g. as an illustration in a collection of Polish (Bowring), Latin (Kitchener, Crosse), or Jesuit (Mahony) poetry or simply in a collection of translations (de Crespigny). It is quite telling that Caroline de Crespigny could not translate Sarbiewski's poems from the originals and apparently mistook the poet for a more famous Pole, King John III Sobieski.

Naturally, this division is not fully exclusive. In every period we can find authors who were drawn to Sarbiewski regardless of or even against the contemporary fashion. For Abraham Cowley Sarbiewski is the master of the Horatian form, for John Pinkerton he is a master of Latin verse in general, while for John Sheehan Sarbiewski is primarily a religious poet, a fellow Roman Catholic. However, the vast majority of the translators and translations included in the volume, fits into one or other of the six waves mentioned above.

The Romantic and early Victorian poets were the last to show an interest in Sarbiewski's poetry. The change was caused on the one hand by the new literary tastes brought by the later nineteenth century, and on the other by educational reforms of the period. Latin ceased to play such an important role in the school curricula (although it remained for decades an important part of university education) and Neo-Latin poetry was soon afterwards largely forgotten. Nevertheless, in the late Victorian period some major English poets continued to write at least some of their verse in Latin, including especially the prolific poet and prose writer Walter Savage Landor (1775–1864) and the Jesuit priest, scholar, and visionary poet Gerard Manley Hopkins (1844–1889).

The English translators of Sarbiewski's poems exhibit a great variety of attitudes towards the original which we have attempted to suggest in the title of the present volume. George Hils is generally praised for the fidelity of his translations to the original. The opposite end of the spectrum may be exemplified by the translations of Mary Masters which were characterized by Robert Cummings as 'elaborations, ineptly handled, [which] renders [them] ridiculous' (2005: 500), even though they were allegedly corrected by her much more famous friend Dr. Johnson. Benlowes's *Theophilia* falls completely beyond the scope of translation criticism as this English poet rather freely treated his source as a store of phrases and images which he inserted in his work.

The range of English authors whose interest in Sarbiewski's works resulted in translations or emulations is truly amazing; we have managed to locate forty-three authors of one hundred and fifty-one translations, and twenty-five anonymous translations. The present collection includes translations of fifty-six out of Sarbiewski's one hundred and thirty-three odes and epodes, most in multiple versions. This makes it the largest collection of Sarbiewski's poetry in English translation published since the first ever publication of Hils' volume in 1646. A ratio of two out of five may not be too impressive but we should bear in mind that three groups of Sarbiewski's poems – Marian poetry, poems addressed to various Roman Catholic religious and political leaders (such as the pope Urban VIII – I 1, I 3, I 5, I 10, I 21, I 22), and fellow Jesuits, and finally those commenting on current events of the 1620s, for various reasons could hardly appeal to an English reader. If we count them out, almost every poem of Sarbiewski which could find an audience in Great Britain was actually translated and usually in several versions.

Each of the chapters opens with a biographical note on the translator or, in the case of anonymous works, the source. As the poets in question range from such world-renowned names as those of Coleridge and Burns, through such people who were famous in their times but now are known to few such as Cowley and Bowring, to virtually unknown and never published authors such as Wodehouse and Chatwin, the content of the notes reflects their relative fame. Those notes which refer to the best-known authors include little if any purely biographical material, which may be found quite easily in generally accessible sources. Rather, they concentrate on issues more directly connected with the relations of a given author and Sarbiewski. The less known the author, the more biographical information offered; naturally, this is not always the case as some of them are truly unknown or forgotten. This material, however, has usually been limited to purely introductory issues intended to help locate a specific translator and translation within its historical and literary context. A more complete presentation of the history of the English fascination with the 'Christian

Horace' and his poetry will be the subject of a separate study by Krzysztof Fordoński *Sons of Casimir. British Translations of the Poetry of Maciej Kazimierz Sarbiewski.*

On Editing Sarbiewski

Some remarks on the edition of the following poems are necessary, as a closing part of the present introduction. The present edition was prepared for all readers interested in the works of Maciej Kazimierz Sarbiewski, and more broadly in Neo-Latin, Baroque, and religious poetry, to mention but a few possible interests. Such readers for whom English is not necessarily their first language cannot be expected to approach these poems with a knowledge of the peculiarities of old vocabulary, punctuation, and spelling; consequently, a certain degree of modernization seemed advisable. We have also taken into consideration the most recent development of the Internet. A reader interested in the original spelling will quite easily find most of the source texts in various databases accessible online.

Naturally, it was not our intention to give these translations, dating from the mid-seventeenth to the mid-nineteenth century, a uniformly modern outlook. On the contrary, we aimed at retaining as much as possible of their original form and character. Furthermore, there is no single governing norm as to how such modernization should be applied throughout the volume. The changes have thus been strictly limited to those we felt were necessary. This means that they apply predominantly to the earliest translations, while in the eighteenth- and the nineteenth-century texts only obvious mistakes and errors have been corrected.

We had to take into consideration the fact that the texts we included came from very many different kinds of sources, ranging from critical editions, private editions, newspapers and magazines to private manuscripts, and consequently on occasion they were rather imperfect. In the case of the three manuscripts, Sir Philip Wodehouse, Lucy Hutchinson, and John Chatwin, this is the first time they are published, hence our original intention to include them without any emendations. Wodehouse, however, wrote in such a peculiar style and language that, after long consideration, we decided to modernize the spelling and publish the original version in a separate critical edition. The three poems of Hutchinson and Chatwin are included without any changes.

Grammar has not been altered, on the assumption that any reader of poetry should be acquainted with the grammatical forms which English poetic language retained until the end of the nineteenth century, such as the second person singular verb endings and pronouns. The use of capital letters and original punctuation was also left intact wherever possible. One change made consistently is a space added before and after a dash as it could otherwise be mistaken for a hyphen, and before or after an apostrophe which replaces an omitted letter beginning or ending a word e.g. *'bout* for *about* and *o' th'* for *of the*.

Omitted letters are all marked with apostrophes. We generally avoided filling such gaps. This may at times make reading somewhat more difficult but such alterations would destroy the rhythm of a given line. Naturally, omissions caused by neglect rather than by intent were corrected. Original shortenings such as *w'are*, *w'have* or *y'have* were replaced by modern *we're*, *we've* and *you've* respectively, as they do not alter the syllable count. However, *'s* for *his* was retained. In numerous places erroneous *it's* were replaced with *its* and vice versa as appropriate in the given context.

Spelling has been modernized with moderation, mostly in such instances where retaining the original orthography might result in a misunderstanding, for example, *waste* replaces *waist*, or where words might be incomprehensible, for example, *oaks* for *okes* or *choir* for *quire*. Various spellings of the same word, for example, *to day*, *to-day* and *today* were replaced by one modern form. The ending *-ie* when it should be pronounced as a diphthong is uniformly rendered as *-y* (e.g. *sky* replaces *skie*). No such changes apply in the case of words at the end of lines forming a rhyme, which would be destroyed by such an alteration. In such cases modern spelling is given in the footnotes. A similar policy has been adopted in relation to old spelling forms which differ from the modern ones but do not obscure the meaning (e.g. *Affrick* for *Africa*), however, this old orthography suggests a different number of syllables in pronunciation. The most profound changes have been introduced in the translations of George Hils (e.g. the removal of devoiced *e* at the end of words culminating in a consonant) but we felt justified by the fact that the original version of the text is readily available in a 1953 reprint.

All chapters end in notes in which is given the source, providing information about the original publication. Naturally, such lists of sources are seldom exhaustive; we tried to concentrate on those we actually used, sometimes giving an alternative which might be more easily accessible or an earlier edition in a magazine which preceded publication in book form which we most often quote.

We realize that regardless of all our continued efforts this collection is still incomplete and we will be extremely grateful to hear of any other English-language translations of Sarbiewski's œuvre which we may add to a subsequent edition of this work.

Krzysztof Fordoński, Piotr Urbański

Acknowledgments

Work on this volume started in 1995 when Piotr Urbański received a scholarship from the Andrew W. Mellon Foundation for research at The Warburg Institute, London. It was Professor Thomas A. Birrell who suggested proper direction for the research of which this volume is the result.

The completion of the first edition of this work was made possible thanks to a financial grant awarded by the Ministry of Science and Higher Education of the Republic of Poland.

The research necessary for the present second enlarged and corrected edition was made possible thanks to the Andrew W. Mellon Foundation Research Fellowship held by Krzysztof Fordoński at the Institute for Advanced Studies in the Humanities, University of Edinburgh, in 2009.

The authors would like to express their gratitude to David K. Money for his exceptional support and editorial help. We would also like to thank Philip J. Ford, Jacqueline Glomski, Brenda Hosington, Jill Kraye, Susan Manning, Alan Stewart, Philip West, and Lorne Whiteway, as well as Polish specialists in Neo-Latin studies: Jerzy Axer, Andrzej Borowski, Elwira Buszewicz, Jan Malicki, Marian Szarmach, and the late Stefan Zabłocki.

Furthermore, we are grateful to MHRA for being kind enough to publish this much expanded and revised edition. We would also like to extend our gratitude for assistance and consideration to the English Editor for the series Catherine Maxwell, our Reader Elizabeth Maslen, and Gerard Lowe, Publishing Manager MHRA, without whom *Casimir Britannicus* could not have been published.

Last but not least, our personal words of gratitude go to our parents, as well as Robert Cieślak and Piotr Olichwer.

Krzysztof Fordoński, Piotr Urbański

List of Abbreviations

Lyr. – M. K. Sarbiewski, *Lyricorum lib. I, II, III, IV*
Ep. – M. K. Sarbiewiski, *Epodon liber*
Epig. – M. K. Sarbiewski, *Epigrammatum liber unus*

Poems

Translation of a Latin Epigram on Casimire

Ye Muses, for your darling Son prepare
A Garland worthy of Apollo's Hair;
Or rather, crown the Bards of low degree,
And weave the Garland, if my due, for Me;
For, as the Trees by Orpheus' Lyre are led,
Bays hasten of themselves to grace his head.

George Jeffreys

George Jeffreys (1678–1755) a playwright and poet of some renown. Educated at Trinity College, Cambridge (BA 1698, MA 1702) he was *lector linguae Latinae* (1704–1709) at the college. Jeffreys was the author of two tragedies *Edwin* (1724) and *Merope* (1731) as well as a collection of poems (1754) from which this translation was taken. Jeffreys was also the translator of several odes by Horace posthumously published in a volume edited and co-authored by William and John Dumcombe (1757 and 1767).

From: *Miscellanies in Verse and Prose. By George Jeffreys, Esq.* London: Printed for the Author. MDCCLIV.

1

George Hils

Very little is known about George Hils (Hills, Hill) of Newark-upon-Trent. He was born approximately in 1606 and received his BA in Trinity College, Cambridge in 1626/1627. In the mid-1640s he lived in London, probably moving in literary circles of the city. After 1650 he became the headmaster of Magnus School in his native Newark, a post which he held until 1655. His literary output we know is also extremely limited. It consists of three liminary verses (two in English and one in Latin) included in editions of *Poems & ca.* by James Shirley (1646), and *Comedies and Tragedies* by Francis Beaumont and John Fletcher (1647), and a volume of translations from Sarbiewski entitled *The Odes of Casimire* (1646) which is quoted here in its entirety.

The Odes of Casimire
Translated by G. H.

To the Censuring Reader

A Word or two to thee, and I have done; and in English, for it may be, 'tis that which makes thee a reader. I know thou wilt start up Critick, if not Cynick; and therefore to prevent thee, I thus Apologize for myself to those of better judgement and affection. I confess I have not been so precisely careful in every Ode, as to render line for line (a thing so strictly stood upon by some late translators) for indeed the exuberant torrent of Elegance, came so fast upon me, that I was forced to make my banks larger; choosing rather to make my fault in the excess, then defect. I ingenuously acknowledge that I am not worthy to blow a coal of that divine fire, which spreads such glorious flames through every Ode; and indeed (if it were possible to expect any mercy from thee) thou mightest excuse me in this bold attempt; for I want those true Promethean helps, that heretofore fetch'd down this fire, and dealt it freely amongst us; Those courteous sons of Maia, that with their powerful rods could break the bars, and easily uncharm the knottiest Authors. Well, if thou takest no pleasure in reading, I did profit in writing, and I had rather, of the two, that thou shouldst be idle. The young Thing was never intended for the Press, but the violence of some friends ravish'd her from me, in her virgin bloom, and now she's grown common: use her and me as courteously as thou canst, however I bid thee farewell.

G.H.

When the hateful forces of the Thracians departed out of Pannonia. Ode 1. Lib. 1.

[Lyr. I 1]

The threats of cruel War now cease:
Instead of them safety and peace,
Banished th' unhallowed earth, do please
    'Return in their white Wain;
Faith joined with Truth, and Plenty too
O'er pleasant fields do nimbly go;
The precious Ages past, do flow
    With liberal streams again.
Clear days, such years as were of old
Recalled are, of th' ancient mold*,
The Heavens hail Pearls, and molten Gold
    Doth rain down-right in showers;
Whilst I with my Prophetique string
Thy Winter festivals do sing,
The whole world doth with Echoes ring
    Old Saturn's age is ours.
Our Fathers' pure and golden rule
Exiled as far as farthest Thule,
Justice from bright Olympus' school
    Comes boldly back again.

---

* I.e. mould.

George Hils

The streams which Milk and Honey yield,
Their passage cut through open field,
And the full banks with Nectar swelled
    Do drown the flow'ry plain.
The glad Corn in the restless stalk
Waves, and the fields as we do walk,
So fruitful reel, to any balk
    The Heat no spite doth owe.
The Herdsman's Pipe to 's wand'ring Goats,
Provokes the Grasshoppers hoarse notes;
The tired Herd with strained throats,
    Makes Hills and Woods to low.
The Mountains leap, and rough Rocks smile
For gentle Peace rejoiceth still
Such solitary rooms to fill
    Hills set apart, lone Towns.
Ceres with yellow Chaplet, and
The Summer rich with ears doth stand,
Great Prince of our appeased Land,
    Thee to encompass round.
The Myrtle begs with humble shade
To serve thee, and the Laurel's glade;
The lofty Oak doth rise; Its head
    The trembling Pine doth bow;
He that o'er Stars and earth hath power,
Beholding us, from his bright Tower,
Calms all, and sets thee father o'er
    The covetous world below.
The Laurel sings long life to thee,
Let Fates and destinies agree
To twine thy thread, which cannot be
    Cut till th' appointed time.
May she amidst those glorious fires,
For thy sake, pitying our desires,
'Bout whom the beauteous star inquires,
    And flowing measures swim;
May she, I say, our Country's grief
Cure, and the chaste complaints relieve
Of all our youth, and willing ears
    Apply to th' prayers of all our Peers.

To Aurelius Lycas.
That he would not complain too much of adverse fortune.
Ode 2. Lib. 1.

[Lyr. I 2]

Unmanly howlings, Lycus, leave,
Thy sad breast, do not vex, nor grieve;
Thy rugged brow from clouds set free,
Although with usual beams on thee
The Sun not shines; or fortune late
Hath thrown the hardest chance of Fate.
With th' waves, that South winds toss today,
The cheerful Eastern gales will play;
The Sun that now hangs down his head,
With joy from blushing Thetis' bed
In th' morn will rise. Laughter and woe
Keep time, and in their courses go.
Clear merriment succeeds wet eyes,
And joys in midst of sorrows rise.
Thus pleaseth it the Fates, that flow
With various hazards here below.
He who his Oxen tir'd, did drive,
Doth laws today, to th' City give:
And the same yokes he took from those,
Upon the Citizens impose.
The day-star great, that man doth see,
Whom th' Evening saw in low degree.
But if the things that serious are
With Fortunes pastimes to compare
Doth please you; See, this Countryman
Betakes himself to 's farm again,
Of 's jeering neighbours th' only sport,
And with those Axes which in th' Court
He ruled all with, Cleaves his wood,
Whose Halves are made of Laurel good.
And if a want of wood there grows,
The Fasces on the fire throws.

George Hils

To Tarquinius Lavinus.
Ode 13. Lib. 1.

[Lyr. I 13]

As if the Sun that once doth set,
    From th' blushing East a new birth doth not get;
As if that those whom Fortune's frown
    By the swift violence of her wheel, throws down,
She would not raise again with ease,
    So active in such nimble sports as these.
Despair not (Sir) whose footsteps now
    Thou'rt said to kiss, and lick the dust of 's shoe,
Let Fortune her light wheel but turn,
    And then, Tarquinius, thou shalt soon discern
From his proud height, him downward thrust,
    His trampled robes smoking in mire and dust.
Thy jeers and laughter then forbear,
    His all-bespattered looks thou shalt not fear,
Nor trample on, rememb'ring how
    Fortune a double ball doth often throw.

To Publius Memmius.
That the shortness of man's life is to be lengthened by good deeds.
Ode 2. Lib. 2.

[Lyr. II 2]

The Valleys, now, all clad in grey
By Winter, when Sol darts his ray
On neighbouring hills, he'll naked lay,
    As heretofore.
But when the winter of thy years
With snow, within thy locks appears,
When hoary frost shall dye thine hairs,
    It parts no more.
Summer, and Autumn's quickly gone,
Th' approaching Spring will pass as soon:
Grey hairs, and chilling cold alone
    With thee will stay.
To thy ill colour, Nard distilled,
Nor the renewed perfumes o' th' field

Of flowers, can any virtue yield,
    Or take 't away.
Thee, whom thy youth hath giv'n today,
At night old age will take away,
Thy time to double, is, to lay
    A fame most bright.
Whom snatch'd by death, his friends bemoan,
He hath liv'd long. Let every one
Write Fame's sole heir; that's free alone,
    From th' rape of night.

A Departure from things human.
Ode 5. Lib. 2.

[Lyr. II 5]

    Lift me up quickly on your wings,
Ye Clouds, and Winds; I leave all earthly things.
    How Devious Hills give way to me!
And the vast air brings under, as I fly,
    Kingdoms and populous states! see how
The Glist'ring Temples of the Gods do bow;
    The glorious Tow'rs of Princes, and
Forsaken towns, shrunk into nothing, stand:
    And as I downward look, I spy
Whole Nations everywhere all scattered lie.
    Oh the sad change that Fortune brings!
The rise and fall of transitory things!
    Here walled towns that threatened Heav'n,
Now old and ruined, with the earth lie even:
    Here stately Palaces, that thrust
Their heads in th' air, lie buried all in dust.
    Here the Air Temp'rate is and mild,
But the fierce people rush to wars, most wild:
    Here in a joyful peace they rest,
But Direful Murraines their quiet fields lay waste.
    Here the whole Land doth scorching lye
Under the glitt'ring Arms o' th' Enemy:
    Under the hovering stroke o' th' Fates
The Armies yet both stand; and fury waits

With doubtful steps, upon the war;
Fresh courage here, the mingled troops prepare,
    Each against other fiercely run,
And mutually they work destruction:
    The slaughtered heaps in reeking gore
With bloody covering spread the fields all o'er;
    Here on safe Seas, as joyful prize
Is stripped away th' Egyptian Merchandise,
    Whilst the full Havens thick beset,
Do furiously with fierce contention fret.
    Mars hath his diverse Causes, and
His several fashioned weapons to command.
    From the Adulteress' smiling looks
Pleasure doth fight, and unto War provokes,
    The doting world with Helen burns.
This sordid man, oh base advantage! turns
    Revenge of words to blows;
Mischief begets itself, from mischief grows.
    Small sins by example higher dare,
Nor doth all sin, always like sin appear.
    There th' Eastern Sea lies covered o'er
With warlike Fleets: Thetis begins to roar
    With storms of flaming Brass, and here
Th' astonished Rocks all trembling stand with fear
    The troubled Sea with winds beset
With stronger waves 'gainst the full shore doth beat.
    Forbear, cruel men to multiply
With fire, Sword – wrack your single destiny.
    Is the large Earth too narrow grown,
Such slaughters, such dire tragedies to own?
    Large Kingdoms there, brought under thrall
With Tumult, stagger, and for fear do fall;
    Where in one Ruin we may see
The dying people all o'erwhelmed lie.
    The silent dust remains, to let
The weary Pilgrim this Inscription set
    (In after times, as he goes by)
'King, Kingdom, People here entombed lie.'
    What should I name the raging Seas,
Whole Havens over-flowing, and with these

    In th' sudden flood whole Cities drowned
The shaken Temples of the Gods that sound?
    Kings' Palaces what should I name
Now sunk i' th' deep, small Cottages i' th' same?
    Vast wealth I see swept down with th' tide
Rich treasure in the Ocean floating glide.
    The active world t' each others harms
Doth daily fight, and the pale Goddess' arms
    The bloody scene with slaughters, wars,
With utter ruins, and with deadly jars;
    Thus there's no Exit of our woes,
Till the last day the Theater shall close,
    Why stay I then, when go I may –
To a house enlightened by the Sun's bright ray?
    Shall I still dote on things humane?*
Lift up your longing Priest, ye Clouds, oh deign
    Lift m' up where th' air a splendour yields
Lights the sun's chariot through the azure fields.
    Am I deceived? or do I see
The following winds on their wings mounting me,
    And now again Great kingdoms lie
Whole Nations perishing before mine eye?
    The earth which always less hath been
Than 's Globe, and now, just now, can scarce be seen,
    Into its point doth vanish, see!
Oh the brimmed Ocean of the Deity!
    Oh Glorious Island richly free
From the cold Harbours of mortality!
    Ye boundless seas, with endless floods of rest
Girt round Sarbinius your panting Priest.

To Publius Memmius.
Ode 7. Lib 2.

              [Lyr. II 7]

    Amidst our loss it were some ease,
If things did fall, with the same stay, and leisure

---

* I.e. human.

They rise; but sudden ruins seize
On our most lofty things, and richest treasure.
    Nothing long time hath happy been.
The restless Fates of peopled Cities, pass:
    In a few hours destroyed we've seen,
In many years what never raised was.
    He gave to Chance long time, that said
One day's enough, whole Kingdoms t' overthrow:
    Each moment holds a people swayed
Under a fatal and exalted blow.
    Being near thy death, then, Publius, spare
To load the Gods, with thy blasphemous plaints;
    That Funerals so frequent are,
Or death so much thy neighbours' houses haunts.
    The hour, that first to thee gave life,
That thou should'st likewise die, gave first to thee.
    He hath lived long, who well doth strive
Sure always of eternal life to be.

To Asterius.
Ode 8. Lib. 2.

[Lyr. II 8]

We're mocked with baits that fortune flings
And fed with th' empty husks of things:
    Shadows, not friends we entertain;
    We're pleas'd with the deceitful train
Of words, and think them deeds. But when
Th' inconstant wheel shall turn again
    To th' parting Goddess, we shall see
    Those friends the self-same words deny.
Things Human under false names please.
Our gifts match not our promises;
    Religion, less to be doth use,
    Than the large language of our vows.

Out of Solomon's Sacred Marriage Song.
Ode 19. Lib. 2.

[Lyr. II 19]

Thou shunnest me, like to a fearful Roe,
    Which, as the stormy North-winds blow,
Or the rough noise o' th' sudden Eastern blast,
    Is snatched away with forceless hast,*
For th' early frost the trembling leaves doth fright,
    Or else the Father of the light
Hath hewn from th' echoing rocks his thund'ring darts,
    He hastens with such doubtful starts.
But till I find thee, I'll not cease, nor rest,
    But cry aloud, Return, O Christ:
And when with swifter speed thou fly'st away,
    Return again, O Christ, I'll say.
The tops of Lebanus, so green and gay,
    The fair tilths of Bethulia,
Encompass thee, old Salem's fruitful Land,
    Or else Capharnia low doth stand.
At length give o'er thy sad and careful flight:
    Thou shalt not 'scape me, th' evening bright
With its so watchful Sentry, thee'll betray,
    And th' Moon with golden horns doth stray.
By th' groans of the neglected shores I'll find
    Thee; and by th' sighs of th' Western wind;
Thee the night's watch, the stars that walk about
    With lively signs will point thee out.

Dirae in Herodem.
Ode 24. Lib. 2.

[Lyr. II 24]

Thou Cursed offspring of that sacred place!
Thou fatal monster of prodigious race!

---

* I.e. haste.

George Hils

A Libyan Lioness in some Affrick* den
Gave nourishment to thee, thou shame of men.
Or mongrel Libard† with a she-Tiger, hurled
Thee, with a mischief, into th' hateful world.
Heir to the fury of thy Sire, and dame‡;
Or some wild Wolf left thee a naked shame:
Under a huge hard rock: some angry storm,
From waves, with things so full of diverse form,
For birds and beasts, spewed th' up a baneful prey;
The Marble quarry, 'midst the raging Sea,
Its rigid veins, from thy rough bosom drew;
Marble, from those rocks hewn, Deucalion threw
Over Gaetulian fields: Megaera first
Fixed th' in thy regal seat, on thee accursed
Then Tisiphon the Sceptre did bestow,
And set the Diadem on thy savage brow:
And as thy princely Ivory, of late
Thou proudly lean'dst upon, close by thee sate§
With stately columns propp'd, fell tyranny,
Her Ensigns, who through Palestine let fly:
And her black sword with bloody trembling hand
Did brandish round, when straight at her command
Hatreds, and strifes appear'd, murder and rage
The horrid ruin of the new-born age,
She drew along; Tumultuous madness, all
The slaughtered peoples' unjust funeral:
Each famous kingdom, inexhausted town
In a large stream of blood by her o'erthrown.
Next followed Her, the plaints, and direful groans
Of sighing parents robb'd of their little ones,
Whole tides of tears, sobs, and lamentings great
And mourning in each corner of the street.
But if this show'r, from this sad cause begun,
In too too narrow rivulets doth run;
Why do revenging storms so much delay

---

*I.e. African.
†I.e. leopard.
‡I.e. dam = mother.
§I.e. sat.

To back the rain? what doth their fury stay?
Why doth the shaken sky with rustling noise
Of the Sun's chariot, bridle in the voice
Of the slow thunder? why the lightning stop
From breaking through the clouds with hideous clap?
Those airy feather'd arrows in the dark
That stray, why do they spare their cursed mark?
Acroceraunia with his three-fork'd flame,
And that huge Hill the Thracian Queen gave name,
Aemathia's craggy trembling rocks may pass
Guiltless; they have not sinned at all, alas!
Unless their Marble, with a prodigious birth,
This direful Monster teemed, t' infest the earth:
Break then the mountains, break ye lightnings,
Throw headlong down ye fruitful rocks of Kings.
May he expire! oh may the murderer fall!
Most execrable, cruel, tragical!
Upon his kingdom's pile, and flaming yew
Let his high carcass blaze; the air anew
May th' monster purge from his infectious breath,
The mock of wrangling furies, and of death.
Oh break your entrails, sluggish earth, and down
Let the high ruins of the rocks be thrown;
'Gainst which the waves o' th' raging Sea may roar
And Nereus with his Quicksands Boiling o'er:
We're heard. The climbing surges strike the stars
And the big Ocean all her strength prepares;
Her foam, and slimy mud sh' hath heaped together
Devouring waves toss'd with the worst of weather:
The firmament doth shake, and Hell so near
Through the earth's large chinks, which gapeth doth appear:
The shatt'red world now falls on 's impious head,
Go, Tyrant with thy death unpardoned,
Even Hell itself pollute, possess, alone,
Cocytus, and sulphureous Acheron.

Out of Solomon's Sacred Marriage Song. Cant. 2.
Stay me with flagons etc. I charge O ye daughters of
Jerusalem, that ye stir not up, nor wake etc.
Behold he commeth leaping upon the Mountains, etc.
Ode 25. Lib. 2.

[Lyr. II 25]

Stay me with saffron, underneath me set
      Full banks of Roses, beds of violet;
Refresh me with the choicest fruit, and spread
      The whitest Lilies round about my head:
For the delay of the seen-pow'r divine
      In sacred flames, consumes this breast of mine,
Ye Daughters of that holy City, ye!
      Ye Sisters! I, 'tis I, that humbly pray!
O, I entreat you, by each Hind, and Roe,
      That straying o'er the tops of Hills do go,
Ye stock of ancient Isaac, ye that move
      With nimble foot through Lebanus sweet grove,
O'er Carmel's fragrant top! Ye Nymphs so fair
      The glory of the noble Hills that are,
Molest not my beloved with your cries,
      Amongst the twining Violets that lies:
Do not with claps of hands, or noise of feet,
      Awake her, from her careful slumbers yet:
Until my Spouse, of her own self, shall rise
      And wipe away the soft sleep from her eyes;
Until the golden day-star shall release
      All things from silent rest, and gentle peace.
Behold from tops of yonder hills doth come
      The blessed offspring of 's fair mother's womb,
The only issue of 's bright father too,
      On the thick tops o' th' groves doth leaping go,
The unshorn head of Lebanus so high
      He leaps, and the great backs of Mountains by,
The stately dwellings of the woods he skips.
      And down again with nimble foot he trips:

Like to a frighted*, and swift running Roe,
    Beholding Lions in a vale below,
With an amazed haste, and deep fetch'd breath
    Through uncouth places runs t' escape his death.

To Egnatius Nollius.
That we ought to be of an even and upright mind against the inconstancy of fortune.
Ode 4. Lib. 3.

[Lyr. III 4]

Art thou blown on, with gentle gale,
Or in rough waters forced to sail?
Still conquer Fortune, make but sports
Of her and her uncertain Arts.
Laughs she? Turn bravely away thy face.
Weeps she? Bring 't back, with smiling grace:
When she's most busy, be thou then
Retired, and always thine own man.
Thus close shut up, thine own free state
Thou best mayst rule, chief Magistrate;
When the fierce Fates shall most molest,
The serene palace of thy breast.
When light mischance, thy fort, or thee
Shall visit; meet it merrily:
Good luck, and peace, in that house stay
Where mourning, first, hath led the way.
In dext'rous chance, this hurt we see,
It makes us soft: Extremity –
This, prosperous hath, whereso'er it hits,
It hardens, and for danger fits.
The grief that hath been of such length,
Doth 'bate its violence and strength.
By bearing much, make fortune free;
She learns, by custom, light to be.

---

* I.e. frightened.

To Marcus Silicernius.
That those are the true riches which are fetch'd from the goods of the mind.
Ode 6. Lib. 3.

[Lyr. III 6]

A rash believer of their ticklish play,
    With Fates, I ne'er join'd greedy hands in haste,
From the strict course of private jars, that they
    With me, in such an equal peace should rest.
I know not what tomorrow's fortune brings
    Heir to myself alone. The wealth she gave
Lies in my outmost rooms, 'mongst worst of things;
    Which, without force, she may for taking have.
Things can be ta'en away, I ne'er thought mine;
    Not poorer I, if mine own self complete.
I kingdom, Marcus, of myself I find
    If the great custom of mine own estate –
Within me I could in just numbers cast.
    A great part of my mind lies close, more wide
Than the rich Indies are, to which at most
    But thrice a year, we can but sail or ride.
But my rich mind, oft to itself a guest,
    By its own self is daily visited;
Not 'bout to buy Toys for a room, or feast,
    If of itself it's seen, it's richly fed.

To Aurelius Fuscus.
That all human things are frail and uncertain.
Ode 12. Lib. 3.

[Lyr. III 12]

If the first bark, Fuscus, thou would'st but pare
    From empty things, the rest will flow,
    And vanish quite like vernal snow;
Which melts away, with the mild breath o' th' air.
Valour from beauty severed, slowly moves.
    Mere outsides please: had Paris seen
    Fair Helen's heart, how foul 't had been,
How ill requiting to the Trojan Loves,

Ne'er, through the midst of Nereus' broils, had he
    Or the winds' anger, borne away
    O' th' Grecian bed that beauteous prey.
But Nature's Lord, the mutual yoke, we see,
Of things hath ord'red well, that black with white,
    Sad things with joyful covered lye.
    And from this various mixture, he
The best would choose, from Heav'n must learn the right.

To Caesar Pausilipius.
The kingdom of a wise man.
Ode 3. Lib. 4.

[Lyr. IV 3]

The large-commanding Thracians we
Have fear'd. More large command hath he,
Who all alone himself retires,
And keeps sure guard o'er his desires.
Thy unwarlike breast, with shield of proof
Forbear to fortify, throw off
From thy unpractised sides the shirt
Of Mail, so hard about thee girt.
Let not the Quiver and the bow
Such homage to thy soft neck doe.*
Whether 't be Dane, or Pict, ta'en out
From farthest Britain, hems th' about
Or Goth, ne'er labour much to know
Thine own Commander, Champion too.
We are – 'tis true a kingdom small;
But, Pausilipius, he that shall
His flattering self, t' himself subdue,
A business great doth undergo;
If his own laws he can persuade,
And doth perform them being made.
An host, makes no King's title good,
Nor Robes deep dyed in people's blood,

---

* I.e. do.

A high brow set with stars of gold,
Or Gems more glorious to behold.
He who hath tamed all coward fears,
And his own Guard himself prepares,
Who practised, in fair combat, first
Dares Chance and Fortune do their worst;
That man's a King. He doth not feign
His looks to th' votes o' th' vulgar strain.
The popular stage, and public shows
Ne'er moves him, nor the air that blows
With swift applause; He's blest whose sprite,[*]
Fall Fortune sad, or fall the light,
Hath ne'er expressed, to th' standers by,
A low complaint, or haughty cry;
But, lest the curious Fates displease
He should, holds modestly his peace.
At his first wounds, who nor groans, nor quakes,
A Conquest with his silence makes:
He that mischance knows how to hide,
The worst of ills, can best abide.
He, though the Sea should everywhere
Hang up its waves i' th' flitting air;
And the rough winds on him, should press
Flames mixed with billows, nay whole Seas,
From the high Court of 's lofty mind
In th' midst of th' ruin, sport can find;
Sets to his neck to th' falling sky,
And props the world most valiantly:
To the now gasping Age safe heir,
Leans on the Earth's sad sepulchre,
Whence, 'midst the fragments of the sky
He sees most clearly from on high,
How much more great those things appear,
He treads on, than indeed they are,
Being then prepared, and ready dressed
To die Olympus' certain guest.

---

[*] I.e. spirit.

Where, when by th' Fates he's gladly brought,
Whether disease, it matters not,
Or enemies' sword, doth thrust him on,
When his last journey he must run.
To th' Port we are but once brought in
To which, we've have always sailing been:
Whether, as mighty Princes, we
In gallant ships have spread the Sea;
Or, as the common sort of men,
In smaller Barks, have carried been.
May my poor bottom to that brink
Me happy bring; why should I shrink –
Safe on th' Aeternal shore to stand,
If with such trash I can shake hand?

To Q. Dellius.
That our life ought not to be instituted so much by popular example, as by the guiding of reason.
Ode 10. Lib. 4.

[Lyr. IV 10]

We err (my Dellius) if we take
    That baser path of life, the people make;
In highest and remotest Hills
    Virtue sequesters up herself, and dwells.
There where the way more beaten lies,
    Less certain, and more slipp'ry always 'tis.
From fruitless order, errors grow;
    Custom, not reason, draws the people now.
Men live by Chance, our time we spend
    I' th' way, like Truants, and forget the end,
Where 'midst the throng of passers by,
    The noise of the mad rout, the hateful cry
Of envy, calls, we're drawn amain
    B' example; others we draw back again.
No man is ill to himself alone,
    Nor no man' life is only called his own:
Whilst that the rambling rout treads o'er
    With after steps, the heels of them before,

They that go foremost are design'd
     A mischief oft to those that come behind.
Parnassus, and chaste Helicon
     Sublimes and takes me from the vulgar throng:
From whence, the false mistakes I view
     And wand'ring minds of the too slothful crew;
And from on high I fearless see,
     With sport, the dangers that below me lye;
Thus warily with joy I live,
     And b' other men's mischances I can thrive.

To Sigismundus Laetus.
He commends the despising of vain-glory, and silence.
Ode. 11. Lib. 4.

[Lyr. IV 11]

Why fleeting glory follow we,
     Laetus, with weapons all in vain?
When like a Moor, or Parthian, she
     Flies at her back with wounded Train.
The Talking-people's love, denies
     Under one roof a guest to fix:
With 's empty ear, one takes up lies,
     And them with truths, doth subtly mix,
Another sticks, and thinks to build
     His nest: but when he plainly sees
His empty breast with noise beguiled,
     Aloft with silent wings, he flees.
True praise would not be known; the Sun
     Forbids from being seen below
By his own light: and he that can
     Eclipse himself, doth brighter show.
He that in silence, of his mind
     The sacred Treasury contains;
Safety i' th' vulgar noise doth find:
     In 's doubtful Court, and wisely reigns.
Still banks thy Pinnace well may pass,
     But when with hoarse rocks they do roar,
Remember wisely to forecast
     And turn 't aside with wary Oar.

To Ianus Libinius. He excuses his retiredness.*
Ode 12. Lib. 4.

[Lyr. IV 12]

What 'tis detains me here, and why –
I hide myself from every eye.
How in so poor a house I spend
My hours, you've often asked me, friend;
When the free Courts of free-born men,
Fall out, which first shall let me in.
I enjoy myself, what need I more?
Of every sense I lock the door;
And close shut up, a task I find
In the retiring house o' th' mind:
The Theatre of my life I view
My own spectator and judge too –
Whether the tale I first begun
In well digested Acts I've spun;
In every scene, if every clause
Goes neatly off, with heav'n's applause:
Each Action scanned, is there set free
Or sentenc'd by authority –
If there, with 'well Done', I escape,
I'm blessed without the people's clap.
I hate the common road of praise,
Or what the gaping vulgar raise,
Which with a pleasant gale awhile
Fame hurries, but doth soon beguile:
Now Envy's sting it feels, ere long
Th' Artillery of some spiteful tongue:
Thus chas'd, with weaken'd wings it dies;
Or torn, on the bare ground it lies.
A private fame, a mean house, where
I live concealed from popular air,
Best fits my mind, and shelters me:
Virtue t' her own praise deaf should be.
Our emulation, things afar off command,
But Envy haunts things that are near at hand.

---

* I.e. solitude.

To Caesar Pausilippius.
That adversity is to be endured with a constant mind.
Ode 13. Lib. 4.

[Lyr. IV 13]

If mournful eyes could but prevent
The evils they so much lament
Sidonian Pearls, or Gems more rare,
Would be too cheap for ev'ry tear.
But moist'ned woes grow fresh, and new,
As Corn besprinkled with the dew.
Tear follows tear, and fruitful grief
Hath from itself, its own relief.
The man whom Fortune doth espy
With drooping spirit, and moist'ned eye,
She often strikes; ill Fate, amain
Runs Scarr'd no notice being ta'ne*.
Bewail not then thyself, dear friend,
Or evils that on thee attend;
What they expel, tears cherish oft;
Hard things deny to yield to soft.
Mischance is conquered, when she spies
A valiant patience with dry eyes.

To Crispus Laevinius.
Being asked why he sung so often as he travelled, he answers.
Ode 14. Lib. 4.

[Lyr. IV 14]

As cheerfully I walk with thee,
My shoulders from all burdens free,
Our native soil again to see
     Rich to myself I sing,
Whilst care strikes thee, and thy Muse dumb,
The heavy weight of thy vast sum,
Or what estate in time to come
     The faithless rout may bring.

---

* I.e. taken.

He's rich that nothing hath; He that
In 's certain hand holds his estate,
That makes himself his constant mate
      Where need commands him go,
What can I want, that naught desire?
Than Pindus' vale, I reach no higher:
O sacred Grove! O pleasant choir
      In those cool shades below!
What paths soe'er my steps invite
Ye Delphian hills, my sole delight
Do go with me; in weary plight,
      And veil me with good grace.
Let th' Goth his strongest chains prepare,
The Scythian hence me captive tear,
My mind being free with you, I'll stare
      The Tyrants in the face.

To Munatius.
That nothing in human affairs is not full of tediousness.
Ode 15. Lib. 4.

[Lyr. IV 15]

Nothing Munatius, nothing I sing 't again,
That's mortal, nothing from th' uncured pain
      Of tediousness is free. The Sun
      Which bright to our forefathers shone
To us, but little healthful, doth appear,
And though not guilty of one spot, not clear:
      Whatsoe'er immortal thing we see
      In high Olympus, silly we
Do overcast with Envy's shade; here one
From his own native Hills the rising Sun
      Disclaims; or th' ancient Moon, that strikes
      Her beams through his father's glass, dislikes.
Each year we change our air, and soil, so light;
Him, Holland's warmer Climate doth invite:
      Another differs, and doth cry
      Ausonia's clearer Suns please me.
In vain all this, if faithful sicknesses
Wait close behind, if secret griefs ne'er cease,

All's one, whether in Chariot
Thou goest, or in Venetian boat.
Poor exiles! Then, things left do please us most,
Who a sure building can from virtue boast,
To him the smoke of 's father's Hall
Doth never hurt his eyes at all.
Virtue oft-times, rich in a rustic ease
Confines herself to her own private bliss;
And in the guiltless straw, her throne
With great delight can lean upon.

Out of Solomon's Sacred Marriage Song. Chap. 1.7.
Tell me (ô thou whom my soul loveth) where thou feedest,
where thou makest thy flocks to rest at noon etc.
Ode. 19. Lib. 4.

[Lyr. IV 19]

Thou said'st, farewell my Spouse, and went'st away
More fleet than Clouds with liquid paces stray:
Oh what a longing, Jesu thus
With thy delay thou mak'st in us?
'Tis now high noon, the scorching Sun doth burn
In th' midst o' th' pole, the mower spares the corn,
The Shepherd, with his flocks, is glad –
And painted birds, to seek cool shade.
But Jesu! where art thou? what region 's blest
By holding thee so long in silent rest?
What darksome shade denies my love?
Or with thick boughs what shady Grove?
Knew I on what green Turf thou dost repose
Thy fainting limbs, what wind with soft breath blows,
What stream, with bubbling, passing by
Disturbs thy sleep, or wakens thee;
Oh! lest the too much noise should raise thee, I
Would let fall streams of tears should qualify;
My warmer sighs thou mix'd should'st find
With the cold blasts of th' Eastern wind.

Out of Salomon's Sacred marriage song.
My beloved spake and said unto me, rise up my love, my Dove, my fair one, and come away; for lo the winter is past, the rain is over and gone: the flowers appear on the earth, the time of singing of birds is come, and the voice of the Turtle is heard in our Land. The figtree putteth forth etc.
Ode 21. Lib. 4.

[Lyr. IV 21]

Do I mistake? or from Elysium clear
    My life's-call do I hear?
Sister arise, and harness thy sweet pair
    Of Doves, thyself more fair;
Mount and drive hither, here let thy Chariot stop,
    From Libanus' high top;
At thy approach the falling showers do fly,
    Tempestuous storms pass by,
The lightning's quench'd under thy harmless feet,
    Winter turns Spring to see 't.
While in the sacred Green, a bow'r we see
    Doth spread itself for thee.
The Earth new Turfs itself for thee to tread,
    The straying stars fresh fields make glad.
Here with their dams, of Kids th' amazed flocks
    Hang on steep sides of Rocks;
Here as they swim, the wanton Hinds do play
    In the cool streams all day.
The Lion with the Libard* down is laid
    Tame and well governed;
Each with his Lamb about the Mountains skip,
    O'er Hills they lightly trip.
By these a spacious brook doth slowly glide,
    Which with a spreading tide
Through bending Lilies, banks of Violets
    From th' hollow Pumice sweats.
The rivers gently flow, and a still sound
    From mossy Rocks doth bound.

---

* I.e. leopard.

The sporting fish dance in the crystal Main,
    The Birds sweetly complain,
The air, if doleful comforts please, doth ring
    With mournful murmuring.
For when the Doves echo each other's cry
    That sound doth hither fly.
As they with widowed notes themselves do please,
    Just so, our joys increase.
No want appears; th' officious Vine doth stand
    With bending clusters to our hand.
Here, thou shalt pick sweet Violets, and there
    Fresh Lilies all the year:
The Apple ripe drops from its stalk to thee,
    From taste of death made free.
The luscious fruit from the full Figtree shall
    Into thy bosom fall.
Meanwhile, the Vine no pruning knife doth know,
    The wounded earth no plough.
The Corn grows green alone, and th' unhurt land
    Doth white with harvest stand.
The grass affords a stately bed, the Plane
    Spreads thee to entertain.
Arabian mists sweat from the gummy tree
    Of Balm, and all for thee;
Which through the air, a rich perfume do throw,
    Fanned with each neighb'ring bough.
Arise my Sister dear, why dost thou stay,
    And spend th' unwilling day?
Behold thy harness'd Doves, at thy delay
    Do sigh, come, drive away.
Put on, and hither drive thy beauteous pair
    Of Doves, thyself more fair.

To Ianusius Skuminus.
When he performed the Funeral obsequies of his most dear Wife. Ode 30. Lib. 4.

[Lyr. IV 30]

What though the Gods have promised she shall be
    Enfranchised to Eternity?

Yet (valiant Sir) so great a loss still cries
    For a just tribute from your eyes;
View but her pious mind, that tow'r of state
    Not shaken by sad storms of Fate,
Her humble innocent soul, her guiltless fear,
    Her modesty chief Regent there;
The prudent thrift of her presaging mind
    Her constant zeal, pure and refin'd;
And who can then forbear t' embalm her Hearse
    With the daily precious dew of tears?
'Tis not in Fate to promise length of days,
    To things of such esteem and praise;
Nor can the stars suffer so ripe a birth
    To be long sullied with dull earth.
Load not the Heavens then with unjust complaints,
    For taking back one of their Saints.
The courage of her richly temp'red breast
    Made her for them a fitter guest:
Such jewels of her mind sparkle about her
    The stars themselves can't shine without her.
Thus Tanaquil; thus Claudia's virgin band
    Steered the unwilling Bark to land.
Thus she, that durst her Husband's fate abide,
    And Cloelia over Tiber's tide;
Too early cropped, survive in Poesie,[*]
    And keep perpetual jubilee.
'Tis not in Art to fetch her back again,
    Or charm the spirits with Orpheus' strain,
To break the bars of Adamant, or scale
    The Rampiers[†] of th' Elysian wall,
No Orisons prevail, sent from the breast
    Of great Apollo's choicest Priest.
Yet in the arched entrance, chinks there be,
    Which may befriend the covetous eye;
Through these to th' hidden mysteries I peep,
    And (if the spirits nor dream, nor sleep)

---

[*] I.e. poetry.
[†] I.e. ramparts.

I saw, or else methought, I there had seen
    Her, wand'ring o'er a spacious Green,
With walls of Diamond, gates of purest glass,
    No Crystal more transparent was:
Each blade of grass was gold, each tree was there,
    A golden Periwig did wear.
The swelling banks of Violets did curl
    Themselves with Gems, and Orient Pearl;
The glorious nothing, of the Trigon glass –
    And all Apelles' Art, which pass.
Through the sweet vales a Choir of Damsels sing
    Eternal Paeans to their King.
The stars with sparkling light stand round I see,
    Twinkling to their shrill melody.
Her and her tender darling, then I spy,
    I' th' midst of that blest company;
With looks more fresh and sweet, than are the Roses
    Of which her Garlands she composes —
Two flow'ry Chaplets, which with Gems set round
    Her own and Nephew's temples crown'd.
But here a veil was drawn, I must not pry
    Nor search too far with mortal eye,
Nor would you more. It may suffice that she
    Hath changed frail flesh for blessed Eternity.

To Albertus Turscius.
Of his Dreams, and Lyricks.
Ode 32. Lib. 4.

[Lyr. IV 32]

Whether a shorter sleep, or whether
    A long one (Turscius) joins mine eyes together
In my soft dreams, methinks, I see
    To my light shoulders wings set on, and I
With joy transported, upward soar,
    The flow'ry Meadows, and the pastures o'er;
Where the green Grove its cool shade yields
    To th' stately grass plots, and ripe swelling fields:
Straight, 'midst the river Swans, up higher
    A winged fowl above the clouds I aspire;

The lively Lakes below, I sleight,
    And with sweet strains a bird I counterfeit.
See, now methinks, the clouds in throngs
    The lightning leaps too, at my ravishing songs;
Iris about my neck hangs round,
    And with her diverse coloured bow, I'm bound.
Being now myself, and newly waked,
    My not unwelcome dreams, just now off shaked;*
Thrice o'er my Lute, I scarce had run
    With nimble finger neat division;
Remembering Horace, Thee, my guide,
    When my high Genius through th' air doth ride;
Now o'er the scatt'red Islands, then
    O'er Seas, with dry feet passing back again;
Nothing that's mortal of me, now
    I bear, and naught to my dull bulk I owe.
Yet Turscius thou hast often told,
    And warn'd me, lest than Icarus of old
By a true fall indeed, I make
    A louder tale, and change the name o' th' Lake.
In vain: Remembering Him, I had
    A care, and counsel, to my folly, add:
For when I sleep, in bed I lye,
    And if I write, my secure chair holds me.

To Quintus Tiberinus.
Ode 34. Lib. 4.

[Lyr. IV 34]

Thou shalt not Tiberinus, call
Him rich, whose every Acre shall
Outvie the Eastern glebe, whose field
Fair Fortune's clearest stream doth gild.
Nor him, whose birth, and pedigree
Is famed abroad by 's Heraldry;
He who by fleeting glory 's hurl'd
In his rich Chariot through the world.

---

* I.e. shaken.

He's poor that wants himself, yet weighs
Proudly himself; in this scale lays
His lands, in th' other broad one, by,
The false weight of his gold doth lye,
Great to himself, to others small,
That never knows himself at all.
As the false people raise him higher,
Himself in 's shadow he'll admire.
The fairest Gem without true light,
Without true praise great titles, slight:
Blessed Tiberinus, and most free
In thyself alone thou'lt* learn to be.

To Paulus Coslovius
Ode 35. Lib. 4.

[Lyr. IV 35]

The Western winds, with the warm breath o' th' Spring,
Return, and o'er our fields their soft gales fling:
    The flow'ry-garnish'd Meadows by,
      With freshest colours painted lie.
The River, which the gainful ships so throng,
With welcome silence gently glides along,
    Although the neighbouring Hill doth ring
      With the shrill notes of birds that sing;
Although the Swain on the green bank that sits
Old Sonnets with his Oaten Pipe repeats,
    Although the Seaman doth not fail
      At length to strike his full blown sail.
To thy Palladian labours interpose
Such changes Paullus; when the Sun forth shows
    And with his golden presence smiles
      On the high tops of highest Hills,
We'll mount the back of green Luciscus, where
He's thickest set with tallest Oaks, and hear

---

* I.e. thou wilt = you will.

The bubbling noise of streams that flow
    From Fountains that close by him go.
Thence from the midst o' th' hill all Vilna shall
Our prospect be, our eye shall lower fall —
    On Vilia's cooler streams, that wind,
    And with embraces Vilna bind.
From thence, far off, the Temples we'll behold,
And radiant 'Scutcheons all adorn'd with gold;
    Then we'll look o'er that double tower,
    Th' extent of great Palaemon's power.
How in a settled peace, and kingdom's rest
The easy people raise themselves, so blessed!
    Three Temples in three years we've seen
    To th' Citizens have reared been;
Where Gediminian Rocks themselves extol
With their plain tops, and then the Capitol.
    Those buildings, whose proud turrets stretch
    Themselves to th' Clouds, and stars do reach:
Great things to greater growth do thus increase,
And with least pains, improve themselves by peace.
    Here, tops of Hills, themselves behold,
    In all their flow'ry pride unfold.
The Poplar now that shakes, when th' East winds blow,
Stood clothed in grey, under the ling'ring snow:
    The Springs that now so nimbly rise,
    Were all of late locked up, in Ice.
The fields that now with blushing Roses spread,
Lay barren, and in hardest frost all hid:
    The birds which chirping sit i' th' Spring;
    When Winter comes, forget to sing.
Break off delays then, and from grievous care
A constant day, set by; which th' ev'ning fair
    Doth promise, and the next day's Sun
    With his white Steeds will freely run.

To Paulus Iordanus Ursinus, Duke of Bracciano.
He commends the pleasantness of the Country, where, in the feasts of September, he retired from Rome.
Ode 1. Lib. Epod.

[Ep. 1]

Appear ye spriteful Choir with choicest sports,
    All pastime fit for Phoebus' Courts;
And Thou, great Master of the Revels, join
    The Graces, to thy Daughters nine;
Wit pure and quaint, with rich conceits and free
    From all obscene scurrility:
Here free from care, nimbly let's dance around
    Upon Bracciano's softer ground.
A gentle Cliff from a steep Hill doth rise
    That even to Heaven, mounts by degrees,
And safe, with uncouth passage, leans upon
    The solid backs, of Rocks and stone:
Whence 'midst the Bulwark'd Forts, we may descry
    A displayed Banner from on high,
Which to th' Imperial force a terror was,
    A terror to great Borgias,
When through the brazen troops of 's threat'ning foes,
    His fearful thunderbolts he throws,
Pursuing routed Caesar, whom he brought
    To that he promised him, to naught.
Great Ursin here puts reins to th' Tuscan pow'r
    The grace of Heroes and the flow'r;
Heir to his father's worth, chief guide and stay
    And praise of great Oenotria.
A Bow'r grows green, set round with trembling Oaks
    Which fans the Heavens with gentle strokes.
It clothes the Hills, and spreads itself all over
    To th' open Theatres a cover.
Close joined to th' walls, the Nymphs' cool Arbour stands,
    Which to the Sunny shore commands;
By these a bank of Vines, which th' neighbour Trench
    With milder waves doth daily drench.
Nowhere the Lakes with fuller Sea doth roar,
    Either of Larius that boils o'er,

Or rough Albanus whose troubled waves do mix
    With the unnavigable Styx:
Not stormy Julia, when her swelling pride
    Most rageth in her highest tide:
Benacus doth not raise more froth, when he
    Assaults the rocks with fiercest Sea.
With rugged tops the bending mountains round
    Upon the slow calm streams look down.
Romanus here his snowy back uprears,
    And draws down envy from the stars:
The lofty head of Cyminus here shakes
    The Oak with trembling leaves which quakes,
And holds off Boreas, when his rawer blasts
    'Gainst the weak Southern winds he casts,
Commands the Country far, and out he sets
    His Winter sides against Heavens threats.
Meanwhile a pleasant calm doth smooth the Lake,
    The waves 'gainst one another break,
Mild Thetis self, with her own self finds sport,
    And waters do the waters court:
Through which a ship doth cut, with pleasant gales,
    Or nimble Bark with swelling sails:
The large-finn'd Crystal cattel as they go
    Are forced whether they will or no
With ready dragnet; then with lines of hair
    They round the Lake, or Nets more rare.
Rich Polla's stately house there shines, and here
    Full stored Fish-ponds do appear:
The friendly Fords which toward the Sea do lye
    Water Trebonian Vineyards by.
Here neat Aurelius' farm looks gay, chief Lord
    And Master of that healthful Ford,
Whose water cures diseases, whose quick springs
    Do purge out all infectious things.
Where Flora makes the banks, and gives the name
    To Fountains, proud of so much fame;
From lively stones perpetual waters flow,
    And wash the fields wheresoe'er they go,
Their father Tiber, and their King they found
    And flow to Rome, with homage bound.

Nature doth purely there advance each part,
        Not any place is help'd by Art:
As yet the virgin furrow, th' Hills yet stand
        Untouched, by any tender hand.
Chaste Tethys, Bacchus courts, Thetis doth woo
        Bacchus again, and Ceres too.
Hence Evius cheerful rises, and doth twine
        With th' Elm, that closely clings to th' Vine,
With 's plenteous horn he swells, his locks hang by –
        With flowing Clusters tangled lye.
Not Lesbos him, nor the sweet smelling grace,
        Of rich Campania's fruitful race
Delights; the purple Grape not so fair shows,
        In the Falernian sun that grows.
He'll not prefer Faliscus' sandy ground,
        Nor Rhaetia, that doth so abound;
The yellow Tilths of happy Cyprus, he
        Ne'er loved so much, nor Rhodos by:
As in his own — in his own channels he
        Hugging himself, doth proudly lye.
Sole Empress Ceres of the fertile lands
        Whose large possessions she commands:
The fields with yellow waves do ebb and flow,
        The ripe ears swim, when winds do blow.
No vapour, here, Heaven's cleared face doth stain,
        No cloudy fleece stretched out with rain:
The Northern blasts are still, and all at peace,
        And the hoarse noise o' th' woods doth cease:
The stubborn Africk winds that use to stray
        About th' unruly sandy Sea,
Are all hushed up, and no Alarum sound
        To th' other winds, entrenched round;
Only the Evening fair, a gentle gale
        Of winds that each year never fail:
The bright Sun darting through th' enlightened Air
        His beams, doth guild the Mountains clear,
The hours drive on heav'n's torch, that shines so bright,
        And Phoebus father of the light —
With a peculiar influence bedews
        The Hills all o'er, when night ensues.

The warm Favonian winds with whistling gale
    Do merrily the boughs assail,
And with their temperate breath, and gentle noise,
    Sweet pleasing slumbers softly raise.
The prattling Nests meanwhile no silence keep,
    Their wandering guests ne'er sleep.
To 's mate, the Turtle 'mongst the branches groans,
    And with complaints breaks hardest stones,
The Nightingale, the pleasant Groves about
    Refresheth with her warbling note,
Bewails her loss to th' woods, i' th' cruel fields
    'Gainst Tereus her cries she yields:
And what the mournful birds do so complain,
    The shrill woods answer back again.
The Oak, the Alder tells; the Poplar tree
    The Ash; and that, the Elm stands by.
The Groves rejoice with th' Echo they afford
    And tell them back — ev'n word for word.
Jordanus here, hither thyself command,
    Great Ruler of th' Oenotrian land.
Withdraw thyself from cares, from all resort
    So cloyed with City, and with Court,
So full of great affairs, at length thy breast
    Convey to thy domestic rest.
Here thou may'st pass thy Ford, in gloomy shade,
    On each side, by thine own trees made,
And here between thy Mounts, with tall Oaks set,
    A large walk thou shalt get:
Or in December, when the fields look white,
    And th' Hills, with th' earliest snow doth light;
Sometime th' entangled game, with twining net
    In th' wood, with fear thou shalt beset:
Sometimes with courser fleet, pursue full sore,
    The Buck thou mayst, sometimes the Boar;
With thy thrown dart the red Deer thou shalt stick,
    And th' frightened ravenous Wolves shalt strick*,

---

* I.e. strike.

And if that Star o' th' sacred dignity
      The glory of all Italy,
Will also from his cares, himself make free,
      And keep his Festivals with thee;
Each Citizen of thine, and every guest
      With the completest joy is blessed.

To the Fountain Sona, When he returned.
Ode 2. Lib. Epod.

[Ep. 2]

O Fount more clear then spotless glass,
More pure, then purest snow e'er was,
The Nymphs' desire, and Country's grace,
Thou joy of this my Native place.
Tir'd with a tedious journey, I,
And press'd with cares that grievous lye,
From the far Tuscan Land made free
Thus low I bow myself to thee:
Oh, if thou canst, vouchsafe to be
Press'd and with hollow palm drawn dry!
So let thy peace no wandering beast
Disturb, no broken bough, thy rest:
So when thou cut'st with prattling noise
The Meads, and leap'st, men hear thy voice;
May th' whistling leaves of Poplar trees
With their unwelcome murmurs cease —
To thee, and thy Priest's Lute: if naught
Urban approves, in vain is thought
T' Blandusia thou canst nothing owe;
Nor to mild flowing Sirmio.

A Palinode.
To the second Ode of the book of Epodes of Q. H. Flaccus.
The praise of a Religious Recreation.
Ode 3. Lib. Epod.

[Ep. 3]

But, Flaccus, now more happy he appears,
      Who, with the burden of his cares,

Far off hath left his father's ground, set free
  From the fierce wrangling Lawyer's fee;
No scorching heat, nor blasts of Winter Jove,
  Doth hurt his fruit, or him can move:
He shuns all strifes, and never doth resort
  The sinful gates o' th' greedy Court.
But either doth bewail those days and nights,
  Lost by him in profane delights;
Or else retired, strives to collect and find
  The dispersed flock of 's wand'ring mind;
Having first fairly poised the recompense
  And gains of a good conscience.
At evening, when the harbinger of night
  The torches of the sky doth light,
How he admires th' immortal rays break forth,
  And their bright Orbs, more large than earth;
How through his trickling tears, he helps his sight.
  Unto the open Courts of light,
Which with thyself, ô Christ, thyself in pray'r
  H' Adores, t' Eternal life an heir!
The Stars with golden wheels, are hurried by,
  And let their prostrate exile lye,
Over whose face, the plenteous tears do stray,
  Which chase all drowsy sleep away;
As soon as Phoebus' head begins t' appear,
  Lately in Indus' streams made clear,
From depth of soul, less then himself he lies,
  And bends the angry pow'rs with cries:
Or when the Sun shines clear, the air serene,
  And April Festivals begin,
His eyes, so used to Heaven, he down doth throw,
  On a large prospect here below:
He views the fields, and wondering stands to see
  In 's shade the shining Deity.
See how (says he) each herb with restless leaves
  To th' stars doth strive and upward heaves:
Remov'd from heaven they weep, the field appears
  All o'er dissolved in pious tears:
The white-flower'd Woodbine, and the blushing Rose
  Branch into th' air with twining boughs;

George Hils

The pale-fac'd Lily on the bending stalk,
      To th' stars I know not what doth talk;
At night with fawning sighs they express their fears
      And in the morning drop down tears.
Am I alone, wretch that I am, fast bound
      And held with heavy weight, to th' ground?
Thus spoke he to the neighbouring trees, thus he
      To th' Fountains talk'd, and streams ran by,
And after, seeks the great Creator out
      By these fair traces of his foot.
But if a lightsome Countryhouse that's free
      From care, such as Luciscus' be,
Or Nemicini's, if Besdan's fruitful field
      Can Grace to his rude table yield,
To his plain board with country dainties set,
      In August's dry and parching heat;
Even at his door, under a private shade
      By a thick pleasant Poplar made,
Provision of all sorts, expect their guest,
      A shell with salt, pure and the best,
New bread, for which, 'midst the thin briars, the Maid
      Picks Strawberries, and 's gladly paid.
Cheese newly pressed, close by, the friendly Can
      With Cup clean washed, doth ready stan'.[*]
With me the Lucrine dainties will not down,
      The Scare, nor Mullet that's well grown;
But the Ring-dove plump, the Turtle[†] dun doth look,
      Or Swan, the sojourner of th' brook,
A mess of Beans which shuns the curious palate,
      The cheerful and not simple sallet;[‡]
Clusters of grapes last gathered, that miss
      And nothing owe to th' weighty press.
Then after noon he takes a kind of pride
      To th' Hills to walk, or River side,

---

[*] I.e. stand.
[†] I.e. turtle-dove.
[‡] I.e. salad.

And 'midst the pleasant Oaks, a shade doth find,
    T'avoid the blasts of th' Southern wind;
To th' darksome shore, by the deep pool he goes,
    And through, with nimble Boat he rows;
Sometimes the sporting fish, his bait thrown in,
    He plucks up with his trembling line.
Meanwhile th' spacious woods with echoing note
    Do answer to the Bull's wide throat,
The shady rivers bleat; the Nightingale
    I' th' bushes chirps her doleful tale.
With 's hastening pipe the shepherd drives away
    His flock, which through the thickets stray:
To which as from the field they pass along,
    Each mower sings by course, his song;
O'er yielding furrows, carts full pressed with corn
    Groan, and are like to break the barn.
Our work once done, we do not silent sit,
    When knots of our good fellows meet;
Nor is our talk prolong'd with rude delay;
    In harmless jests we spend the day;
Jests dipp'd in so much salt, which rubbing shall
    Only make fresh our cheeks, not gall.
If that rich churl, this had but seen, when he
    A Country man began to be,
The money which i' th' Ides he scraped in
    Next month he'd not put out again.

Epig. 4. *Let my beloved come into his Garden.* Cant. 5.

[Epig. 4]

Love takes the tools of a rude Country clown,
    His own Artill'ry, and his torch lays down;
With staff in 's hand, Oxen to th' Plow he set
    For tillage, and such honest labour fit;
Straight, as he turned up hearts with easy share,
    And grace i' th' virgin-furrows did appear,
'Mongst thousand others, one flower, quoth he, is miss'd:
    That none may wanting be, come thou: O Christ.

Who is thy Beloved?
Out of Cant. 5. Lib. Epig. 37.

[Epig. 37]

What is that Spouse of thine? that fairest He?
    The barb'rous people said, of late, to me.
A Pen I took, and in a Tablet drew
    Whatsoe'er, O Christ, in thy blessed orb I view.
Roses, and Gold I paint, Gems, Groves, Corn-land,
    Green Gardens, Lakes and Stars with nimble hand;
Would you needs learn, what might my fairest be?
    Look o'er this tablet, pray, O such was He.

Epig. 40.

[Epig. 40]

Thou run'st, and running cry'st, why dost thou stay
My Spouse? Thou would'st be ta'en, not get away.

Epig. 48. To — bearing Lilies in her hand.

[Epig. 48]

These Lilies which on virgin stalks do bend,
    From whence do they their chaster leaves extend?
The Paestan beds such flow'rs did ne'er bring forth,
    Nor Pharian fields e'er gloried in such worth:
Alcinous' purple banks ne'er teemed with these,
    Nor rich Carystos watered by the Seas.
Since then these flow'rs no native place do know,
    Who can deny from her chaste hand they grow.

Ex. Lib. Epigr. 51.
To Iohan de Lugo, when after a long sickness, he returned to his intermitted Lecture of Repentance.

[Epig. 51]

With hairs uncomb'd Repentance late did mourn,
    When with so fierce a Fever thou wert torn:
She's said, to let loose reins t' untamed grief,
    T' afford her moist'ned bosom, no relief,

But when th' desks again, thy sickness tamed,
> Thou mounted'st, she's said her careless hair t' have comb'd
T' have bridled in her conquer'd grief, and smile,
> Of tears, her open'd bosom to beguile.
Who cannot then be glad, thou being safe?
> When tears rejoice, and grief itself doth laugh.

The voice of Christ upon the Cross:
I Thirst.

[Epig. 110]

Alas I thirst, great King, thou loud dost groan;
> I have no pleasant Wine for Thee, thirst on,
Yet oh I thirst, thou cry'st: a Cup to thee
> Woes me! I'll give: but mixed with gall 't must be.
Drink this, my Spouse: perhaps thou'lt ask to whom?
> To me, O Christ, to th' health o' th' world let 't come.

From: *The Odes of Casimire. Translated by G.H.,* London: Printed by T.W. for Humphrey Moseley, at the signe of the Princes Armes in Pauls Churchyard, 1646.

Note: The volume was reprinted (without English and Latin prefaces by Hils) by The Augustan Reprint Society, Los Angeles in 1953.

2

Sir Philip Wodehouse

Sir Philip Wodehouse (1608–1681), third Baronet, of Kimberley in Norfolk, was a politician (MP for Norfolk in 1654–1658 and for Thetford after 1660) and a poet. A volume of his manuscripts preserved in the library of the University of Leeds includes the following collection of never previously published translations of Sarbiewski's epigrams dating probably from the 1660s or the 1670s. Apart from several original compositions, mostly moral or satirical, the manuscript includes also an impressive collection of translations from other Classical and Neo-Latin poets and philosophers – verse adaptations of Augustine, Horace, Ovid, Petronius, Seneca, and Virgil, partly the work of Sir Philip himself, and partly that of his son Edmund.

[Epig. 54]

[Epig. 54]

Bragg Ansa, whilst the Crohates* took repast
Going to fight the Ottoman in hast,
Lively my harts (says he) Let's cheer it up,
Let's dine, God us bespeaks, In heav'n we'll sup.
But when he hears Bellona's clangour, larum, guns,
And Trumpets tantarars, to town he runs,
He being asked, why he'd refuse to sup in heav'n?
False fool replies: I must keep fast this Eav'n.†

---

* Probably: Croats, in the original Sarmatians i.e. Poles.
† I.e. evening.

[Epig. 34]

[Epig. 34]

Low Love and Death for prize of praise contend
Both in their Armour and artill'ry shined.
Death pleads, I vanquish bodies with my darts:
Love pleads, with flames 'tis I who vanquish hearts.
But Death replies, My Victories are more
Then Love rejoins, My glories yours outdo.
They fought, but that he judged, They equal were,
Who was in both Conquered, and Conqueror.

[Epig. 33]

[Epig. 33]

Why seek wee shade by day, or light by night?
Since Love is our Umbrella and our light?

Epig. 8 Canz. Through Towns and Streets. M. Magdalen

[Epig. 8]

She moans and moves the stars with sad lament
Her tender cheeks with silver streams besprent*
Through towns, and streets, o're hills and vales she hyes†
Through plains and deserts, in pursuit she flies
To speed her course, her weeping what avails?
With wind of sighs in her own tears she sails.

Epigr. 14

[Epig. 14]

Without thee I, through darks and deserts stray
Jesus! I am impatient of delay.
O happy Magdalen! whose braided hair
To bind thee to his knees thy tyalls‡ were!

---

* I.e. sprinkled over.
† I.e. to hasten; to go in haste.
‡ I.e. ties.

As constant handmaid she thy love retains
Whilst thou his Captive, and he thine remains
My Jesus look on me
    Let me thy Magd'len be
I carry me with Thee
    Or tarry thou by Me.

Epig. 10

[Epig. 10]

That thou woudst suck my breasts
    My Spouse, Thou sing'st to me:
So I thy Bride that was
    Should now thy Mother be.
I well remember, I
    Thy breasts have suckt times past:
So Thou who wert my Spouse
    Ev'n there my mother wast.
We often at one breast
    Have suckt, both one, and t'other:
So I thy sister was
    And thou wert then my brother.
O Love! O only Love!
    From thee all love does move,
Whilst to thy self, Thou'rt small
    Thou'rt all in all, to all.

Epig. 15

[Epig. 15]

Love throws his bow, and arrows on a bough
There hang my arms! To other sport let's go.
He to an ally hyes, as smooth as Ice
And with a scourge-sticks furnished in a tryce
But wants a Top*. He takes my Heart, and then
He whips it round, till It ev'n sings again.

---

* I.e. spinning top.

Epig. 5

Starv'd Mammes cast upon the dreary stage,
      To Savage Lions in their hungry rage,
The brutes abhor to touch so tender age.
      Pure Pity does their angry jaws assuage.
Whence so abstemious? Who'st them dismay?
      The Martyr taught it, and the beasts obey.

Note: Another version of the final verse:
His powerful doctrine t' was, which they obey.

Epig. 6

The Judge condemn'd thee to the greedy gripe*
Of Lions' paws: as thou wert not ripe.
They Civil were, and truly more humane
Their nat'rals† they unlearnt. In brave disdain
They scorn to prey upon a harmless child
Though th' horrid Judge forbade them to be mild:
Since Lions know the innocent to spare
They the right Judges, you the Lion are.

Epig. 11

The dying Lilies pray to heav'n for rain
And sun-burnt roses do for drink complain.
Love calls Favonius, and he pow'rs upon
The field, a florid resurrection.
Flow'rs Aromatic! which Olympus' dew
And Vesta's breath (refreshing winds) renew.

---

* I.e. grip.
† I.e. natural tendencies.

Sir Philip Wodehouse

Epig. 74 To Cæcilian.

[Epig. 74]

Thou singst of Ma'dlen's* tears, and Afra's fires
Thou sendst them fresh, my judgement thou requires
In brief take this. Thy Ma'dlen worthy tears,
Thy Afra worthy fires, to me appears.

Epigr. 16

[Epig. 16]

I Thirst! Thou cry'st: Water these rocks have none
My Eyes run rivers, drink thou these alone.

Epig. 64

[Epig. 64]

Quinct's buys a mule whose sight was wholly gone
Eye, that had none: and he had never a one.

Quintus a mule it stark blind did buy
The beast had none and he not half an eye

Note: Both variants cancelled in the MS.

From: Leeds University Library, Brotherton Collection, MS Lt 40. Published by kind permission of the Brotherton Collection, Leeds University Library.

---

* I.e. Magdalen (pronounced as two syllables).

Peter Paul Rubens's illustration for the title page of
Lyricorum libri IV, Antwerp 1632.

3

Sir John Denham

Sir John Denham (1615–1669) was a poet, translator (e.g. a part of the *Iliad* published as *The Destruction of Troy* in 1656, Cato's *De senectute* as *Cato Major of Old Age*, 1669), courtier and gambler, a fierce supporter of Charles I and the Royalist party. His literary career began with the tragedy *The Sophy* (1641) but he is most often remembered for his descriptive poem *Cooper's Hill* (1642), long considered as one of the most famous poems in the English language, and one which uses a descriptive technique adapted from Sarbiewski's ep. 1 (Urbański 2000: 190). Dr Johnson wrote that Denham was 'deservedly considered as one of the fathers of English poetry' (1779: 11) but he was quite critical of his actual achievement, an opinion which later generations of critics supported. Although nothing is known of his talents as an architect, immediately after the Restoration Sir John became the Surveyor of the Works, a post he inherited from Inigo Jones and left to Sir Christopher Wren. He was also elected MP for the most notorious rotten borough Old Sarum in 1661 and a Fellow of the Royal Society in 1663.

The following translation and another by John Hall of Durham (see chapter 9) come from *Lachrymae Musarum*, first published in London in 1649 and reprinted in 1650. It is a volume of 35 elegies by various authors in English and Latin commemorating the death of the nineteen year-old Henry Lord Hastings. The volume is remembered mostly because it includes the first published poem by John Dryden and one of the few works of Andrew Marvell published in his lifetime. Each of the two quoted elegies included in the volume opens with a passage paraphrased (without attribution) from Sarbiewski's ode 13 of the 4th book of lyrics, in both cases the rest of the poem does not resemble Sarbiewski's work.

An Elegie Upon the death of Lord Hastings.

[Lib. 4 Ode 13]

Reader, preserve thy peace: those busie eyes
Will weep at their own sad Discoveries;
When every line they adde, improves thy loss,
Till, having view'd the whole, they sum a Cross,
Such as derides thy Passions best relief,
And scorns the succours of thy easie Grief.

From: R[ichard] B[rome] (ed.), *Lachrymae Musarum: The Tears of the Muses; Exprest in Elegies; Written By divers persons of Nobility and Worth, Upon the death of the most hopefull Henry Lord Hastings ... Collected and set forth by R. B.*, London: Printed by T. N. and are to be sold at the blue Anchor in the New Exchange, 1650.

4

Richard Lovelace

Richard Lovelace (1618–1657) was a Metaphysical poet, playwright, and soldier; he was, and still is, considered the perfect Cavalier. At the age of sixteen he wrote his first play *The Scholar* (of which only the prologue and epilogue survive) staged at the Whitefriars Theatre. In 1639–1640 he took part in the Bishops' War against Scotland. His military experiences were the material for his second play *The Soldier*, never acted and now lost. In 1642, Lovelace was imprisoned when he presented a royalist petition to the House of Commons, at that time in open conflict with the King. When released, he went into exile, for a time fighting for the French against the Spaniards. Upon his return to England he was imprisoned again, and he used the opportunity to prepare for publication his only volume of poetry *Lucasta* (1649) in which, among others, his translation of Sarbiewski's Lyr. IV 13 was included. Susan A. Clarke (2005: 125) argues that the translation was written immediately after the battle of Carmarthen in 1644. If we accept her theory, this is the earliest English translation of any poem by Sarbiewski.

To his Dear Brother Colonel F. L. immoderately mourning my Brother's untimely Death at Carmarthen.
[Lyr. IV 13]

If Tears could wash the Ill away,
A Pearl for each wet bead I'd pay
But as dew'd Corn the fuller grows,
So water'd eyes but swell our Woes.

One drop another calls, which still
(Grief adding Fuel) doth distill;
Too fruitful of herself is Anguish,
We need no cherishing to Languish.

Coward Fate degen'rate Man
Like little children uses, when

He whips us first until we weep,
Then 'cause we still a-weeping keep.

Then from thy firm self never swerve;
Tears fat* the Grief that they should sterve†;
Iron decrees of Destiny
Are never wiped out with a wet Eye.

But this way you may gain the field.
Oppose but sorrow and 'twill yield;
One gallant thorough-made Resolve
Doth Starry Influence dissolve.

From: Richard Lovelace, *Lucasta: Epodes, Odes, Sonnets, Songs etc. to Which is Added a Aramantha, A Pastoral*, London: Thomas Harper 1649.

---

* I.e. fatten

† I.e. starve

5

Abraham Cowley

Abraham Cowley (1618–1667) was one of the most famous English poets of his age. He was a child prodigy; at the age of ten he wrote *Tragicall History of Piramus and Thisbe*, an epic romance in a six-line stanza. His first volume of poetry *Poetical Blossoms* was published in 1633. Cowley excelled in his classical studies, while in Cambridge he started an epic poem about king David in Latin (later completed in English as *Davideis*) as well as other Neo-Latin works such as *Sex Libri Plantarum* and the play *Naufragium Joculare*. His academic career was cut short by the Civil War and Cowley spent the most part of the Commonwealth period in exile with the Royal Family in Paris. It was there that he was first acquainted with the works of Pindar whom he translated into English (*Pindarique Odes* in his *Miscellanies*, 1656, among which the following unattributed translation first appeared). Cowley translated numerous Classical and Neo-Latin authors throughout his life (the translation presented below belongs to his early period); an interesting selection of excerpts from Anacreon, Claudian, Horace, Martial, Seneca, and Virgil was included in his last volume *Essays, in Verse and Prose* published posthumously in 1668. The popularity which Cowley enjoyed in his lifetime was eclipsed by that of Milton almost immediately after the former's demise, a fact which was sealed by Johnson's biography in *The Lives of the Poets*.

The Extasie

[Lyr. II 5]

I leave Mortality, and things below;
I have no time in Complements to waste,
        Farewell to ye all in haste,
        For I am called to go.
    A Whirlwind bears up my dull Feet,
    Th' officious Clouds beneath them meet.
        And (Lo!) I mount, and (Lo!)
How small the biggest Parts of Earth proud Title show!

Where shall I find the noble British Land?
Lo, I at last a Northern Spec espy,
        Which in the Sea does lie,
        And seems a Grain of th' Sand!
    For this will any sin, or Bleed?
    Of Civil Wars is this the Meed?
        And is it this, alas, which we
(Oh Irony of Words!) do call Great Britanie?

I pass by th' arched Magazines, which hold
Th' eternal stores of Frost, and Rain, and Snow;
        Dry, and secure I go,
        Nor shake with Fear, or Cold.
    Without affright or wonder
    I meet Clouds charged with Thunder,
        And Lightnings in my way
Like harmless Lambent Fires about my Temples play.

Now into a gentle Sea of rolling Flame
I'm plunged, and still mount higher there,
        As Flames mount up through air.
        So perfect, yet so tame,
    So great, so pure, so bright a fire
    Was that unfortunate desire,
        My faithful Breast did cover,
Then, when I was of late a wretched Mortal Lover.

Through several Orbs which one fair Planet bear,
Where I behold distinctly as I pass
        The hints of Galileo's Glass,
          I touch at last the spangled Sphere.
    Here all th' extended Sky
    Is but one Galaxy,
        'Tis all so bright and gay,
And the joint Eyes of Night make up a perfect Day.

Where am I now? Angels and God is here;
An unexhausted Ocean of delight
        Swallows my senses quite,
          And drowns all What, and How, or Where.
    Not Paul, who first did thither pass,
    And this great World's Columbus was,
        The tyrannous pleasure could express.
Oh 'tis too much for Man! But let it ne're be less.

The mighty Elijah mounted on so high,
That second Man, who leapt the Ditch where all
        The rest of Mankind fall,
          And went not downwards to the sky.
    With much of pomp and show
    (As Conquering Kings in Triumph go)
        Did he to Heav'n approach,
And wondrous was his Way, and wondrous was his Coach.

'Twas gaudy all and rich in every part,
Of essences of Gems, and Spirit of Gold
        Was its substantial mold;
          Drawn forth by Chymique Angels art.
    Here with Moon-beams 'twas silvered bright,
    There double-gilt with the Sun's light
        And mystique Shapes cut round in it,
Figures that did transcend a Vulgar Angels wit.

The Horses were of temper'd Lightning made,
Of all that in Heavens beauteous Pastures feed,
        The noblest, sprightful'st breed,
           And flaming Mains their Necks arrayed.
    They all were shod with Diamond,
    Not such as here are found,
        But such light solid ones as shine
On the Transparent Rocks o' th' Heaven Chrystalline.

Thus mounted the great Prophet to the skies;
Astonisht Men who oft had seen Stars fall,
        Or that which so they call,
           Wondered from hence to see one rise.
    The soft Clouds melted him a way,
    The Snow and Frosts which in it lay
        A while the sacred footsteps bore,
The Wheels and Horses Hoofs hizzed as they past them ore.

He past by th' Moon and Planets, and did fright
All the Worlds there which at this Meteor gazed,
        And their Astrologers amazed
        With th' unexampled sight.
    But where he stopt will ne're be known,
    Till Phoenix Nature aged grown
        To a better Being do aspire,
And mount herself, like Him, to Eternity in Fire.

From: *The Works of Mr. Abraham Cowley. Consisting of Those which were formerly Printed: And Those which he Design'd for the Press, Now Published out of the Authors Original Copies*, London: Printed by J.M. for Henry Herringman, at the Sign of the Blew Anchor in the Lower Walk of the New Exchange. 1668.

6

Sir Edward Sherburne

Sir Edward Sherburne (Sherborne) (1618–1702), a minor Metaphysical poet and translator. Sherburne took an active part in the Civil War supporting the King, he fought in the battle of Edgehill. Following the execution of Charles I in 1649, Sherburne retired to his relatives' country estates and it was there that he studied and translated French, Italian, and Neo-Latin poets. The result of this work was the volume of *Poems and Translations. Amorous, Lusory, Morall, Divine* (1651). In later years Sherburne translated also Classical authors such as Manilius (*Sphere of Marcus Manilius Made an English Poem*, 1675), Seneca (*Troades: or the Royal Captive*, 1679 and *Tragedies*, 1702) and Theocritus. As he was a royalist and converted to Roman Catholicism his fortune suffered in the turmoil of the latter half of the seventeenth century. The final years of his life were spent in relative poverty. Sherburne's original creation was rather small in size, and his poetry is not very highly esteemed.

On Captain Ansa, a bragging Run-away.
Casimire

[Epig. 54]

Whilst timorous Ansa led his Martial Band
'Gainst the Invaders of his Native Land,
Thus he bespake his Men before the Fight:
Courage my Mates, let's dine, for we tonight
Shall Sup (says he) in Heaven: this having said,
'Soon as the threatening Ensigns were displayed,
And the loud Drums and Trumpets had proclaimed
Defiance 'twixt the Hosts; he, (who ne'er shamed
At Loss of Honour) fairly ran away,
When being asked, how chance he would not stay
And go along with them to sup in Heaven?
Pardon me Friends (said he) I fast this Even.

Amphion, or a City well ordered.
Casimer

[Lyr. IV 36]

Foreign Customs from your Land,
Thebans by fair Laws command:
And your good old Rites make known
                Unto your own.

Piety your Temple grace;
Justice in your Courts have Place;
Truth, Peace, Love, in every Street
                Each other meet.

Banish Vice, Walls guard not Crimes.
Vengeance o'er tall Bulwarks climbs:
O'er each Sin, A Nemesis
                Still waking is.

Truth resembling craft, Profane
Thirst of Empire, and of Gain,
Luxury, and idle ease,
                Banish all these.

Private Parsimony fill
The Public Purse: Arms only Steel
Know, and no more: Valour fights cold
                In plundered Gold.

War, or Peace do you approve,
With united Forces move:
Courts which many Columns rear
                Their falls less fear.

Safer Course those Pilots run,
Who observe more Stars than One.
Ships with double Anchors tied
                Securer ride.

Strength united firm doth stand
Knit in an eternal Band:
But proud Subject's private hate
                Ruins a State.

This as good Amphion sings
To his Harp's well-tuned strings,
Its swift Streams clear Dirce stopped,
                Cytheron hopped,

Stones did leap about the Plains,
Rocks did skip to hear his Strains,
And the Groves the Hills did crown
                Came dancing down.

When he ceased, the Rocks and Wood
Like a Wall about him stood;
Whence fair Thebes, which seven Gates close
                Of Brass, arose.

To the Eternal Wisdom
Upon the Distraction of the Times

[Lyr. IV 28]

O Thou Eternal Mind! Whose Wisdom sees,
And rules our Changes by unchanged Decrees,
As with Delight on thy grave Works We look,
Say; art thou too with our light Follies took?
For when thy bounteous Hand, in liberal Showers
Each where diffused, thy various Blessing powers.*
We catch at them with strife as vain to sight,
As Children, when for Nuts they scrambling, fight.
This snatching at a Sceptre breaks it; He,
That broken does e're he can grasp it see.
The poor World seeming like a Ball, that lights
Betwixt the hands of Pow'rful Opposites:

---

* I.e. pours.

Which while they cantonize in their bold Pride,
They but an Immaterial Point divide.
O whilst for Wealthy Spoils these fight, let Me,
Though poor, enjoy a happy Peace with Thee.

Draw Me, and I will follow Thee

[Epig. 14]

Through devious Paths, without thee, Lord! I run,
And soon, without Thee, will my Race be done.
Happy was Magdalen, who like a Bride,
Herself to Thee by her fair Tresses tied.
So she thy Presence never did decline,
Thou her dear Captive wert, and she was Thine.
Behold another Magdalen in Me!
Then stay with Me, or draw me after Thee.

If a Man should give all the substance of his House for Love, he would value it as nothing. **Cant. 8.**

[Epig. 2]

Love I'd of Heaven have bought; when He, (this who
Would think?) both Purchase was, and Seller too.
I offered Gold; but Gold he did not prize.
I offered Gems; but Gems he did despise.
I offered All; All he refused yet: why,
If All won't take, take what is left, said I.
At this he smiled, and said; in vain divine
Love's Price thou beat'st; give nothing and she's thine.

Mary Magdalen weeping under the Cross

[Epig. 16]

I thirst, my dear, and dying Saviour cries:
These Hills are dry: O drink then from my Eyes.

The Message

[Epig. 18]

Dear Saviour! that my Love I might make known
To thee, I sent more Messengers than one.
My heart went first, but came not back; My Will
I sent thee next, and that stayed with thee still.
Then, that the better thou might'st know my Mind,
I sent thee Int'lect; that too stays behind.
Now my Soul's sent: Lord! if that stay with thee,
O what a happy Carcass shall I be!

From: *Poems and Translations. Amorous, Lusory, Morall, Divine: By Edward Sherburne Esq.*, London: Printed by W. Hunt, for Thomas Dring, at the Sign of the George, near Cliffords-Inn in Fleetstreet. 1651.

7

Lucy Hutchinson

Lucy Hutchinson (1620–1681) was a biographer, poet, and translator. She was a Puritan, her husband John was a colonel in the service of the Commonwealth. Hutchinson left both original works (mostly religious poetry), translations from Latin (she was the first English translator of the complete text of Lucretius' *De rerum natura* published 1996), and memoirs such as *Memoirs of the Life of Colonel Hutchinson* (published 1806). It is only in recent times that Hutchinson has started to enjoy the appreciation she deserves. In her lifetime her greatly varied and interesting oeuvre was known only to her relatives and friends except for the anonymously published biblical epic poem *Order and Disorder* (five cantos 1679, the whole text 2001). Hutchinson's manuscripts have not been fully researched yet, it is possible that she translated more poems of Sarbiewski.

Casimiri Epig. Lib. Unus. Ep. XXXIV
Love is strong as Death. Can. 8.6.

[Epigr. 34]

Once Love and Death about their triumphs strove
Death brought his quiver forth and so did Love
All bodies fall (sayd Death) by my sure darts
My flaming shafts (sayd Love) doe vanquish hearts
My victory greater is (sayd Death) than thine
Yet is (sayd Love) thy glory lesse than mine
Darts had persued but that God umpiring sayd
Both equall Victors were, both vanquished.

From: Lucy Hutchinson *Commonplace Book* in Hutchinson Manuscripts in the Nottinghamshire Record Office (ref: DD/HU/1). Published by kind permission of Nottinghamshire County Archives.

8

Henry Vaughan

Henry Vaughan (1621–1695), poet, writer and translator of devotional works, the twin brother of Thomas Vaughan (1621–1666), the alchemist and hermetic philosopher. Henry Vaughan did not excel in his early life. He probably studied at Oxford (data inconclusive) but soon moved to London in order to study law. This attempt ended quickly when the Civil War broke out, Henry joined the royalist army and fought in the battle of Rowton Heath (1645). After the King's defeat Vaughan returned permanently to his native Wales where he began to practice quite successfully as a doctor although he had neither studied medicine nor claimed to have done so. His first volume of poetry, *Poems, with the Tenth Satire of Juvenal Englished*, appeared in 1646, the second, *Silex Scintillans* followed in 1650, *Olor Iscanus* in 1651 (from which the following selection of translations from Sarbiewski is taken), and a new enlarged edition of *Silex* appeared in 1655. His last volume of poems, *Thalia Rediviva* (1678), was published after a volume of prose and devotional meditations, and offered a selection of less interesting verse. Vaughan's poetry reveals his interest in the occult, which so much fascinated his twin brother. His poetry may not be as accomplished technically as that of some of his contemporaries yet his visions of the world and nature are unique (and they may have influenced William Wordsworth's poetry). His translations published in *Olor Iscanus* include works by Juvenal, Ovid, Boethius, and Horace. Their common theme is that of banishment or retirement, suggesting that they should be read, including the following translations from Sarbiewski, as a poignant political statement in the days immediately following the defeat of the royalists and execution of Charles I.

Casimirus, Lib. 4. Ode 28.

[Lyr. IV 28]

Almighty Spirit! Thou that by
Set turns and changes from thy high
And glorious throne, dost here below
Rule all, and all things dost foreknow;
Can those blind plots we here discuss
Please thee, as thy wise Counsels us?
When thou thy blessings here dost strow,
And pour on Earth, we flock and flow
With Joyous strife, and eager care
Struggling which shall have the best share
In thy rich gifts, just as we see
Children about Nuts disagree.
Some that a Crown have got and foiled
Break it; Another sees it spoiled
E're it is gotten: Thus the world
Is all to piece-meals cut, and hurled
By factious hands, It is a ball
Which Fate and force divide 'twixt all
The Sons of men. But o good God!
While these for dust fight, and a Clod,
Grant that poor I may smile, and be
At rest, and perfect peace with thee.

Casimirus, Lib. 2. Ode 8.

[Lyr. II 8]

It would less vex distressed man
If Fortune in the same pace ran
To ruin him, as he did rise;
But highest states fall in a trice.
No great Success held ever long:
A restless fate afflicts the throng
Of Kings and Commons, and less days
Serve to destroy them, then to raise.
Good luck smiles once an age, but bad
Makes Kingdoms in a minute sad,
And every hour of life we drive,
Has o're us a Prerogative.

Then leave (by wild Impatience driv'n
And rash resents,) to rail at heav'n,
Leave us unmanly, weak complaint
That Death and Fate have no restraint.
In the same hour that gave thee breath,
Thou hadst ordained thy hour of death,
But he lives most, who here will buy
With a few tears, Eternity.

Casimirus, Lib. 3. Ode 22.

[Lyr. III 22]

Let not thy youth and false delights
Cheat thee of life; Those heady flights
But waste thy life, which posts away
Like winds unseen, and swift as they.
Beauty is but mere paint, whose die
With time's breath will dissolve and fly,
'Tis wax, 'tis water, 'tis a glass
It melts, it breaks, and away does pass
'Tis like a Rose which in the dawn
The air with gentle breath doth fawn
And whisper too, but in the hours
Of night is sullied with smart showers.
Life spent, is wished for but in vain,
Nor can past years come back again.
  Happy the Man! Who in this vale
Redeems his time, shutting out all
Thoughts of the world, whose longing Eyes
Are ever Pilgrims in the skies,
That views his bright home, and desires
To shine amongst those glorious fires.

Casimirus Lyric. Lib. 3. Ode 23.

[Lyr. III 23]

'Tis not rich furniture and gems
With Cedar-roofs, and ancient stems,
Nor yet a plenteous, lasting flood
Of gold, that makes man truly good.

Leave to Inquire in what fair fields
A River runs which much gold yields,
Virtue alone is the rich prize
Can purchase stars, and buy the skies.
Let others build with Adamant,
Or pillars of carved Marble plant,
Which rude and rough sometimes did dwell
Far under earth, and near to hell.
But richer much (from death released)
Shines in the fresh groves of the East
The Phoenix, or those fish that dwell
With silvered scales in Hiddekel.
Let others with rare, various Pearls
Their garments dress, and in forced Curls
Bind up their locks, look big and high,
And shine in robes of Scarlet-die.
But in my thoughts more glorious far
Those native stars, and speckles are
Which birds wear, or the spots which we
In Leopards dispersed see.
The harmless sheep with her warm fleece
Clothes man, but who his dark heart sees
Shall find a Wolf or Fox within
That kills the Castor for his skin.
Virtue alone, and naught else can
A difference make 'twixt beasts and man,
And on her wings above the spheres
To the true light his spirit bears.

Casimirus, Lib. 4. Ode 15.

[Lyr. IV 15]

Nothing on Earth, nothing at all
Can be exempted from the thrall
Of peevish weariness! The Sun
Which our forefathers Judged to run
Clear and unspotted, in our days
Is taxed with sullen, Eclipsed rays.
Whatever in the glorious sky
Man sees, his rash, audacious Eye

Dares Censure it, and in mere spite
At distance will condemn the light.
The wholesome mornings, whose beams clear
Those hills our fathers walked on here
We fancy not, nor the Moon's light
Which through their windows shined at night,
We change the Air each year, and scorn
Those Seats, in which we first were born.
Some nice, affected wand'rers love
Belgia's mild winters, other remove
For want of health and honesty
To Summer it in Italy;
But to no end: The disease still
Sticks to his Lord, and kindly will
To Venice in a Barge repair,
Or Coach it to Vienna's air,
And then (too late with home Content,)
They leave this willful banishment.
   But he, whose Constancy makes sure
His mind and mansion, lives secure
From such vain tasks, can dine and sup
Where his old parents bred him up.
Content (no doubt!) most time doth dwell
In Country-shades, or to some Cell
Confines itself, and can alone
Make simple straw, a Royal Throne.

Casimirus, Lib. 4. Ode 13.

[Lyr. IV 13]

If weeping Eyes could wash away
Those Evils they mourn for night and day,
Then gladly I to cure my fears
With my best Jewels would buy tears.
But as dew feeds the growing Corn,
So Crosses that are grown forlorn
Increase with grief, tears make tears way,
And cares kept up, keep cares in pay.
That wretch whom Fortune finds to fear,
And melting still into a tear,

She strikes more boldly, but a face
Silent and dry doth her amaze.
Then leave thy tears, and tedious tale
Of what thou doest misfortunes call,
What thou by weeping think'st to ease,
Doth by that Passion but Increase;
Hard things to Soft will never yield,
'Tis the dry Eye that wins the field;
A noble patience quells the spite
Of Fortune, and disarms her quite.

**The Praise of a Religious Life by Mathias Casimirus.
In Answer to that Ode of Horace,**
Beatus Ille qui procul negotiis, etc.

[Ep. 3]

Flaccus not so: That worldly He
Whom in the Country's shade we see
Ploughing his own fields, seldom can
Be justly stilled, The Blessed man.
      That title only fits a Saint,
Whose free thoughts far above restraint
And weighty Cares, can gladly part
With house and lands, and leave the smart
Litigious troubles and loud strife
Of this world for a better life.
He fears no Cold, nor heat to blst
His Corn, for his Accounts are cast,
He sues no man, nor stands in Awe
Of the devouring Courts of Law;
But all his time he spends in tears
For the Sins of his youthful years,
Or having tasted those rich Joys
Of a Conscience without noise
Sits in some fair shade, and doth give
To his wild thoughts rules how to live.
      He in the Evening, when on high
The Stars shine in the silent sky
Beholds th' eternal flames with mirth,
And globes of light more large than Earth,

Then weeps for Joy, and through his tears
Looks on the fire-enameled Spheres,
Where with his Savior he would be
Lifted above mortality.
Meanwhile the golden stars do set,
And the slow Pilgrim leave all wet
With his own tears, which flow so fast
They make his sleeps light, and soon past.
By this, the Sun o're night deceast
Breaks in fresh Blushes from the East,
When mindful of his former falls
With strong Cries to his God he calls,
And with such deep-drawn sighs doth move
That he turns anger into love.
      In the Calm Spring, when the Earth bears,
And feeds on April's breath, and tears,
His eyes accustomed to the skies
Find here fresh objects, and like spies
Or busy Bees search the soft flowers
Contemplate the green fields, and Bowers,
Where he in Veils, and shades doth see
The back Parts of the Deity.
Then sadly sighing says, 'O how
'These flowers with hasty, stretched heads grow
'And strive for heaven, but rooted here
'Lament the distance with a tear!
'The Honey-suckles Clad in white,
'The Rose in Red point to the light,
'And the Lilies hollow and bleak
'Look, as if they would something speak,
'They sigh at night to each soft gale,
'And at the day-spring weep it all.
'Shall I then only (wretched I!)
'Oppressed with Earth, on Earth still lie?'
Thus speaks he to the neighbour trees
And many sad Soliloquies
To Springs, and Fountains does impart,
Seeking God with a longing heart.
      But if to ease his busy breast
He thinks of home, and taking rest

A Rural Cot, and Common fare
Are all his Cordials against Care.
There at the door of his low Cell
Under some shade, or near some well
Where the Cool Poplar grows, his Plate
Of Common Earth, without more state
Expect their Lord. Salt in a shell,
Green cheese, thin beer, Draughts that will tell
No tales, a hospitable Cup,
With some fresh berries do make up
His healthful feast, nor doth he wish
For the fat Carp, or a rare dish
Of Lucrine Oysters; The swift Quist*
Or Pigeon sometimes (if he list)
With the slow Goose that loves the stream,
Fresh, various Salads, and the Bean
By Curious Palates never sought,
And to Close with, some Cheap unbought
Dish for digestion, are the most
And Choicest dainties he can boast.
      Thus feasted, to the flow'ry Groves,
Or pleasant Rivers he removes,
Where near some fair Oak hung with Mast
He shuns the South's Infectious blast.
On shady banks sometimes he lies,
Sometimes the open Current tries,
Where with his line and feathered fly
He sports, and takes the scaly fry.
Meanwhile each hollow wood and hill
Doth ring with lowings long and shrill,
And shady Lakes with Rivers deep,
Echo the bleating of the Sheep.
The blackbird with the pleasant Thrush
And Nightingale in every Bush
Choice Music give, and Shepherds play
Unto their flocks some loving Lay;
The thirsty Reapers in thick throngs

---

* I.e. ring-dove.

Return home from the field with Songs,
And the Carts laden with ripe Corn
Come groaning to the well-stored Barn.
     Nor pass we by as the least good,
A peaceful, loving neighbourhood,
Whose honest Wit, and Chaste discourse
Make none (by hearing it) the worse,
But Innocent and merry may
Help (without Sin) to spend the day.
Could now the Tyrant-usurer
Who plots to be a Purchaser
Of his poor neighbour's seat, but taste
These true delights, o with what haste
And hatred of his ways would he
Renounce his Jewish Cruelty,
And those Cursed sums which poor men borrow
On use today, remit tomorrow!

From: *Olor Iscanus. A Collection of Some Select Poems and Translations, Formerly written by Mr. Henry Vaughan Siluris. Published by a Friend*, London: Printed by T.W. for Humphrey Moseley, and are to be sold at his shop, at the Signe of the Prince's Arms in St. Paul's Churchyard, 1651.

9

John Hall of Durham

John Hall of Durham (1627–1656) was a minor Caroline poet and translator, the author of numerous short poems included in such volumes as *Poems* (1646) and translations such as *The Height of Eloquence* by Longinus. The following translation, just like that by Sir John Denham, quoted in Chapter 3, is a fragment of a much longer elegiac poem included in the volume *Lachrymae Musarum* first published in 1649.

To the Earl of Huntingdon, On the death of his Son.
                                                                    [Lib. 4 Ode 13]
Could any Tears our Miseries remove,
Redeem our Losses, or assuage our Love,
Blest were you, though you paid for ev'ry Tear
As rich a Jewel as the West can bear,
And did, for ev'ry Sigh or Groan, dispense
An od'rous Tempest of Masle Frankincense.
But these impossible Wishes cannot finde
A place; and are but scattered by the Winde.

From: B[rome], R[ichard] (ed.), *Lachrymae Musarum: The Tears of the Muses; Exprest in Elegies; Written By divers persons of Nobility and Worth, Upon the death of the most hopefull Henry Lord Hastings ... Collected and set forth by R.B.*, London: Printed by T.N. and are to be sold at the blue Anchor in the New Exchange, 1650.

10

Lady Mary Chudleigh

Lady Mary Chudleigh (*née* Lee) (1656–1710) poet and essayist, was engaged in literary pursuits from her early childhood. She enjoyed the friendship of numerous important literary personalities of her age, most notably that of John Dryden and John Norris. She was also a friend of several other writing ladies such as Mary Astell and Elisabeth Thomas with whom she exchanged letters and to whom she often dedicated her poems. Although she was a frequent visitor to London, most of her life was spent near Exeter. The published œuvre of Chudleigh is relatively small and includes two collections: *Poems on Several Occasions* (1703), reprinted repeatedly during the next five decades, and *Essays upon Several Subjects in Prose and Verse* (1710), as well as a long verse dialogue, *The Ladies Defence*, published separately in 1701. She felt at home in a variety of Restoration literary forms, from lyric to satiric dialogues and odes. Her favourite subjects were ironically-presented pitfalls of love and marriage. According to family memoirs, apart from the published works, Chudleigh also wrote two tragedies, two operas, a masque, Lucian's dialogues put into verse, and other small poems, yet the manuscripts have apparently been lost to us. Her works are an ample testimony to her interest in classical literature which she probably read in translation. The following translations from Sarbiewski represent some of the very few translated works in her known œuvre.

The Elevation

[Lyr. II 5]

O how ambitious is my Soul,
    How high she now aspires!
There's nothing can on Earth control,
    Or limit her desires.

Upon the Wings of Thought she flies
    Above the reach of Sight,
And finds a way through pathless Skies
    To everlasting Light:

From whence with blameless Scorn she views
    The Follies of Mankind;
And smiles to see how each pursues
    Joys fleeting as the Wind.

Yonder's the little Ball of Earth,
    It lessens as I rise;
The Stage of transitory Mirth,
    Of lasting Miseries:

My Scorn does into Pity turn,
    And I lament the Fate
Of Souls, that still in Bodies mourn,
    For Faults which they create.

Souls without Spot, till Flesh they wear,
    Which their pure Substance stains:
While they th' uneasy Burden bear,
    They're never free from Pains.

The Happy Man

[Ep. 3]

He is the happy Man whose constant Mind
Is to th' Enjoyment of himself confined:
Who has within laid up a plenteous Store,
And is so rich that he desires no more:

Whose Soul is always easy, firm, and brave,
And much too great to be Ambition's Slave:
Who Fortune's Frowns without Concern can bear,
And thinks it less to suffer, than to fear:
Who, still the same, keeps up his native State,
Unmoved at all the Menaces of Fate:
Who all his Passions absolutely sways,
And to his Reason cheerful Homage pays,
Who's with a Halcyon Calmness ever blest,
With inward Joy, untroubled Peace, and Rest:
Who while the Most with Toil, with Guilt, and Heat,
Lose their dear Quiet to be Rich and Great,
Both Business, and disturbing Crowds does shun,
Pleased that his Work is with less Trouble done:
To whom a Grove, a Garden, or a Field,
Much greater, much sublimer Pleasure yield,
Than they can find in all the Charms of Power,
Those splendid Ills which so much Time devour:
Who more than Life, his Friends and Books can prize,
And for those Joys the noisy World despise:
Who when Death calls, no Weakness does betray,
Nor to an unbecoming Fear give way;
But to himself, and to his Maxims true,
Lies smiling down, and bids Mankind adieu.

The Song of the Three Children.
Paraphras'd Casimir II 5

[Lyr. II 5]

Ascend my Soul, and in a speedy Flight
Haste to the Regions of eternal Light;
Look all around, each dazzling Wonder view,
And thy Acquaintance with past Joys renew.
Through all th' Ethereal Plain extend thy Sight,
    On every pleasing Object gaze;
      On rolling World below,
    On Orbs which Light and heat bestow:
And thence to their first Cause their Admiration raise
In sprightly Airs, and sweet harmonious Lays.

Assist me, all ye Works of Art Divine,
Ye wondrous Products of Almighty Pow'r,
    You who in lofty Stations shine,
And to your glorious Source by glad Approaches tow'r:
    In your bright Orders all appear;
    With me your grateful Tribute pay,
Before his Throne your joint devotions lay.
Ye charming Offsprings of the Earth draw near,
And for your Beauties pay your Homage here,
    Let all above, and all below,
All that from unexhausted Bounty flow,
    To Heav'n their joyful Voices raise,
    In a melodious Hymn of Praise.
When Time shall cease, and each revolving Year,
Lost in Eternity shall disappear,
The blest Employment ever shall remain,
And God be sung in each immortal Strain.

Note: The complete paraphrase consists of 90 parts, only the first of which bears similarity to Sarbiewski's Lyr. II 5.

From: *Poems on Several Occasions. Together with the Song of the Three Children Paraphras'd. By Lady Mary Chudleigh,* London: Printed by W.B. for Bernard Lincott and the Middle Temple Gate in Fleetstreet. 1703.

11

John Norris

John Norris (1657–1711) was a philosopher and poet. Educated at Winchester College and Exeter College, Oxford, he was appointed a fellow of All Souls in 1680. In 1689, Norris married and left Oxford, choosing the life of a country parson. He spent the rest of his life with his family, first in Newton St. Loe, Somerset, and from 1692 on in Bemerton, Wiltshire (once the benefice of the poet George Herbert). Norris was a Cartesian Platonist and mystic which made him oppose the philosophy of his contemporary John Locke, once a personal friend. His philosophical works include *An Idea of Happiness* (1683), *Theory and Regulation of Love* (1688), and *Discourse concerning the Immortality of the Soul* (1708). His original poetry and translations were included in *Collection of Miscellanies, consisting of Poems, Essays, Discourses and Letters* (1687) after which year he wrote only two more poems. The volume gained some popularity, reaching nine editions in the following four decades. As was sometimes his custom, Norris supplemented the following translation with lengthy 'Annotations' in which he explains his design in detail.

The Elevation

[Lyr. II 5]

Take wing (my Soul) and upwards bend thy flight
To thy originary Fields of Light.
    Here's nothing, nothing here below
    That can deserve thy longer stay;
    A secret whisper bids thee go
To purer Air, and Beams of native Day.
Th' ambition of the tow'ring Lark out-vy,
And like him sing as thou dost upward fly.

How all things lessen which my Soul before
Did with the grovelling Multitude adore!
               Those Pageant Glories disappear,
                 Which charm and dazzle mortals' Eyes.
               How do I in this higher Sphere,
How do I mortals, with their Joys despise!
Pure, uncorrupted Element I breathe,
And pity their gross Atmosphere beneath.

How vile, how sordid here those Trifles show,
That please the Tenants of that ball below!
               But ha, I've lost the little sight,
                 The Scene's remov'd, and all I see
                 Is one confused dark mass of Night.
What nothing was, now nothing seems to be:
How calm this Region, how serene, how clear!
Sure I some strains of Heavenly Music hear.

On, on, the task is easy now and light,
No steams of Earth can here retard thy flight.
               Thou needst not now thy strokes renew,
                 'Tis but to spread thy Pinions wide
                 And thou with ease thy seat wilt view,
Drawn by the Bent of the Ethereal tide.
'Tis so I find; How sweetly on I move,
Not let by things below, and help'd by those above!

But see, to what new Region am I come?
I know it well, it is my native home.
               Here led I once a life divine
                 Which did all good, no evil know,
                 Ah who would such sweet bliss resign
For those vain shows which Fools admire below?
'Tis true, but don't of Folly past complain,
But joy to see these blest abodes again.

A good retrieve: But lo, while thus I speak
With piercing rays th' eternal day does break.
> The Beauties of the face divine
> Strike strongly on my feeble sight:
> With what bright glories does it shine!
'Tis one immense and ever-flowing Light.
Stop here, my Soul; thou canst not bear more Bliss,
Nor can thy now rais'd Palate ever relish less.

From: John Norris, *A Collection of Miscellanies: Consisting of Poems, Essays, Discourses and Occasionally Written. By John Norris, M.A. and Fellow of All-Souls College in Oxford*, Oxford: Printed at the Theater For John Crossey Bookseller, 1687.

12

Thomas Brown

Thomas Brown (1662–1704) was a professional writer, author of poems, satires, translations, dramas, and works in prose. After some years spent as headmaster of the free school at Kingston upon Thames, Brown moved to London to live by his pen. He left an impressive and various body of work that is, however, of very uneven quality. Remembered now mainly for his witty political satires, Brown wrote three stage plays (e.g. *The Dispensary*, 1697) and a large number of essays. A lifelong friend of Aphra Behn, Brown assisted in her literary career. He translated copiously from Latin and Greek, French, Italian, and Spanish. The list of the translated authors includes, among others, Catullus, Cicero, Horace, Martial, Persius, Pliny, Petronius, and Lucian. In his lifetime he published only one volume of poetry, *Miscellany Poems* (1699). His *Works* were published posthumously in four volumes between 1707 and 1711. The following translation first appeared in *Miscellany Poems and Translations by Oxford Hands* in 1685 and it was probably Brown's literary debut.

Casimire, Ode 23. Book 4.
To the Grasshopper

[Lyr. IV 23]

  Blest Epicure of Race Divine,
  Who, drunk with Heaven's dewy Wine,
  On some cool shady Tree dost sit,
  And sing upon the top of it;
Whilst with the cheerful Music of thy Voice
Thou mak'st thyself, and silent Woods rejoice.

Now since the tedious Winter's past,
And welcome Summer's come at last
(Which with swift Wheels still hurries on,
And still is eager to be gone)
Chide the Sun's haste, with mirth the day prolong,
Make Phoebus stop his course to hear thy Song.

As the most happy glorious day
Just brings itself, and shows us joy;
So bliss but smiles on us, and then
Snatches itself away again:
Our empty joys too fleeting still appear,
But solid griefs too long and tedious are.

From: *Miscellany Poems and Translations by Oxford Hands*, London: Printed for Anthony Stephens, Bookseller near Theatre in Oxford, 1685.

Note: The volume includes also a translation of Sarbiewski Lyr. IV 25 signed T.B. It is impossible, however, to state with any finality whether it is the work of Thomas Brown or Dr T. Blow who is also listed among the authors. This poem was not included in Brown's *Works*, consequently, it is included here in Chapter 14 among other anonymous translations from the volume.

13

John Chatwin

John Chatwin (c. 1667 – after 1685) was a poet and student of Emmanuel College, Cambridge (BA 1685). Although only one of Chatwin's poems saw publication in his lifetime, over two hundred pages of his verse survive in manuscript. The following two translations from Sarbiewski were found in MS. Rawl. poet. 94 in the Bodleian Library, University of Oxford. The volume was written in about 1682–1685 by John Chatwin and includes an impressive selection of poems written and translated by the author. Among those one finds also the translation of a laudatory poem addressed to Casimire entitled 'On a Nightingale that died betwixt the Strings of a Lyre, translated from a Poem to Casimirus', a further testimony to Chatwin's interest in the works of Sarbiewski.

Ad Rosam
The eighteenth Ode of the Last Book of the Lyricks
of Casimirus
On the Virgin Mary's Annual Coronation

[Lyr. IV 18]

Thou Glorious Rivall of the Sky,
Why in Night's bed dost thou still lye?
Lift up thy head, thou queen of flow'rs,
Gay daughter of celestial pow'rs!
Now no wat'rish clouds appear,
Gentle zephyrs calm the air;
Now the Western Gales do play,
And the Northern Blasts allay.
Arise! But ask not whose bright Face,
Or Hair thy native Beam may grace;
The Lewd, Lascivious, and Prophane
May glory from thy Beauties gain,
Thou sacred Trophy of chaste Love,
Thou Wealth of Vertue fixt Above!

Forbour* the vulgar heads t' adorn,
For Shrines and Altars Thou art born;
The Blessed Virgin's Hair, now unconfin'd,
Which sports with easy soft obsequious Wind,
Thy gay Perfumes, and youthful Leaves shall bind.

In Imitation of the 23rd Ode of the 4th Book of Casimirus Ad Cicadam

[Lyr. IV 23]

Thrice happy Thou! Who on the Poplar's Boughs,
    Sit'st drunk with Heav'n's Ambrosial Dews.
    And with thy Notes thyself, dost please,
And all the num'rous Throng of list'ning Trees.

After long Colds and odious Winters past,
    On nimble Wheels the Summers hast;
    Blame its unkindness, gently say –
The Sun too soon withdraws his chearing Ray.

As ev'ry happy Day itself does show,
    So in a trice it leaves us too,
    No pleasure over long remains
For short-liv'd joyes We meet with lasting pains.

From: MS Rawl. poet 94, fols. 57–59 and 223–226 by kind permission of the Bodleian Library, University of Oxford.

---

* I.e. forbear.

14

"Oxford Hands"

The following poems were included in a collection entitled *Miscellany Poems and Translations by Oxford Hands* printed in London for Anthony Stephens, a bookseller and publisher from Oxford, in 1685. It was one of several such collections appearing in the late seventeenth and the eighteenth century. This volume of over two hundred pages includes a vast selection of translations from various mostly Classical Latin authors such as Catullus, Horace, Martial, Petronius, Persius, and Claudian, as well as a variety of original compositions. The authors and translators such as Francis Willis, Dr T. Blow, Thomas Brown, whose translation is presented in chapter 12, J. Glanvil, and Humphrey Hody were students and fellows of Oxford colleges. Many of the poems included are signed only with initials or as 'anonymous'. Such is the case with most of the following poems, only one of which may be ascribed to an author.

Ode the 18th Book the 4th of Casimire Pariphrastically Translated.
The Rose with which he vow'd to Crown the Virgin Mary with every June.

[Lyr. IV 18]

Fair Rose, whom joyful Heaven does beget
    With seminal showr's, and Bridegroom heat
    Whose shining leaves so flaming are.
    Thou seem'st thyself a very Star;
Spring from Earth's Womb, thy lovely head display,
And blush from thy bright East a Purple day.

To welcome thee ev'n Nature now does gild
    With glittering Pride, each Bush and Field.
    Soft Gales from Heav'n black Clouds do chase,
    And Golden Smiles sit on its face.
The Winter's rage grows calm, and flies away;
The West-winds sport, and clap their wing for Joy.

Spring gentle Flow'r; and ask not whose bright Hair
    Shall thy gay, comely Honours wear:
    For thou whose blush speaks thee to be
    The Child of Virgin Modesty,
Ought'st not alas! thy Beauties to bestow,
On any common, or unhallow'd Brow.

Then Crown no more the prophane Vulgar's Head,
    Thou'rt fit to be on Altars laid.
    See how the sacred Virgins Hair
    Flows loosely thro' the flowing Air;
She sues by thy rich Purple to be Crown'd,
By thee she longs to have her Temples bound.

Out of Casimire
To Quintus Tiberinus
Ode the 34th Book the 4th.

[Lyr. IV 34]

No – never think him truly rich, or great,
    Whose fertile soil and large Estate
    Far more luxurious Crops, and Harvests yields
    Then the most fruitful Eastern Fields;
Tho' Fortune with rich Tides his Land o'reflows,
And Golden Seeds for Grain in his bright Furrow sows.

    Nor him whose Birth, whose Arms, and Father's Name,
    Have made the Heir to wealth, and fame.
    Whom Glory in her Chariot glittering bright
    With Golden rays, and gemmy light,
    Has born in Pomp, and a Triumphant shew,
Thro' wond'ring cities, & all earth's vast kingdoms too.

    He's poor that wants himself, who proud to weigh
    Himself against his Vanity,
    He with his Titles, ponderous Baggs and all
    His massy Gold can't turn the Scale;
    And tho' he adds his Lands, and whole Estate
In his own lighter Scale, he can't make up the weight.

He scarcely knows himself, and he seems great
    Only in his own vain conceit;
Who, being puffed up with the false esteem
    The Giddy crowd bestows on him,
Wonders to see his Size so monstrous made,
In the Gigantic bulk of his own stalking shade.

Let no false glittering treasure cheat thy sight,
    With its deluding foolish light;
Scorn swelling Titles without solid praise,
    Which nothing but Ambition raise.
Like Boys' thin Bubbles for a while they fly,
    They shine, look big, then burst and die.
Get thou true Wealth from Virtues of thy own,
And learn thou to be Happy from thyself alone.

Casimire Ode the 25th Book the fourth.
A Dialogue between the Child Jesus and the Virgin-Mother, taken partly out of the First, Fourth, Fifth, Sixth and Seventh Chapters of the Canticles.

[Lyr. IV 25]

Child

O Virgin-Mother! fairer to behold
    Then Stars Heav'ns glittering Diamonds are,
More glorious then refulgent rays of Gold,
    More bright more clear than Crystal far,
More pleasing then rich Scarlet to the sight,
More fair then Lilies clod in Virgin white.

Virgin

Dear Child, then Purple Hesperus more clear,
    More shining then the Midnight Moon,
Lovelier then Meadows that Spring's Livery wear,
    More radiant then the Sun at noon:
A Sea of Milk does all thy Limbs o'reflow,
And thou'rt more pure then Beds of Winter Snow.

Child
Your sparkling eyes two Silver streams surpass,
    That near to Essebon do stray,
Which when they long have bubbl'd o're the grass,
    And sported long in wanton play,
Wonder to find their wand'ring Streams supprest,
To bounds confin'd, and husht in calms of rest.

Virgin
Your shining Eyes as clear, and spotless look
    As two white Doves in Milk washt o're,
Which sit upon the Bank of some fair Brook,
    Or some transparent Rivers shore:
Yet from those Balls of Snow bright flashes fly,
More swift then Lightning darted from the Sky.

Child
Your comely Locks with circling glories deck
    The shaded Beauties of your Face,
They add new whiteness to your snowy Neck,
    And with loose pride your Shoulders grace;
Like Gilead's new-washt Fleeces they appear,
But they with Sun-beams gilt are not so fair.

Virgin
As some green Palm about whose flourishing head,
    Its verdant leaves for hair does grow,
So round your Cheeks your golden Tresses spread,
    And down in Waves of Curls they flow;
Like Ravens wings they shine which glisten bright,
And cast a lustre from their very night.

Child
As from the Comb the Honey drops distil,
    So from your Lips words gently fall,
With golden sweets the ravisht Ear they fill,
    And show'r down blessings upon all;
Or like Bride's long veil loos't from her hair,
They dance and revel in the sportive air.

Virgin
Within your mouth soft Accents gently glide,
    And in swoll'n tides of Nectar swim,
Like generous Wine in a charg'd Bowls full tide,
    Which sparkling bright o'relooks the brim.
Your words are like fair Lilies when made wet,
And all with liquid gems of Dew beset.

Child
Your two white Breasts may with twin-Roes compare,
    That in sweet beds of Flowers stray;
And feeding on the Lilies, wanton there
    'Till night shuts in declining day;
Which now grown old, weary and panting lies,
And all its vital flames extinguisht, dies.

Virgin
Your Breasts more bright then purple Clusters show,
    Clusters that fruitful Cyprus bears,
Or those that Engaddus Vineyards grow,
    When crown'd with Grapes its head appears:
Those bunches of soft gems that load the Vine,
Are not so beauteous as those Breasts of thine.

Child
Who looks upon your Cheeks may see,
    Such various lively colours spread
As blushing Apples show upon the tree,
    All painted gay with streaks of red:
But in your Breast there heav'nly Beauties lie,
Too glorious to be seen by Mortal Eye.

Virgin
Who sees your face with wonder there shall view
    Borders of Flowers in order stand;
Here Roses blow and palefac'd Lilies too,
    All set by artful Nature's hand:
And he that choicest Flow'rs, or Spices seeks,
May have them in the Flowrets of your Cheeks.

Child
Who loves not thee his monstrous Breast has fill'd
    With more inhumane cruelty
Then the most salvage woods and deserts yield,
    Where Beasts on blood and slaughter prey:
Fierce Tigers, Serpents, Bears and Panthers seem,
All mild and gentle things compar'd to him.

Virgin
Who loves not thee is more inconstant known
    Then fickle Gales of veering wind;
He's more relentless then the Marble Stone,
    Deafer then Seas, and more unkind:
The craggy Mountains raging fire and Sea
Are not so rough, so merciless as he.

Ode the 15th of the First Book of Casimire imitated, encouraging the Polish Knights after their last Conquest to proceed in their Victory.

[Lyr. I 15]

Believe, ye after ages yet to come,
    Believe the mighty Conquest won.
Jo! the mighty Conquest's won, and we
Have purchas'd a triumphant Victory.
    The Turks they fly now basely all,
    Their scatter'd Troops ignobly fall;
Gasping they beg your fatal Arms to cease,
And with their Blood they bargain for a Peace.

What trembling fear did through their Army spread;
    And wing'd with fear how swift they fled,
When our great King in Honours noble race
Before him did their flying Heroes chase
    Like Jove he then his Thunder threw,
    All kill'd whole Myriads as they flew.
Terribly bright his Sword, like Lightning, kills;
And num'rous deaths increase the neighb'ring Hills.

What great amazements now the Tartars seize;
      One faints for fear, another dies.
The cruel Tartars, which no pity knew,
On bended knees did now for pity sue;
      When they beheld the Danube's Flood
      Roll down in Tides of their own Blood;
And how the Bospher to the Ocean fled,
In blushing streams to hide his Captive head.

When they saw all their Chiefs, their men of War,
      And Janissaries fly for fear;
Whilst they beneath their shelt'ring Arms did bow,
And strove now only to defend the blow;
      They could not now their Spears command,
      They dropped from their weak trembling hand.
So meaner Beasts of Prey to Lions yield,
And leave the Spoil and Trophies of the Field.

When Buda, Gran, and ev'ry Fortress near
      Of their inglorious flight did hear,
The noise of Arms, and groans of dying Men;
Their fresh disgrace they echo'd back again.
      When the sad news Byzantium knew,
      The great Byzantium trembled too;
Its lofty Tow'rs now seem'd to rock with fear,
As if our King play'd all his Thunder there.

Shall we thus crown'd with Laurels and success,
      Lie all dissolv'd in sloth and ease?
Have we in vain with our Blood Honours bought?
In vain for future ages glories sought?
      Shall our example sloth create,
      And make our Sons degenerate?
Our sprightly youth useless in War become,
And sleep in peace and slavery at home.

Alas 'twill be a most upbraiding shame
      (A hated truth I'd blush to name)
To see that sprightly fire and gen'rous heat
(Which did our great Fore-fathers animate)

"Oxford Hands"

    In us to languish and decay,
    In us to die and faint away:
And all their Warlike rage in us to wast,
And ev'ry age grow worse still then the last.

Or let us (who in all the Glories share,
    Our Ancestors e're got in War)
Pull down the Trophies in our Temples hung;
(For which we lately Io Paean! sung)
    Th' Imperial Flag (which our great King
Late from the Turkish Camp did bring)
The Arms, the Swords, the Helmets and rich spoil,
The just rewards of our great Leader's toil.

Let us pull down all those bright Arms, that be
    Our Monuments of Victory,
And sacred Statues, which the likeness give
Of our great Fathers, in which still they live;
    And let us all their Honours raze,
    And burn the Records of their praise;
Least ev'n their Images should blush to know
A Race so much unlike themselves, as you.

Or if we hope our Glories to increase
    And would not live in lazy Peace;
With sacred Oaths let's in a League combine;
With brave Lorrain and Staremburg let's join:
    And let us once again act o're,
    Those Triumphs we obtain'd before;
Whilst the curst Infidels to make it good,
Shall Seal and shall Cement it with their Blood.

O mighty Prince of everlasting Fame,
    Whom Kings and Emp'rors joy to name,
Whom Glory on swift Wings to Heaven bears,
And fixes thy bright Praise amongst the Stars;
    Thou Bulwark of the German Throne,
    Thou Pride and Glory of thy own.
Stop thou not here, but as thou hast begun,
To greater Conquests lead thine Armies on.

March thro' thick Groves of Spears with thy drawn Sword
    And to quick Victory give the word,
And let thy Glutton Blade (which twice before,
Has been made drunk with Turkish Hero's gore)
    Be nobly the third time embru'd
    In a vast Sea of Turkish Blood;
And with thy Troops pull the proud Sultan down,
Tho' Mahumet should stand to guard his Throne.

From: *Miscellany Poems and Translations by Oxford Hands*, London: Printed for Anthony Stephens, Bookseller near Theatre in Oxford, 1685.

15

Isaac Watts

Isaac Watts (1674–1748) a Nonconformist preacher, poet, and hymn-writer, praised as the 'father of English Hymnody', and credited with writing 750 hymns. Watts was also a respected religious thinker and philosopher, his *Philosophical Essays on Various Subjects* (1733) and *The Rational Foundation of a Christian Church, and the Terms of Christian Communion* (1747) and other treatises were widely read in the eighteenth century. He was very much involved in the development of education; among other works he addressed to children his *The Art of Reading and Writing English* (1721) and *Catechisms* (1730). He was also the author of successful textbooks such as *Logick: or the Right Use of Reason in the Enquiry after Truth* (1725) followed by *The Improvement of the Mind* (1741). As a student of Thomas Rowe's dissenting academy in Little Britain, the City of London, Watts got to know the future poets John Hughes and Samuel Say. Watts wrote most of his own poetry, both in English and Latin, in his younger years; he published four collections of verse. He expressed his views on poetry and hymn-writing in prefaces to his collections such as 'A short essay toward the improvement of psalmody' published in the second edition of his collection *Horae lyricae* (the first edition in 1706, expanded to three volumes, 1709, and then repeatedly corrected and reprinted). An excerpt from such a preface, one of ample testimonies of Watts' special fascination with the works of Sarbiewski, is quoted below. His translations (apart from an impressive selection of Sarbiewski's poems published originally in *Horae Lyricae*,) are mainly biblical texts, of which the most famous are *Psalms of David Imitated* (1719). Among his hymns the Christmas carol 'Joy to the World' enjoys the most lasting popularity.

The Preface to *Horae Lyricae*

The imitations of that noblest Latin Poet of modern ages, Casimir Sarbiewski of Poland, would need no excuse, did they but arise to the beauty of the original. I have often taken the freedom to add ten or twenty lines, or to leave out as many, that I might suit my song more to my own design, or because I saw it impossible to present the force, the fineness, and the fire of his expression in our language. There are a few copies wherein I borrowed some hints from the same author, without the mention of his name in the title. Methinks, I can allow so superior a genius, now and then, to be lavish in his imagination, and to judgment: The riches and glory of his verse make atonement in abundance. I wish some English pen would import more of his treasures, and bless our nation.

Seeking a Divine Calm in a Restless World
Casimire, Book IV. Ode 28
O Mens, quae stabili fata Regis vice, & c.

[Lyr. IV 28]

Eternal Mind, who rulest the fates
Of dying realms, and rising states,
    With one unchanged decree,
While we admire thy vast affairs,
Say, can our little trifling cares
    Afford a smile to thee?

Thou scatters honours, crowns, and gold;
We fly to seize, and fight to hold
    The bubbles and the oar:
So emmets struggle for a grain;
So boys their petty wars maintain
    For shells upon the shore.

Here a vain man his sceptre breaks,
The next a broken sceptre takes,
    And warriors win and lose;
This rolling world will never stand,
Plundered and snatched from hand to hand,
    As power decays or grows.

Earth's but an atom; Greedy swords
Carve it amongst a thousand lords,
    And yet they can't agree:
Let greedy swords still fight and slay,
I can be poor; but, Lord, I pray
    To sit and smile with thee.

Breathing Towards the Heavenly Country
Casimire. Book I. Ode 19. Imitated.
Urit me Patriae Décor, & c.

[Lyr. I 19]

The beauty of my native land
    Immortal love inspires;
    I burn, I burn with strong desires,
    And sigh, and wait the high command.
    There glides the moon her shining way,
And shoots my heart through with a silver ray,
    Upwards my heart aspires:
    A thousand lamps of golden light
Hung high, in vaulted azure, charm my sight,
And wink and beckon with their amorous fires,
O ye the fair glories of my heav'nly home,
    Bright sentinels who guard my Father's court,
    Where all the happy minds resort,
    When will my Father's chariot come?
Must ye for ever walk the ethereal round?
    For ever see the mourner lie
    An exile of the sky,
    A pris'ner of the ground?
Descend some shining servants from on high,
    Build me a hasty tomb;
    A grassy turf will raise my head;
    The neighbouring lilies dress my bed;
    And shed a cheap perfume.
Here I put off the chains of death,
    My soul too long has worn:
Friends, I forbid one groaning breath,
    Or tear to wet my urn;

Raphael, behold me all undrest,
Here gently lay this flesh to rest;
Then mount, and lead the path unknown,
Swift I pursue thee, flaming guide, on pinions of my own.

On Saint Ardalio, who from a Stage-Player became a Christian, and suffered Martyrdom

[Epig. 100]

Ardalio jeers, and in his comic strains
The mysteries of our bleeding God profanes,
While his loud laughter shakes the painted scenes.

Heaven heard, and straight around the smoking throne
The kindling lightning in thick flashes shone,
And vengeful thunder murmur'd to be gone.

Mercy stood near and with a smiling brow
Calmed the loud thunder; 'There's no need of you;
'Grace shall descend, and the weak man subdue.'

Grace leaves the skies, and he the stage forsakes,
He bows his head down to the martyring axe,
And as he bows, this gentle farewell speaks;

'So goes the comedy of life away;
'Vain earth, adieu; heaven will applaud today;
'Strike, courteous tyrant, and conclude the play.'

Strict Religion Very Rare

[Lyr. II 5]

I'm borne aloft, and leave the crowd,
I sail upon a morning cloud
    Skirted with dawning gold:
Mine eyes beneath the opening day
Command the globe with wide survey,
Where ants in busy millions play,
    And tug and heave the mould.

'Are these the things' my passion cried,
'That we call men? Are these allied
    'To the fair worlds of light?
'They have 'ras'd out their Maker's name,
'Grav'n on their minds with pointed flame
    'In strokes divinely bright.

'Wretches! they hate their native skies;
'If an ethereal thought arise,
    'Or spark of virtue shine,
'With cruel force, they damp its plumes,
'Choke the young fire with sensual fumes,
    'With business, lust, or wine.

'Lo! how they throng with painting breath
    'The broad descending road
'That leads unerring down to death,
    'Nor miss the dark abode.'
Thus while I drop a tear or two
On the wild herd, a nobler few
Dare to stray upward, and pursue
    Th' unbeaten way to God.

I meet Myrtillo mounting high,
I know his candid soul afar;
Here Dorylus and Thyrsis fly,
    Each like a rising star,
Charin I saw, and Fidea there,
I saw them help each other's flight,
    And bless them as they go.
They soar beyond my lab'ring sight,
And leave their loads of mortal care,
    But not their love, below.
On heav'n, their home, they fix their eyes,
    The temple of their God:
With morning incense up they rise
Sublime, and through the lower skies
    Spread the perfumes abroad.

Across the road a seraph flew
'Mark (said he) that happy pair,
'Marriage helps devotion there:
'When kindred minds their God pursue
'They break with double vigour through
    'The dull incumbent air.'
Charmed with the pleasure and surprise,
    My soul adores and sings,
'Blessed be the power that springs their flight,
'That streaks their path with heav'nly light,
'That turns their love to sacrifice,
    'And joins their zeal for wings.'

To William Blackbourn, Esq.
Casimir. Lib. II. Ode 2. Imitated.
Quae tegit canas modo Bruma valles, & c.

[Lyr. II 2]

Mark how it snows! How fast the valley fills!
And the sweet groves the hoary garment wear;
Yet the warm sun-beams bounding from the hills
Shall melt the veil away, and the young green appear.

But when old age has on your temples shed
Her silver-frost, there's no returning sun;
Swift flies our autumn, swift our summer's fled,
When youth, and love, and spring, and golden joys are gone.

Then cold, and winter, and your aged snow,
Stick fast upon you; not the rich array,
Not the green garland, nor the rosy bough
Shall cancel or conceal the melancholy grey.

The chase of pleasures is not worth the pains,
While the bright sands of health run wasting down;
And honour calls you from the softer scenes,
To sell the gaudy hour for ages or renown.

'Tis but one youth, and short, that mortals have,
And one gold age dissolves our feeble frame;
But there's a heav'nly art t' elude the grave,
And with the hero-race immortal kindred claim.

The man that has his country's sacred tears
Bedewing his cold hearse, has lived his day;
Thus, Blackbourn, we should leave our names our heirs;
Old time and waning moons sweep all the rest away.

To Mrs. B. Bendish
Against Tears

[Lyr. IV 13]

Madam, persuade me tears are good
To wash our mortal cares away:
These eyes shall weep a sudden flood,
And stream into the briny sea.

Or if these orbs are hard and dry,
(These orbs that never use to rain)
Some star direct me where to buy
One sov'reign drop for all my pain.

Were both the golden Indies mine,
I'd give both Indies for a tear:
I'd barter all but what's divine:
Nor shall I think the bargain dear.

But tears, alas! are trifling things,
They rather feed than heal our woe;
From trickling eyes new sorrow springs,
As weeds in rainy seasons grow.

Thus weeping urges weeping on;
In vain our miseries hope relief,
For one drop calls another down,
Till we are drown'd in seas of grief.

Then let these useless streams be staid,
Wear native courage on your face:
These vulgar things were never made
For souls of a superior race.

If 'tis a rugged path you go,
And thousand foes your steps surround,
Tread the thorns down, charge through the foe;
The hardest fight is highest crown'd.

The celebrated Victory of the Poles, over Osman the Turkish Emperor, in the Dacian battle
Translated from Casimire. Book IV. Ode 4. with large Additions

[Lyr. IV 4]

 Gador the old, the wealthy and the strong,
Cheerful in years (nor of the heroic muse
Unknowing, nor unknown) held fair possessions
Where flows the fruitful Danube: Seventy springs
Smiled on his seed, and seventy harvest-moons
Fill'd his wide granaries with autumnal joy:
Still he resumed the toil: and same reports,
While he broke up new ground, and tired his plough
In grassy furrows, the torn earth disclosed
Helmets, and swords (bright furniture or war
Sleeping in rust) and heaps of mighty bones.
The sun descending to the western deep
Bid him lie down and rest; he loosed the yoke,
Yet held his wearied oxen from their food
With charming numbers, and uncommon song.

 Go, fellow-labourers, you may rove secure,
Or feed beside me: taste the greens and boughs
That you have long forgot; crop the sweet herb,
And graze in safety, while the victor Pole
Leans on his spear, and breathes; yet still his eye
Jealous and fierce. How large, old soldier, say,
How fair a harvest of the slaughtered Turks
Strewed the Moldavian fields? What mighty piles

Of vast destruction, and of Thracian dead
Fill and amaze my eyes? Broad bucklers lie
(A vain defence) spread o'er the pathless hills,
And coats of scaly steel and hard habergeon,
Deep-bruised and empty of Mahometan limbs.
This the fierce Saracen wore, (for when a boy,
I was their captive, and remind their dress)
Here the Polonians dreadful marched along
In august port, and regular array,
Led on to conquest: Here the Turkish chief
Presumptuous trod, and in rude order ranged
His long battalions, while his populous towns
Poured out fresh troops perpetual, drest in arms,
Horrent in mail, and gay in spangled pride.

    O the dire image of the bloody fight
These eyes have seen, when the capacious plain
Was thronged with Dacian spears; when polished helms
And convex gold blazed thick against the sun
Restoring all his beams! but frowning war
All gloomy, like a gather'd tempest, stood
Wavering, and doubtful where to bend its fall.

    The storm of missive steel delayed a while
By wise command; fledged arrows on the nerve;
And scimitar and sabre bore the sheath
Reluctant; till the hollow brazen clouds
Had bellowed from each quarter of the field
Loud thunder, and disgorged their sulph'rous fire.
Then banners waved, and arms were mixed with arms:
Then javelins answer'd javelins as they fled,
For both fled hissing death: With adverse edge
The crooked falchions met; and hideous noise
From clashing shields, through the long ranks of war,
Clang'd horrible. A thousand iron storms
Roar diverse: And in harsh confusion drown
The trumpet's silver sound. O rude effort
Of harmony! not all the frozen stores
Of the cold North, when poured in rattling hail
Lash with such madness the Norwegians plains,

Or so torment the ear. Scarce sounds so far
The direful fragor, when some southern blast
Tears from the Alps a ridge of knotty oaks
Deep fang'd, and ancient tenants of the rock:
The massy fragment, many a rood in length,
With hideous crash, rolls down the rugged cliff
Resistless, plunging in the subject lake
Como, or Lugaine; th' afflicted waters roar,
And various thunder all the valley fills,
Such was the noise of war: the troubled air
Complains aloud, and propagates the din
To neighbouring regions; rocks and lofty hills
Beat the impetuous echoes round the sky.

 Uproar, revenge, and rage, and hate appear
In all their murderous forms; and flame and blood
And sweat and dust array the broad campaign
In horror: hasty feet, and sparkling eyes,
And all the savage passions of the soul
Engage in the warm business of the day.
Here mingling hands, but with no friendly gripe,
Join in the fight; and breast in close embrace,
But mortal, as the iron arms of death.
Here words austere, or perilous command,
And valour swift t' obey; bold feats of arms
Dreadful to see and glorious to relate,
Shine through the field with more surprising brightness
Than glittering helms of spears. What loud applause
(Best meed of warlike toil) what manly shouts,
And yells unmanly, through the battle ring!
And sudden wrath dies into endless fame.

 Long did the fate of war hang dubious. Here
Stood the more num'rous Turk, the valiant Pole
Fought here; more dreadful, though with lesser wings.

 But what the Dahees, or the coward soul
Of a Cydonian, what fearful crowds
Of base Cilicians 'scaping from the slaughter,
Or Parthian beasts, with all their racing riders,

What could they mean against th' intrepid breast
Of the pursuing foe? Th' impetuous Poles
Rush here, and here the Lithuanian horse
Drive down upon them like a double bolt
Of kindled thunder, raging through the sky
On sounding wheels; or as some mighty flood
Rolls his two torrents down a dreadful steep,
Precipitant, and bears along the stream
Rocks, woods, and trees, with all the grazing herd,
And tumbles lofty forest headlong to the plain.

    The bold Borussian smoking from afar
Moves like a tempest in a dusky cloud,
And imitates th' artillery of heav'n,
The lightning and the roar. Amazing scene!
What showers of mortal hail, what flaky fires
Burst from the darkness! while their cohorts firm
Met like the thunder, and an equal storm,
From hostile troops, but with a braver mind.
Undaunted bosoms tempt the edge of war,
And rush on the sharp point; while baleful mischiefs
Deaths, and bright dangers flew across the field
Thick and continual, and a thousand souls
Fled murmuring through their wounds. I stood aloof,
For 'twas unsafe to come within the wind
Of Russian banners, when with whizzing sound,
Eager of glory and profuse of life,
They bore down fearless of the charging foes
And drove them backward. Then the Turkish moons
Wander'd in disarray. A dark eclipse
Hung on the silver crescent, boding night,
Long night, to all her sons: at length disrob'd
The standards fell; the barbarous ensigns torn
Fled with the wind, the sport of angry heav'n:
And a large cloud of infantry and horse,
Scattering in wild disorder, spread the plain.

    Not noise, nor number, nor the brawny limb,
Nor high-built size prevails: 'Tis courage fights,
'Tis courage conquers. So whole forests fall

(A spacious ruin) by one single axe,
And steel well sharpened: so a generous pair
Of young-wing'd eaglets fright a thousand doves.

   Vast was the slaughter, and the flow'ry green
Drank deep of flowing crimson. Veteran bands
Here made their last campaign. Here haughty chiefs
Stretch'd on the bed of purple honour lie
Supine, nor dream of battle's hard event.
Oppress'd with iron slumbers, and long night.
Their ghosts indignant to the nether world
Fled, but attended well: for at their side
Some faithful Janissaries strew'd the field,
Fall'n in just ranks or wedges, lines or squares,
Firm as they stood; to the Warsovian troops,
A nobler toil, and triumph worth their fight,
But the broad sabre, and keen poll-axe flew
With speedy terror through the feebler herd,
And made rude havoc and irregular spoil
Amongst the vulgar bands that own'd the name
Of Mahomet. The wild Arabians fled
In swift affright a thousand different ways
Through brakes and thorns, and climb'd the craggy mountains
Bellowing; yet the hasty fate o'ertook the cry,
And Polish hunters clave the timorous deer.

   Thus the dire prospect distant fill'd my soul
With awe; till the last relics of the war
The thin Edonians, flying had disclos'd
The ghastly plain: I took a nearer view,
Unseemly to the sight, nor to the smell
Grateful. What loads of mangled flesh and limbs
(A dismal carnage!) bath'd in reeking gore
Lay welt'ring on the ground; while flitting life
Convuls'd the nerves still shivering, nor had lost
All taste of pain! Here an old Thracian lies
Deform'd with years and scars, and groans aloud
Torn with fresh wounds; but inward vitals firm
Forbid the soul's remove, and chain it down
By the hard laws of nature, to sustain

Long torment: his wild eye-balls roll; his teeth
Gnashing with anguish, chide his ling'ring fate.
Emblazon'd armour spoke his high command
Amongst the neighbouring dead; they round their Lord
Lay prostrate; some in flight ignobly slain,
Some to the skies their faces upward turn'd
Still brave, and proud to die so near their prince.

    I moved not far, and lo, at manly length
Two beauteous youths of richest Ott'man blood
Extended on the field: in friendship join'd,
Nor fate divides them: hardy warriors both;
Both faithful: drowned in show'rs of darts they fell,
Each with his shield spread o'er his lover's heart,
In vain: for on those orbs of friendly brass
Stood groves of javelins; some, alas, too deep
Were planted there, and through their lovely bosoms
Made painful avenues for cruel death.
O my dear native land, forgive the tear
I dropt on their wan cheeks, when strong compassion
Forc'd from my melting eyes the briny dew,
And paid a sacrifice to hostile virtue.
Dacia, forgive the sigh that wish'd the souls
Of those fair infidels some humble place
Among the blest. 'Sleep, sleep, ye hapless pair,
'Gently, I cry'd, worthy of better fate,
'And better faith.' Hard by the general lay,
Of Saracen descent, a grisly form
Breathless, yet pride sat pale upon his front
In disappointment, with a surly brow
Louring in death, and vext; his rigid jaws
Foaming with blood bite hard the Polish spear.
In that dead visage my remembrance reads
Rash Caracas: In vain the boasting slave
Promis'd and sooth'd the Sultan threat'ning fierce
With royal suppers, and triumphant fare,
Spread wide beneath Warsovian silk and gold;
See on the naked ground all cold he lies,
Beneath the damp wide cov'ring of the air
Forgetful of his word. How heaven confounds

Insulting hopes! with what an awful smile
Laughs at the proud, that loosen all the reins
To their unbounded wishes, and leads on
Their blind ambition to a shameful end!

    But whither am I borne? This thought of arms
Fires me in vain to sing to senseless bulls,
What generous horse should hear. Break off, my song,
My barbarous muse be still: Immortal deeds
Must not be thus profan'd in rustic verse:
The martial trumpet, and the following age,
And growing fame, shall loud rehearse the fight
In sounds of glory. Lo, the evening-star
Shines o'er the western hill; my oxen, come,
The well-known star invites the labourer home.

To the Discontented and Unquiet
Imitated partly from Casimire, Book IV. Ode 15.

[Lyr. IV 15]

Varia, there's nothing here that's free
From wearisome anxiety:
And the whole round of mortal joys
With short possession tires and cloys:
'Tis a dull circle that we tread,
Just from the window to the bed,
We rise to see and to be seen,
Gaze on the world a while, and then
We yawn, and stretch to sleep again.
But Fancy, that uneasy guest,
Still holds a longing in our breast:
She finds or frames vexations still,
Herself the greatest plague we feel,
We take strange pleasure in our pain,
And make a mountain of a grain,
Assume the load, and pant, and sweat
Beneath th' imaginary weight.
With our dear selves we live at strife,
While the most constant scenes of life
From peevish humours are not free;

Still we affected variety:
Rather than pass an easy day,
We fret and chide the hours away,
Grow weary of this circling sun,
And vex that he should ever run
The same old track; and still, and still
Rise red behind yon eastern hill,
And chides the moon that darts her light
Through the same casement every night.

    We shift our chambers, and our homes,
To dwell where trouble never comes:
Silvia has left the city crowd,
Against the court exclaims aloud,
Flies to the woods; a hermit-saint!
She loathes her patches, pins, and paint,
Dear diamonds from her neck are torn:
But Humour, that eternal thorn,
Sticks in her heart: She's hurry'd still,
'Twixt her wild passions and her will:
Haunted and hagg'd where-e'er she roves,
By purling streams, and silent groves,
Or with her furies, or her loves.

    Then our own native land we hate,
Too cold, too windy, or too wet;
Change the thick climate, and repair
To France or Italy for air;
In vain we change, in vain we fly;
Go, Silvia, mount the whirling sky,
Or ride upon the feather'd wind
In vain; if this diseased mind
Clings fast, and still sits close behind.
Faithful disease, that never fails
Attendance at her lady's side,
Over the desert or the tide,
On rolling wheels, or flying sails.

    Happy the soul that virtue shows
To fix the place of her repose,

Needless to move; for she can dwell
In her old grandsire's hall as well,
Virtue that never loves to roam
But sweetly hides herself at home.
And easy on a native throne
Of humble turf sits gently down.

    Yet should tumultuous storms arise,
And mingle earth and seas, and skies,
Should the waves swell, and make her roll
Across the line, or near the pole,
Still she's at peace; for well she knows
To launch the stream that duty shows,
And makes her home where'er she goes.
Bear her, ye seas, upon your breast
Or waft her, winds, from east to west
On the soft air; she cannot find
A couch so easy as her mind,
Nor breathe a climate half so kind.

To John Hartopp, Esq; now Sir John Hartopp, Bart.
Casimire, Book I. Ode 4. imitated
Vivae jucundae metuens juventae, & c.
July 1700.

[Lyr. I 4]

    Live, my dear Hartopp, live today,
Nor let the sun look down and say,
    'Inglorious here he lies,'
Shake off your ease, and send your name
To immortality and fame,
    By ev'ry hour that flies.

Youth's a soft scene, but trust her not:
Her airy minutes, swift as thought,
    Slide off the slipp'ry sphere;
Moons with their months make hasty rounds,
The sun has pass'd his vernal bounds,
    And whirls about the year.

Let folly dress in green and red,
And gird her waist with flowing gold,
Knit blushing roses round her head,
Alas! the gaudy colours fade,
    The garment waxes old.
Hartopp, mark the withering rose,
And the pale gold how dim it shows!

Bright and lasting bliss below
    Is all romance and dream;
Only the joys celestial flow
    In an eternal stream,
The pleasures that the smiling day
    With large right-hand bestows,
Fals'ly her left conveys away,
    And shuffles in our woes.
So have I seen a mother play,
    And cheat her silly child;
She gave, and took a toy away,
    The infant cry'd and smil'd.
Airy chance, and iron fate
Hurry and vex our mortal state,
And all the race of ills create;
Now fiery joy, now sullen grief,
Commands the reins of human life,
    The wheels impetuous roll;
The harnest hours and minutes strive,
And days with stretching pinions drive —
    — down fiercely on the goal.

Not half so fast the galley flies
    O'er the Venetian sea,
When sails, and oars, and lab'ring skies
    Contend to make her way.
Swift wings for all the flying hours
    The God of time prepares,
The rest lie still yet in their nest
    And grow for future years.

To Thomas Gunston, Esq. 1700
Happy Solitude
Casimire, Book IV. Ode 12. Imitated
Quid me latentem, & c.

[Lyr. IV 12]

    The noisy world complains of me
    That I should shun their sight, and flee
    Visits, and crowds, and company.
    Gunston, the lark dwells in her nest
        Till she ascend the skies;
    And in my closet I could rest
Till to the heavens I rise.

    Yet they will urge, 'This private life
    'Can never make you blest,
    'And twenty doors are still at strife
        'T' engage you for a guest.
Friend, should the towers of Windsor or Whitehall
    Spread open their inviting gates
    To make my entertainment gay;
    I would obey the royal call,
        But short should be my stay,
    Since a diviner service waits
T' employ my hours at home, and better fill the day.

    When I within myself retreat,
    I shut my doors against the great;
    My busy eye-balls inward roll,
    And there with large survey I see
    All the wide theatre of me,
And view the various scenes of my retiring soul;
There I walk o'er the mazes I have trod,
While hope and fear are in doubtful strife,
    Whether this opera of life
Be acted well to gain the plaudit of my God.

There's a day hast'ning, 'tis an awful day!
When the great Sov'reign shall at large review
    All that we speak and all we do,
The several parts we act on this wide stage of clay:

      These he approves, and those he blames,
And crowns perhaps a porter, and a prince he damns.
O if the Judge from his tremendous seat
         Shall not condemn what I have done,
         I shall be happy though unknown,
Nor need the gazing rabble, nor the shouting street.

         I hate the glory, friend, that springs
         From vulgar breath, and empty sound;
      Fame mounts her upward with a flatt'ring gale
            Upon her airy wings,
Till Envy shoots, and Fame receives the wound;
            Then her slugging pinions fail,
         Down Glory falls and strikes the ground,
            And breaks her batter'd limbs.
Rather let me be quite concealed from Fame;
            How happy I should lie
            In sweet obscurity,
Nor the loud world pronounce my little name!
         Here I could live and die alone;
         Or if society be due
To keep our taste of pleasure new,
         Gunston, I'd live and die with you,
            For both our souls are one.

      Here we could sit and pass the hour,
         And pity kingdoms, and their kings,
         And smile at all their shining things,
   Their toys of state, and images of power;
         Virtue should dwell within our seat,
         Virtue alone could make it sweet,
Nor is herself secure, but in a close retreat.
         While she withdraws from public praise
            Envy perhaps would cease to rail;
         Envy itself may innocently gaze
            At beauty in a vail:
         But if she once advance to light,
         Her charms are lost in Envy's sight,
And Virtue stands the mark of universal spite.

Salvation in the Cross
Hymn Book II, 4.

[Ep. 5]

Here at thy cross, my dying God,
I lay my soul beneath thy love,
Beneath the droppings of thy blood,
Jesus, nor shall it ever remove.

Not all that tyrants think of say,
With rage and lightning in their eyes,
Nor hell shall fright my heart away,
Should hell with all its legions rise.

Should worlds conspire to drive me thence,
Moveless and firm this heart should lie;
Resolved, for that's my last defence,
If I must perish, there to die.

But speak, my Lord, and calm my fear;
Am I not safe beneath thy shade;
Thy vengeance will not strike me here,
Nor Satan dares my soul invade.

Yes, I am secure beneath thy blood,
And all my foes shall lose their aim:
Hosanna to my dying God,
And my best honours to his name.

From: *The Works of The Late Reverend and Learned Isaac Watts, DD. Published by himself and now collected in Six Volumes ... Now first published from his manuscripts, and, by the Direction of his Will, revised and Corrected by D. Jennings, D.D. and the late P. Doodridge, D.D.* Vol. IV, London: Printed for T. and T. Longman at the Ship, and J. Buckland at the Buck, in Paternoster Row; J. Oswald at the Rose and Crown in the Poultry; J. Waugh at the Turks's Head in Lombard Street; and J. Ward at the King's Arms in Cornhill. 1753.

Isaac Watts

Imitation of an Ode of Casimir

[Lyr. II 15]

'Twas an unclouded sky: the day-star sat
On highest noon' no breezes fanned the grove;
Nor the musicians of the air pursued
Their artless warbling; while the sultry day
Lay all diffused and slumbering on the bosom
Of the white lily, the perfumed jonquil,
And lovely blushing rose. Then first my harp,
Labouring with childish innocence and joy,
Brake silence, and awoke the smiling hour
With infant notes, saluting the fair skies,
(Heaven's highest work) the fair enamel'd meads,
And tall green shades along the winding banks,
Of Avon gently flowing. Thence my days
Commenced harmonious; there began my skill
To vanquish care by the sweet-sounding string.
      Hail, happy hour, O bless'd remembrance, hail!
And banish woes for ever. Harps were made
For Heaven's beatitudes: there Jesse's son
Tunes his bold lyre with majesty of sound,
To the creative and all-ruling Power
Not unattentive: while ten thousand tongues
Of hymning seraphs and disbodied saints,
Echo the joys and graces round the hills
Of Paradise, and spread Messiah's name.
Transporting bliss! Make haste, ye rolling Spheres,
Ye circling Suns, ye winged Minutes, haste,
The meanest son of harmony to join
In that celestial concert.

The Hebrew Poet

This Ode represents the Difficulty of a just Translation of the Psalms of David in all their Hebrew Glory; with an Apology for the Imitation of them in Christian Language. –
The first Hint borrowed from Casimir, Jessaea quisquis, &c. Book iv. Ode 7.

[Lyr. IV 7]

Show me the man that dares and sings
Great David's verse to British strings:

Sublime attempt! but bold and vain
As building Babel's tower again.

The Bard* that climb'd to Cooper's Hill,
Reaching at Zion, shamed his skill,
And bids the sons of Albion own,
That Judah's Psalmist reigns alone.
Bless'd Poet! now, like gentle Thames,
He sooths our ears with silver streams:
Like his own Jordan, now he rolls,
And sweeps away our captive souls.

Softly the tuneful shepherd leads
The Hebrew flocks to flowery meads:
He marks their path with notes divine,
While fountains spring with oil and wine.

Rivers of peace attend his song,
And draw their milky train along:
He jars; and, lo! the flints are broke,
But honey issues from the rock.

When, kindling with victorious fire,
He shakes his lance across the lyre,
The lyre resounds unknown alarms,
And sets the Thunderer in arms.

Behold the God! the' almighty King
Rides on a tempest's glorious wing:
His ensigns lighten round the sky,
And moving legions sound on high.

Ten thousand cherubs wait his course,
Chariots of fire and flaming horse:

---

* Sir John Denham, who gained great reputation by his poem called Cooper's Hill, failed in his translation of the Psalms of David. [Note by Isaac Watts.]

Earth trembles; and her mountains flow,
At his approach, like melting snow.

But who these frowns of wrath can draw,
That strike Heaven, Earth, and Hell, with awe?
Red lightning from his eyelids broke;
His voice was thunder, hail, and smoke.

He spake; the cleaving waters fled,
And stars beheld the ocean's bed:
While the great master strikes his lyre,
You see the frighted floods retire:

In heaps the frighted billows stand,
Waiting the changes of his hand:
He leads his Israel through the sea,
And watery mountains guard their way.

Turning his hand with sovereign sweep,
He drowns all Egypt in the deep:
Then guides the tribes, a glorious band,
Through deserts to the Promised Land.

Here camps with wide embattled force;
Here gates and bulwarks stop their course:
He storms the mounds, the bulwark falls,
The harp lies strow'd with ruin'd walls.

See his broad sword flies o'er the strings,
And mows down nations with their kings:
From every chord his bolts are hurl'd,
And vengeance smites the rebel world.

Lo! the great Poet shifts the scene;
And shows the face of God serene:
Truth, Meekness, Peace, Salvation, ride,
With guards of justice, at his side.

No meaner Muse could weave the light,
To form his robes divinely bright;

Or frame a crown of stars to shine
With beams for Majesty divine.

Now in prophetic light he sees
Ages to come, and dark decrees:
He brings the Prince of Glory down,
Stripp'd of his robe and starry crown,

See Jews and Heathens fired with rage;
See, their combining powers engage
Against the' Anointed of the Lord,
The Man whom angels late adored;

God's only Son: Behold, he dies!
Surprising grief! The groans arise!
The lyre complains on every string,
And mourns the murder of her King.

But Heaven's Anointed must not dwell
In death: the vanquish'd powers of Hell
Yield to the harp's diviner lay;
The grave resigns the' illustrious prey.

MESSIAH lives! MESSIAH reigns!
The song surmounts the airy plains,
To' attend her Lord with joys unknown,
And bear the Victor to his throne.

Rejoice, ye shining worlds on high,
Behold the Lord of Glory nigh:
Eternal doors, your leaves display,
To make the Lord of Glory way.

What mortal bard has skill or force
To paint these scenes, to tread this course,
Or furnish through the' ethereal road
A triumph for a rising God?

Astonish'd at so vast a flight
Through flaming worlds and floods of light,

My Muse her awful distance keeps,
Still following, but with trembling steps.

She bids her humble verse explain
The Hebrew harp's sublimer strain;
Points to her Saviour still, and shows
What course the Sun of Glory goes.

Here he ascends behind a cloud
Of incense,* there he sets in blood;†
She reads his labours and his names
In spicy smoke, and bleeding lambs.

Rich are the graces which she draws
From types, and shades, and Jewish laws;
With thousand glories long foretold
To turn the future age to gold.

Grace is her theme, and joy, and love:
Descend, ye blessings, from above,
And crown my song. Eternal God,
Forgive the Muse that dreads thy rod.

Silent, she hears thy vengeance roll,
That crushes mortals to the soul,
Nor dares assume the bolt, nor sheds
The' immortal curses on their heads.

Yet since her God is still the same,
And David's Son is all her theme,
She begs some humble place to sing
In concert with Judea's king.

From: Isaac Watts – Thomas Yalden, *The British Poets. Including Translations. In One Hundred Volumes. XLVI. Watts, Vol. II. Yalden,*

---

* Christ's Intercession. [Note by Isaac Watts.]

† His Sacrifice. [Note by Isaac Watts.]

Chiswick: Printed by C. Whittingham, College House; For J. Carpenter, J. Booker, Rodwell and Martin, G. and W.B. Whittaker, R. Jennings, G. Cowie and Co. N. Hailes, J. Porter, B. E. Lloyd and Son, C. Smith, and C. Whittingham, 1822.

16

Thomas Yalden

Thomas Yalden (1670–1736) was a scholar, priest, lecturer in philosophy, and fellow of Magdalen College, Oxford (1699-1713) where he became the lecturer in moral philosophy. Yalden became Doctor of Divinity in 1708 and he made a considerable career in the Church of England, supported by his Tory friends such as Addison and Sacheverell. His poetry, however, was not very highly esteemed. As the author of odes on political themes and thus a follower of Abraham Cowley, Yalden was considered inferior. He was also the author of satirical poems such as *Aesop at Court, or, State Fables* (1702). His poetry was judged 'if not below mediocrity, not above it' (Yalden 1833: VI), although he deserved his biography to be included in Dr Johnson's *The Lives of the Poets*. Yalden copiously translated and imitated Latin and Greek poets – most notably Horace, Homer, and Ovid.

Against Immoderate Grief: An Ode in Imitation of Casimire. To a Young Lady Weeping

[Lyr. IV 13]

Could mournful sighs, or floods of tears, prevent
    The ills unhappy men lament;
    Could all the anguish of my mind
Remove my cares, or make but Fortune kind;
    Soon I'd the grateful tribute pay,
    And weep my troubled thoughts away;
To wealth and pleasure every sigh prefer,
And more than gems esteem each falling tear.

But since insulting cares are most inclined
    To triumph o'er th' afflicted mind;
    Since sighs can yield us no relief

And tears, like fruitful showers, but nourish grief
        Then cease, fair mourner, to complain,
        Nor lavish such bright streams in vain:
But still with cheerful thoughts thy cares beguile,
And tempt thy better fortunes with a smile.

The generous mind is by its sufferings known
        Which no affliction tramples down;
        But when oppressed, will upward move,
Spurn down its clog of cares, and soar above.
        Thus the young royal eagle tries
        On the sun's beams his tender eyes,
And if he shrinks not the offensive light,
He is for empire fit, and takes his soaring flight.

Though cares assault thy breast on every side,
        Yet bravely stem the impetuous tide;
        No tributary tears to fortune pay,
Nor add to any loss a nobler day:
        But with kind hopes support thy mind,
        And think thy better lot behind;
Amidst afflictions let thy soul be great,
And show thou dar'st deserve a better state.

Then, lovely mourner, wipe these tears away,
        And cares, that urge thee to decay;
        Like ravenous age, thy charms they waste,
Wrinkle thy youthful brow, and blooming beauties blast:
        But keep thy looks and mind serene,
        All gay without, all calm within;
For Fate is awed, and adverse fortunes fly
A cheerful look, and an unconquered eye.

From: *The Poetical Works of Thomas Yalden*, London: William Mark Clark, 1833.

17

Samuel Say

Samuel Say (1676–1743) was a Nonconformist minister, active in Lowestoft, Suffolk, and London. He was a friend of John Hughes and Isaac Watts, his fellow students from the London Academy. Say seems to have been quite indifferent to any fame to be won by publishing and in his lifetime only a few of his sermons appeared. His poems, according to the 'Preface' to his *Poems on Several Occasions*, composed in his younger years (those dated were written mostly in the 1690s) and described by himself as 'youthful rubbish', were published only posthumously in 1745, edited by William Duncombe. The volume included a number of original compositions and a selection of translations both from Latin, such as the poems quoted below, but also *Epistles* of Horace and poems of Catullus and Ovid, and into Latin, such as the opening lines of John Milton's *Paradise Lost*. The poems must have enjoyed some degree of popularity as a new edition appeared in 1754, while the translations from Sarbiewski quoted below were reprinted in 1785 by *The Gentleman's Magazine*.

**To his Harp:
In Imitation of the Ode of Casimire.**

[Lyr. II 3]

Sonorous Daughter of the Box!
On this high Poplar hang, my Lyre,
While Heaven thus smiles, and Vernal Airs
    Play, wanton, with the leaves.

Thy trembling Strings a whispering Breeze
Soft shall attune; while, I beneath,
On this green Bank supinely lie,
    Thus carelessly diffus'd.

The riling Brook, that murmurs by,
Shall lull my Thoughts, till gentle Sleep

Seize me, with pleasing Golden Dreams
        Of my Cecilia blest!
But ah! – what sudden Clouds Above
Fly Shadowing! How dark the Air!
What Sound of clattering Hail I hear!
        Rise, luckless Damon, Rise.

How soon, alas! thy Joys decay!
How swift all Pleasures haste away!

Occasion'd by the Tenth Ode of the Second Book of Casimire

[Lyr. II 10]

Blest in Myself, the World I give
        The Ch---ds and D-----bs to possess;
Contended with my Mite, permit
        The miserable Rich
To enjoy their large, their countless Sums.

        Let them unlock the Iron Chest,
        Nor fear to touch the hoarded Gold;
        Hoarded for Heirs that ne'er shall rise,
            Or rise, with lavish Hand,
            T' unearth the buried Store;
The labour of Life, defeated in an hour!
        Whom Glory raises to the Stars,
        I nor enquire, nor know; but live
        Retir'd within Myself, and bar
        My Door upon the World; yet dare,
            Fearless of prying Eyes
        Permit Myself to Open View,
        Bold, and securely Confident
        In conscious Virtue! --- Me the Muse
        Shall Upwards bear, from whence Sublime
        I'll scorn this Earth: Among the Gods,
            Almost a God Myself,
(Refin'd, and rais'd by Influence Divine)
            Familiar I converse!
        And what the Pow'rs command Above,

Will here, Below, in lofty Sounds rehearse —
>> No Man, nor Me of Mortal Race
>> Deem Now, nor at old Hampton born,
Native of Heaven, though here a while I dwell;
>> Commission'd from on high; design'd
>> The Scourge and Terror of Mankind;
>>> In Vengeful Verse to lash
>> The flagrant Vices of the Age!
>> Me, with impatient Virtue fir'd,
>> Of Temper too Severe and Fierce,
>> The Fates, that made no Purple King
>> In Royal Laziness to reign;
A Laurell'd Bard, to Punish Guilt, ordain!

1698.

An Emblem of the Shortness of Human Pleasure
To the Grasshopper

[Lyr. IV 23]

Little Insect, that on high,
> On a Spire of springing Grass,
Tipsy with the Morning Dew,
> Free from Care thy Life dost pass:

So may'st Thou, Companion sole,
> Please the lonely Mower's Ear;
And no treach'rous winding Snake
> Glide beneath, to work Thee Fear,

As in Chirping, Plaintive Notes
> Thou the hasty Sun dost chide,
And with murm'ring Music charm,
> Summer long with Us t' abide.

If a pleasant Day arrives
> Soon a pleasant Day is gone:
While we reach to seize our Joys
> Swift the Winged Bliss is flown.

Pain and Sorrow dwell with Us;
    Pleasure scarce a Moment reigns:
Thou thyself find'st Summer short;
    But the Winter long remains.

From: *Poems on Several Occasions: and Two Critical Essays, viz. The First, On the Harmony, Variety, and Power of Numbers, whether in Prose or Verse. The Second On the Numbers of Paradise Lost by Mr Samuel Say*, London: Printed by John Hughs, near Lincoln's-Inn-Fields, 1745.

18

John Hughes

John Hughes (1678-1720) was a poet, playwright, composer, essayist, librettist, and translator. His younger brother was the poet Jabez Hughes (1684-1731), while his sister Elizabeth married another writer William Duncombe. Graduate of a dissenting academy, where he studied with Isaac Watts, Hughes made a living principally as a secretary to several government commissions. He was also an active playwright and composer; he wrote his first opera, *Amalasunt, Queen of the Goths, or, Vice Destroys Itself* (1697, staged before 1700), before he turned eighteen. Hughes would often write songs (music and lyrics) or poems which would be set to music e.g. *An Ode in Praise of Musick* to the music of Philip Hart (1703), cantata texts (George Frederick Handel's *Venus and Adonis*) and librettos (Handel's *Acis and Galatea*, 1718, with Gay and Pope). His most famous works of this genre were the masque *Apollo and Daphne* (1716, music by John Christopher Pepusch), and the opera *Calypso and Telemachus* (1712, music by John Ernst Galliard). Hughes also wrote the tragedy *The Siege of Damascus* (staged 1720). His essays appeared in the *Tatler*, *Spectator*, and *Guardian*. Hughes translated from French and Latin, ranging from prose (*Letters of Abelard and Heloise*, 1713) to plays such as Molière's *Misanthrope* (1709). He was also the editor of the first critical edition of Edmund Spenser (1715). Samuel Johnson includes Hughes in his *The Lives of the Poets* but Johnson's opinion of his work is rather critical, and it seems that such was the general opinion (expressed e.g. by Pope and Swift) soon after Hughes' demise. The following translation of Sarbiewski's ode 'The Ecstasy' was first published as a separate volume in 1720 with 'Advertisement' quoted below which was not reprinted in later editions.

Me vero primum dulces ante Omnia Musae
Accipiant, Coelique Vias & Sidera monstrent.
                    Virg. [Georg. II 475–476]

Advertisement

It may be proper to acquaint the Reader that the following Poem was begun on the Model of a Latin Ode of Casimire entitled *E rebus humanis Excessus*, from which it is plain that Cowley likewise took the first Hint of his Ode call'd the *Ecstasy*. The former Part therefore is chiefly an Imitation of that Ode, though with considerable Variations, and the Addition of the whole second Stanza, except the first three Lines: But the Plan it self seeming capable of a further Improvement, the latter Part, which attempts a short View of the Heavens, according to the Modern Philosophy, is entirely Original, and not founded on any Thing in the Latin Author.

The Ecstasy
An Ode

[Lyr. II 5]

I Leave Mortality's low Sphere.
Ye Winds and Clouds, come lift me high,
And on your airy Pinions bear
Swift thro' the Regions of the Sky.
What lofty Mountains downward fly!
And lo, how wide a Space of Air
Extends new Prospects to my Eye!
The gilded Fanes, reflecting Light,
And Royal Palaces, as bright,
    (The rich Abodes
Of Heav'nly and Earthly Gods)
Retire apace; whole Cities, too,
Decrease beneath my rising View.
And now far off the rolling Globe appears;
    Its scatter'd Nations I survey,
    And all the Mass of Earth and Sea;
    Oh! Object well deserving Tears!

Capricious State of Things below,
That, changeful from their Birth, no fix'd Duration know!

   Here new-built Towns, aspiring high,
     Ascend, with lofty Turrets crown'd;
   There others fall, and mould'ring lie,
Obscure, or only their Ruins found.
Palmyra's far-extended Waste I spy,
   (Once Tadmor, ancient in Renown)
   Her Marble Heaps, by the wild Arab shown,
    Still load with useless Pomp the Ground.
But where is Lordly Babylon? where now
   Lifts she to Heav'n her Giant Brow?
Where does the Wealth of Niniveh abound?
   Or where's the Pride of Africk's Shore?
   Is Rome's great Rival then no more?
In Rome herself behold th' Extremes of Fate,
Her ancient Greatness sunk, her Modern boasted State!
   See her luxurious Palaces arise
    With broken Arches mix'd between!
   And here what splendid Domes possess the Skies!
   And there old Temples, open to the Day,
    Their Walls o'ergrown with Moss display;
   And Columns, awful in Decay,
Rear upon their Roofless Heads to from the various Scene!

   Around the Space of Earth I turn my Eye;
    But where's the Region free from Woe?
   Where shall the Muse one little Spot descry
    That Seat of Happiness below?
   Here Peace would all its Joys dispense,
The Vines and Olives unmolested grow,
   But, lo! a purple Pestilence
   Unpeoples Cities, sweeps the Plains,
   Whilst vanity thro' deserted Fields
   Here unreap'd Harvests Ceres yield,
And at the Noon of Day a Midnight Silence reigns.
   There milder Heat the healthful Climate warms,
    But Slaves to arbitrary Power,
    And pleas'd each other to devour,

The mad Possessors rush to Arms.
I see, I see them from afar,
I view distinct the mingled War!
I see the charging Squadrons prest
   Hand to Hand, and Breast to Breast.
Destruction, like a Vulture, hovers nigh;
  Lur'd with the Hope of human Blood,
She hangs upon the Wing, uncertain where to fly,
But licks her droughty Jaws, and waits the promis'd Food.

Here cruel Discord takes a wider Scene
To exercise more unrelenting Rage;
Appointed Fleets their numerous Pow'rs engage,
  With scarce a Space of Sea between.
Hark! what a brazen Burst of Thunder
  Rends the Elements asunder!
  Affrighted Ocean flies the Roar,
And drives the Billows to the distant Shore:
  The distant Shore,
That such a Storm ne'er felt before,
Transmits it to the Rocks around;
The Rocks and hollow Creeks prolong the rolling Sound.

Still greater Horrors strike my Eyes:
Behold convulsive Earthquakes there
A shatter'd Land in Pieces tear,
And ancient Cities sink, and sudden Mountains rise!
  Thro' opening mines th' astonish'd Wretches go,
    Hurry'd to unknown Depths below.
The buried Ruin sleeps; and nought remains
    But Dust above and desert Plains,
Unless some stone this sad Inscription wear,
  Raised by some future Traveller,
The Prince, his People, and his Kingdom here
  One common Tomb contains.

Again, behold where Seas, disdaining Bound,
  O'er the firm Land usurping ride,
And bury spacious Towns beneath their sweeping Tide!
Dash'd with the sudden Flood the vaulted Temples sound.

Waves roll'd on Waves, Deep burying Deep, lift high
A wat'ry Monument, in which profound
The Courts and Cottages together lie.
   E'en now the floating Wreck I spy,
   And the wide Surface far around
   With Spoils of plunder'd countries crown'd.
Such, Belgia, was the Ravage and Affright
   When late thou saw'st thy ancient Foe
   Swell o'er thy Digues oppos'd in vain,
With deadly Rage, and rising in its Might
Pour down swift Ruin on thy Plains below.
   Thus Fire, and Air, and Earth, and Main
   A never-ceasing Fight maintain,
While Man on ev'ry Side is sure to lose;
And Fate has furnish'd out the stage of Life
   With War, Misfortune, and with Strife;
Till Death the Curtain drops, and shuts the Scene of Woes.

   But why do I delay my Flight?
   Or on such gloomy Objects gaze?
I go to Realms serene with ever-living Light.
Haste, Clouds and Whirlwinds, haste a raptur'd Bard to raise,
   Mount me sublime along the shining Way
   Where Planets, in pure Streams of Aether driv'n,
   Swim thro' the blue Expanse of Heav'n.
And lo! th' obsequious Clouds and Winds obey!
And lo! again the Nations downwards fly,
And wide-stretch'd Kingdoms perish from my Eye.
   Heav'n! what bright Visions now arise!
What opening Worlds my ravish'd Sense surprise!
I pass Cerulean Gulfs, and now behold
New solid Globes their Weight, self-balanc'd, bear
   Unpropp'd amidst the fluid Air,
And all, around the Central Sun, in circling Eddies roll'd.
   Unequal in their Course, see they advance,
   And form the Planetary Dance!
Here the pale Moon; whom the same Laws ordain
   T' obey the Earth, and rule the Main;
Her Spots no more in shadowy Streaks appear;
   But Lakes instead, and Groves of Trees,

The Wond'ring Muse transported sees,
And their tall Heads discover'd Mountains rear.
And now once more I downward cast my Sight,
When, lo! the Earth, a larger Moon, displays
Far off, amidst the Heav'ns, her silver Face,
And to her Sister-Moon by Turns gives Light!
Her Seas are shadowy Spots, her Land a milky White.

What Pow'r unknown my Course still upwards guides,
Where Mars is seen his ruddy Rays to throw
Thro' heatless Skies that round him seem to glow?
And where remoter Jove o'er his four Moons presides?
And now I urge my Way more bold,
Unpierc'd by Saturn's chilling Cold,
And pass his Planetary Guards, and his bright Ring behold.
Here the Sun's Beams so faintly play,
The mingled Shades almost extinguish Day.
His Rays reverted hence the Sire withdraws,
For here his wide Dominions end;
And other Suns, that rule by other Laws,
Hither their bordering Realms extend.

And now far off, thro' the blue Vacant borne,
I reach at last the Milky Road,
Once thought to lead to Jove's Supreme Abode,
Where Stars, profuse in Heaps, Heav'ns glittering Heights ador
Lost in each other's neighb'ring Rays,
They undistinguish'd shine in one promiscuous Blaze.
So thick the lucid Gems are strown,
As if th' Almighty Builder here
Laid up his Stores for many a Sphere
In destin'd Worlds, as yet unknown.
Hither the nightly-wakeful Swain,
That guards his Folds upon the Plain,
Oft turns his gazing Eyes,
Yet marks no Stars, but o'er his Head
Beholds the streamy Twilight spread,
Like distant Morning in the Skies;
And wonders from what Source its dawning Splendours rise.

But, lo! — what's this I see appear?
It seems far off a pointed Flame;
From Earth-wards too the shining Meteor came.
How swift it climbs th' aerial Space!
And now it traverses each sphere,
And seems some living Guest, familiar to the Place.
'Tis He — as I approach more near
The great Columbus of the Skies I know!
'Tis Newton's Soul that daily travels here
In Search of Knowledge for Mankind below.
O stay, thou happy Spirit! stay,
And lead me on thro' all th' unbeaten Wilds of Day;
As when the Sybil did Rome's Father guide
Safe thro' the downward Roads of Night,
And in Elysium blest his Sight
With Views till then to mortal Eyes denied.
Here let me, thy Companion, stray,
From Orb to Orb, and now behold
Unnumber'd Suns, all Seas of molten Gold;
And trace each Comet's wand'ring Way,
And now descry Light's Fountain-Head,
And measure its descending Speed;
Or learn how Sun-born Colours rise
In Rays distinct, and in the Skies
Blended in yellow Radiance flow,
Or stain the fleecy Cloud, or streak the wat'ry Bow;
Or, now diffus'd their beauteous Tinctures shed
On ev'ry Planet's rising Hills, and ev'ry verdant Mead.

Thus, rais'd sublime on Contemplation's Wings,
Fresh Wonders I would still explore,
Still the great Maker's Pow'r adore,
Lost in the Thought — nor ever more
Return to Earth, and Earthly Things;
But here with native Freedom take my Flight,
An Inmate of the Heav'ns, adopted into Light!
So for a while the Royal Eagle's Brood
In his low Nest securely lies,
Amid the Darkness of the shelt'ring Wood,
Yet there with inborn Vigour hopes the Skies,

Till, fledg'd with Wings full-grown, and bold to rise,
　The Bird of Heav'n to Heav'n aspires,
Soars 'midst the Meteors and Celestial Fires,
With generous Pride his humbler Birth disdains,
And bears the Thunder thro' th' Ethereal Plains.

'Advertisement' from: John Hughes, *The Ecstasy. An Ode.* London, Printed And Sold by J. Roberts in Warwick Lane. MDCCXX.
'The Ecstasy: An Ode' from: John Hughes, *Poems on Several Occasions. With Some Select Essays in Prose.* London: Printed for J. Tonson and J. Watts, MDCCXXXV. [Edited by William and John Duncombe].

An Image of Pleasure
In Imitation of an Ode in Casimire.

[Lyr. II 3]

Solace of my Life, my sweet Companion Lyre!
On this fair Poplar Bough I'll hang thee high,
While the gay Fields all soft Delights inspire,
And not One Cloud deforms the smiling Sky.

While whisp'ring Gales, that court the Leaves and Flowers,
Play thro' thy Strings, and gently make them sound
Luxurious I'll dissolve the flowing Hours
In balmy Slumbers on the Carpet Ground.

But see – what sudden Gloom obscures the Air,
What falling Showers impetuous change the Day!
Let's rise, my Lyre – Ah Pleasure false as fair
How faithless are thy Charms, how short thy Stay!

From: John Hughes, *Poems on Several Occasions. With some Select Essays in Prose.* London: Printed for J. Tonson & J. Watts, MDCCXXXV. [Edited by William and John Duncombe].

19

Samuel Philips

Samuel Philips (b. 1684) was the editor of the shortlived *Poetical Courant* appearing weekly in 1705 and 1706 which 'published much poetry, often of an indecent character' (Yost 1936: 10). Philips presents himself as 'late of St. John's College, Oxford', he was probably the student from London matriculated on June 30th 1703 but soon expelled from the university.

Casimire, Ode 13 Book 4. Against Immoderate Grief Paraphrastically Translated

[Lyr. IV 13]

Cou'd heavy Groans, or Tears prevent
    Those Evils, which mistaken Men lament?
Cou'd Sighs my daily Cares remove,
    Or blow Distracting Thoughts away,
Make partial Fortune kinder prove,
    With Joy I'd the blest Tribute pay:
Court Sorrow as a Mistriss, and prefer,
To Gold, and sparkling Gems, each happy Tear.

But we, alas! Torment ourselves in vain,
    Sighs can bring us no Relief,
And Tears, like fruitless Show'rs of Rain,
    Tend only to the nourishment of Grief;
Scarce has the Eye distill'd one gushing Tear,
But Hydra like, a thousand straight appear.

The Generous Soul was never known,
To truckle to jilt Fortune's Frown:
    But, like the Palm, wou'd upwards move
    Whene'er oppress'd, and soar above,
Leaving dull grov'ling Wretches to their Fears,
A Prey to Savage Woe, and tyrannizing Cares.
Learn then, my Friend, henceforth be wise:
    Was I attack'd on every side,

Shou'd Fear betray the Woman in my Eyes?
No! With unusual Chearfulness I'd rise,
    And with redoubl'd Force oppose th' impetuous Tide.
For a brisk Look, and an undaunted Soul,
Can Fortune Awe, and Destiny Controul.

From: *The Poetical Courant,* June 1706

20

Aaron Hill

Aaron Hill (1685–1750) a poet, playwright, entrepreneur, and essayist who enjoyed the greatest popularity as the translator of plays by Voltaire such as *Zaïre* (*The Tragedy of Zara*, 1736) *Alzira* (1736), and *Mérope* (1749). Hill was the manager of the Theatre Royal in Drury Lane and later director of opera at the Queen's Theatre in the Haymarket, as well as the producer and translator of the libretto of Handel's *Rinaldo* (1711). However, he was hardly ever successful in his theatrical or other enterprises. He is remembered as a pivotal character in the history of the English stage both for his various activities and theoretical writings such as *The Art of Acting* (1746). In the 1720s Hill acted as patron and promoter of other writers such as Edward Young, Richard Savage, and James Thomson. Hill left an impressive body of original compositions including epic poems, pastoral operas, plays such as the tragedies *Elfrid* (1710) and the more successful *The Fatal Extravagance* (1721), and farces such as the *The Walking Statue* (1710), as well as satirical poems, of which *The Progress of Wit* (1730), a response to Alexander Pope's *Dunciad*, is the best known.

The Transport
[Lyr. II 5]

    Mount my freed soul! forsake thy loos'ning clay,
Broadly, at once, expand thy wingy zeal,
    Rapture, involved in raptures, feel,
And, thro' yon dazzling regions, cut thy way!
    See! see! as 'twixt the op'ning worlds, I soar,
Millions of beck'ning joys, at once, in view,
    Draw me, still onward, thro' th' unfathomed sky!
    Ravished! o'erwhelmed! amazed! I fly,
'Midst pleasure, which, before,

My boldest flights of fancy never knew!
Oh! thou dim speck! thou dusky earth! farewell!
From height, like this, I see thee, plainly, now!
Thou art, at best, a kind of hope-cool'd hell!
I see, and I detest thy painted pride!
What sun-gilt bubbles all thy grandeurs are!
    What gugaws all thy tinselled ware!
Oh! who that saw thee, hence, could swell with pride!

    Hark! how the starry vaults of heav'n resound!
With shouts, that shake the rolling orbs around!
    Kindly, with earth-assisting care,
Descending angels aid th' o'erloaded air!
And my too weighty burthen, upward, bear!
High-flooding tides of rapture sense confound!

    Where am I now? oh, fiercely glorious view!
    The liquid pavement, sparkling, shines,
    With star-mixed adamant, and flaming gold!
    Now ecstasies, past ecstasies, pursue!
    Glory, refulgent, aching sight confines!
My mem'ry lost, my trembling tongue controlled!
O! who, with mortal eyes, can heav'n's bright king behold!

From: *The Works of the Late Aaron Hill, Esq; in Four Volumes. Consisting of Letters on Various Subjects, and of Original Poems, Moral and Facetious. With an Essay on the Art of Acting*, London: Printed for the Benefit of the Family, 1753.

21

William Duncombe

William Duncombe (1690–1769) was a miscellaneous writer, poet, and editor. He was also a translator from French (Racine's *Athaliah*, 1722) and Latin. Duncombe edited and contributed to *The Works of Horace in English Verse. By Several Hands*, two volumes in 1757 and 1759, but earlier editions of his translations from Horace were published in 1715 and 1721. He left a number of fugitive pieces published by the *Whitehall Evening Post* and the *London Journal*, as well as a tragedy in blank verse *Lucius Junius Brutus* (1732, staged and successfully published 1735). Although his personal fortune was secured with a large lottery win in 1726, when he could leave his post as clerk in the Navy Office, Duncombe continued to write and publish. He edited the works of John Hughes (1735), Henry Needler (1724), and, with his son John, also a poet, Samuel Say (1743). The following translation was published as a liminary verse to an edition of poems by George Jeffreys.

Casimire, Book II. Ode 2. Imitated
[Lyr. II 2]

Tho' Autumn now to Winter yields,
And hides with Snow the neighb'ring Fields;
Yet when the Sun, with piercing Ray,
Darts on the hills, the Snow will melt away.

But soon as Age, around our Brow,
The silver Locks shall thinly sow,
That wintry Mantle will remain,
Nor change its cold unpleasing Dye again.

Swift flies the Summer; Autumn flies;
The blooming Spring, that soon will rise,
With equal speed will pass away;
For all things here are subject to Decay.

Nor can the fragrant Nard renew
On your wan Cheeks the rosy hue;
Nor flow'ry Wreaths, around your head
Tho' daily worn, their glowing tincture spread.

What tho' our hungry Sister-Worm
Demands this frail and fleeting Form?
For You the grateful Muse will claim
A fair reversion of surviving Fame.

Long has he liv'd, around whose Urn
His friends with pious Sorrow mourn.
To Memory your Fame convey;
All else the greedy Moons will snatch away.

November, 1753

From: *Miscellanies in Verse and Prose. By George Jeffreys, Esq.*, London: Printed for the Author, 1754.

22

Anonymous Translations from Various Magazines 1738–1822

The first general-interest magazine in the modern sense was *The Gentleman's Magazine* established in 1731. It was quickly followed by *The London Magazine* (1732) and many others. Most of them followed the model first proposed by Edward Cave in *The Gentleman's Magazine* – touching upon a variety of subjects from commerce and politics to literature. A selection of poetry and prose, both original compositions and translations, sent in by readers, usually closed each issue, although the editors of the more culturally minded magazines gave literature a more prominent place. Translations from the poetry of Sarbiewski found their way into the English magazines as early as in 1738.

The present chapter includes only anonymous translations arranged chronologically which were published in various English magazines. Poems whose authors are known can be found under the names of their translators in respective chapters with information on sources of their publication.

The Ascension. Imitated from Casim.
Ode 5th of his second Book.

[Lyr. II 5]

The glitt'ring toys on India's coast,
The airy bliss that monarchs boast,
    No longer charm my eyes;
I wait thy influence, gentle wind,
To chase the darkness of my mind,
    And waft me to the skies.

How swift my flight, how bright my way!
Mountains resign to little clay,
    And lessen in my view;

Nay empire too, and rolling seas,
Retreat and shrink to narrow space,
    Wrapt in ethereal blue.

But while I grasp, with wide survey,
These mingling scenes of earth and sea,
    I drop the kindly tear;
For fortune on a dazzling throne,
Dares to pronounce the world her own,
    And sports despotic there.

Here smiles, and sends her orders forth,
And cities rise in waste of earth,
    And tow'r into the sky;
Then sudden clouds her brow in frowns,
And haughty palaces and crowns,
    In smoky ruin lie.

Here health descending from the skies,
Sooths every zephyr as it flies,
    And bars what might destroy;
But see, the nation spurns its charms,
Clothes in the dire array of arms,
    With rude impatient joy.

Across a neighb'ring fruitful land,
See peace her golden winds expand;
    But oh! a numerous train
Of purple plagues are stalking there,
Scatt'ring their poisons through the air,
    And slaughters on the plain.

The shield, the sword, the brandished spear,
And all the dreadful pomp of war,
    Blaze through yon plain below;
While fate above with sovereign sway,
Suspends the fury of the fray,
    And waits to give the blow.

Whilst here with savage, fierce delight,
The gloomy potentate of fight
    Two warring hosts confounds,
Nor checks his arm, nor sates his rage,
Till myriads in the bloom of age,
    Rush groaning through their wounds.

The seas that lave the eastern shore,
Beneath contending navies roar,
    And dash themselves to foam,
Trembling to see outrageous fire,
Involving deaths, to heav'n aspire,
    And plunge into their womb.

While ocean in his old abodes,
Seated amongst his kindred gods,
    Admires the sultry waves;
Though trembles when his eyes behold
The roaring brine impetuous rolled,
    In crimson to his caves.

O cease your rage, ye savage brood,
That sport with war, and thirst for blood,
    And yield to milder thought;
Nor let us say that sword and flame,
And shipwreck, things of dreadful name!
    A mixed destruction wrought.

But thus it is (so heav'n allowed)
And nought but ruin, war, and blood,
    In ever-circling trains,
Must rend the world with ceaseless sway,
Till time rolls on the final day,
    That shuts these mortal scenes.

But why should I retard my flight
Tow'rd yon celestial worlds of light,
    To dwell on mortal things?
Ye clouds, that sail the azure seas,

Range the infinitude of space,
> Assist with all your wings.

Else I am charmed with false delight,
And airy visions of the night,
> Or winds, and clouds of gold,
Labour along the fields of day,
Sustain, and ease my painful way,
> And every side enfold.

I can't with all my stress of view,
Discern the sep'rate realms below,
> And earth such little place
Claims for its portion, and so small
Is the whole circle of the ball,
> 'Tis but a point in space.

And now I sail that heavenly flood,
Immensely deep, immensely broad,
> Where I can dart my eye,
To learn and silently adore
The wonders of JEHOVA'S pow'r,
> And grasp infinity.

Here will I bathe my guilty soul,
Nor feel a wave of trouble roll,
> And lose each thought of sense;
Leaving the things of mortal name,
For earth to take, and worms to claim,
> Nor stir a wish from hence.

Ignosce puero.

Note: The original title states erroneously it is a translation of the 6th and not 5th ode.

From: *The London Magazine*, November 1738.

An Ode of Casimire, Ad Cicadam.

[Lyr. IV 23]

Pretty insect, Summer's child,
O'er the meadow's bounding wild,
There from morn to morn dost sup
Balmy life from Nature's cup,
And thine ever-titt'ring strains
Chear thyself and all the plains.

Now the winter's reign is o'er,
Piercing blast and stormy roar;
Now the summer wings its way,
Dress'd with ev'ry golden ray,
Golden rays with joy receive,
Sweetest sunshine has its eve.

Days that purest brightest shone
As a dawn they once have known,
So they headlong rush to night,
And in darkness quench their light;
Sorrows make a tedious stay,
Pleasures glance and glide away.

From: *The Universal Magazine*, May 1759.

Casimire, Ode 26. Ad Auram

[Lyr. IV 26]

Come, gentle Zephyr! with thee bring,
    The coolness of the Thracian breeze,
Attended by the jocund Spring,
    Which now expands the budding trees.

Here, lovely Zephyr! freely rove,
    Wandering amidst the fragrant shade;
Skim o'er the flowery lawn and grove,
    And every rural sweet pervade.

Wanton amongst the blooming flowers,
    Where purling streams to sleep invite;

And rustling leaves and shady bowers,
    With sylvan melody delight.

So may for thee fair Phoebus' ray
    With splendour all the skies adorn;
And silver dews the meads array,
    And glitter on the opening thorn!

Ceres, and the Sicilian plains,
    With richest odours shall abound;
And each reviving gale dispense
    Delicious fragrance all around.

For thee I'll wake the tuneful lyre,
    While gentle breezes waft the sound;
And, if Apollo too, inspire,
    Echo thy praises shall resound.

From: *The Gentleman's Magazine*, April 1780.

Ode to the Air.
Imitated from Mat. Casimir.

[Lyr. IV 26]

By the trembling poplar made,
Lo, this hospitable shade
Calls thee Air, whom tepid spring
Bears along on flutt'ring wing;
Or the southern sprites transport,
In mild cars, from Neptune's court.
    With thee, sportive Zephyr free
Oft shall leap this shaking tree;
Or the tattling boughs beneath
Oft in chiding laugh shall breathe;
Or delight on earth to stray,
Teasing herbs in tender play.
    While yon brooks, inciting sleep,
Bubbling, over flow'rets creep,
Softly fan me as I lie,
And thy tender touch apply

On yon bough-suspended lute,
Waking notes that now are mute.
    Nature with thy sounds beguile:
Every solar ray shall smile:
And, with liquid step, the dew
From each leaf shall drop to you;
Or, silent on the waving grass,
Shall hang its gems where you may pass;
While to you the peaceful field
Double, treble sweets shall yield.
    Here the rose, the violet spreads,
Haste, and brush their scented heads;
Haste, and as I strike these strings, --
With thy trembling, sportive wings,
In sharp whisp'rings touch the wire,
Sweet companion, on the lyre.

X.Y.

From: *The European Magazine, and London Review*, February 1794.

Casimir, Epigram XIII
Lampades eius lampades ignis Cant. VIII. 6.

[Epig. 13]

Yes, my beloved, were I plac'd,
    Like earth revolving on its tree;
Still in thy hand I'd hold me fast –
    Thy trembling spouse would cling to thee.

Were I more ruffled than the flood,
    Rolling its turbid waves below;
My quiet passions, at thy nod,
    Should gently as passions flow.

Or, were I fleeter than the wind,
    Which drives along yon eastern hill,
More swiftly still my ready mind,
    Should yield subjection to thy will.

Yes, I can move with swifter pace
    Than yonder darting fires I see;
Or I would gladly change my place –
    All things become, or – nothing be.

        U.U.

From: *The Gentleman's Magazine*, May 1794

Casimir, Lib. II. Ode VII.
To Publius Memmius

[Lyr. II 7]

    It would be one relief,
    To moderate our grief,
If things would sink as slowly as they rise:
    But lofty towers quickly fall,
    Sudden ruin buries all;
No happiness is long beneath the skies.

Fates of cities and of men
    Are restless and unquiet all, –
Kingdoms may rise in many years – and in
    As many hours they fall.
    Who gives a single day
    To throw an empire quite away,
Gives time enough – a moment's stroke
Rivets the fate of nations, never to be broke.

    Dying man, forbear,
To load just heaven with impious complaints.
    What though death's trophies here and there
Thicken among your neighbours tents:

The moment when your life began,
    You too began to die.*
He has lived long enough, (O happy man),
Whose life has gained him an eternity.

U.U.

From: *The Gentleman's Magazine*, May 1794.

Ode from Casimir

[Lyr. II 3]

O Lute, the box-tree's sweet harmonious child!
    Now shalt thou hang upon this poplar's bough,
While the clear air sports round in laughter wild,
    And breezes kiss the tender leaves below.

And whistling Eurus now on thee shall breathe,
    Touching thy strings his gentle spirits fly,
While I delight, my head reclin'd beneath,
    Thoughtless upon some verdant bank to lie.

Alas! what clouds so sudden veil the skies,
    What sudden showers fall with patt'ring noise;
Th' o'erwhelming glooms increase! I have to rise!
    Thus, thus, with fleeting step, pass all our joys.

X.Y.

From: *The European Magazine*, July 1794.

---

* 'Our life is ever on the wing, / And death is ever nigh; / The moment when our lifes begin, / We all begin to die.' Watts, Book II Hymn 58. 'Quae tibi primum dedit hora nasci, / Haec hora primum dedit.' Casim. [Note by U.U.]

Casimir, Lib. I. Ode XIII.
To Tarquinius Lavinus

[Lyr. I 13]

What though the sun has disappeared –
    Shall he not tomorrow rise
    In the blushing Eastern skies? –
This gloomy darkness then shall all be cleared;
    Fortune, with her rattling wheel,
May push and roll you on the ground;
    She plays her jokes, but still you feel
You're rising as the wheel turns round.
Live, my Tarquin, live in hope,
    And envy not the great,
    Who walks in dignity and state;
The dust beneath his feet you now lick up: –
But Fortune's wheel turns swiftly round;
    Wait till it turns, and turn it must.
    Then, wrapt in smoke and clouds of dust,
His purple and his pomp lie flutt'ring on the ground:
    But still forbear to laugh, forbear to smile –
    Lord of the purple once, though now he's vile –
Feast not your eyes with this, nor trample on his name,
Remember, Fortune sometimes plays a double game.

U.U.

From: *The Gentleman's Magazine*, September 1794.

Casimir, Book IV. Ode XXIII.
To the Cicada.

[Lyr. IV 23]

    Little insect perching high,
      Midst the lofty poplar leaves,
    Drunk with dew-drops of the sky,
Chirp, and regale thyself and all the groves.
      Long winter now is past,
    And summer months run on in haste –
      On rapid wheels they run,
Come, gently chide the swiftly-flying sun.

Happy seasons just appear,
  Then rush away in haste;*
No pleasures long continue here –
  Too long our sorrows last.

U.U.

From: *The Gentleman's Magazine*, May 1795.

To Aurelius Lycus.
Against immoderate Complaint in Adversity.

[Lyr. I 2]

Tho' for a while no beams of splendour glow,
  Tho' clouds impedent round thy glories wait,
Tho' changeful Fortune treacherously throw
  The die most difficult of dreadful Fate;

Still, Lycus, still the grief dull'd note forbear,
  Let not unworthy moans thy song deform,
Burst not thy breast with vap'ry sighs of Care,
  Nor low'r thy eye-brow with Affliction's storm.

Yon Main where now the mad'ning tempests spread.
  Shall soon in sparkling waves with Zephyrs play;
Yon Sun who hides in mantling woes his head,
  Shall sport tomorrow with a rose-deck's ray.

The sprightly Laugh, – the leaden-winged Sigh –
  Ever in quick alternate dance appear:
Beside young Mirth, whose fervid cheeks are dry,
  Is Sorrow seen bedew'd with many a tear.

Alas! in travail hard are short-liv'd Joys,
  Midst hov'ring woes and shrieking mis'ries born:

---

* 'Ut Se quaeque dies attulit optima / Sic quaeque rapit.' Casim. 'The present moments just appear, / Then slide away in haste, / That we can never say, they're here / But always say, they're past.' Watts, Book II. Hymn 58. [Note by U.U.]

Oft mid the stream that rolls with cheerful noise,
    Is heard the drowning cry – the groan forlorn.

He who with panting oxen lately plow'd,
    Now to the Senate new decrees explains;
And now amid the law-enrobed crowd,
    Involves the produce of his wearied pains.

Oft on his wealth the Star of Morning shines,
    Whom Hesperus had mournful left and bare:
Thus wayward Fortune sportingly entwines
    Wild sprigs of Mirth with with'ring boughs of Care.

She bad yon Clown the favour feel of court,
    A winged dream flies o'er his restless sleep;
She gives him now to sneering Envy's sport,
    And bid him seek his cottage and his sheep.

His laurel'd axe by nations late obey'd,
    Now cleaves the wood his clam'rous wants require; –
Restrain'd at home – of wintry storms afraid –
    His loosen'd fasces aid his glimm'ring fire.

                              X.Y.

From: *The European Magazine*, July 1795.

Casimir, Book III. Ode 22.
To Caesar Pausilipius.
Ne nimium adolescentia fidat.

                                      [Lyr. III 22]

    Trust not to youthful joys, my friend,
        Youth rolls on rapid and on restless wheels;
Swifter it rolls than driving wind,
        'Tis gone ere man its motion feels.
        Beauty, fragile as the glass,
        Years destroy as they pass,
            And drive away our good;
    Deceitful charms will melt and run,

Like wax before the burning sun –
How vain are youth and beauty in the bud!

So have I seen the summer rose
Its blushing honours all disclose,
    At the first dawning light;
Warm breezes fanned its dewy leaves –
But storms arise, the tempest heaves,
    It droops, it dies at night.

The Sisters never will restore
The threads of life their hands have drawn:
    Fate forbids us ever more,
T' enjoy again life's early dawn.

Thrice happy is the man
Whose soul's too big to be confined
    Within life's narrow span;
From custom's yoke he frees his mind,
Rises, and leaves a changing world behind;
    While tow'rd yon lucid skies,
        His country, his abode,
        The palace of his God,
Midst shining worlds of light, he lifts his longing eyes!

                            U.U.

From: *The Gentleman's Magazine*, September 1795.

Casimir, Book II. Ode 26.
To the Virgin Mother,
when Poland was afflicted with War, Famine,
and unseasonable Weather.

                                  [Lyr. II 26]

Mary, queen of golden skies,
    Moesian valleys view from far,
Come, descend, and bring supplies,
    Riding in thy cloud-girt car!

With thee bring thy golden boy,
    Hasten on resplendent wing,

Bring attendants from the sky,
>   Health, and Peace, and Plenty, bring!

U.U.

From: *The Gentleman's Magazine*, September 1795.

To Philidius Marabotinus.
Translated from Casimir, Lib. IV. Ode 31.

[Lyr. IV 31]

In yon reflective streamlet's deep repose
>   Mark what soft scenes of beauty sportful play;
Heav'n's tranquil radiance in her bosom glows,
>   The solar orb, and moon's majestic ray.

Such be thy steadfast mind; by rigid lore
>   Taught with unshaken dignity to glow;
Or when tempestuous billows round thee roar,
>   Or soft airs whisp'ring pleasure swiftly blow,

Still let the cloudless lustre gild thy breast,
>   And golden smiles serene its pure abode;
Thus shall it bear in deeper shades impressed,
>   The awful face of Nature and of God.

Sweet is the task retreating Truth to trace,
>   And lead the ling'ring fugitive to day;
To follow Nature with undaunted pace;
>   Nor bent to tort'ring Doubts imperious sway.

But, in the mind's bright mirror to unfold
>   In liquid colours all the lovely scene,
Truth from the watch-tow'rs of the eyes behold,
>   And each fair object in its native mien.

In vain to curb the headlong steed we try,
>   If our more headlong rage no rules o'er-awe;
The car that shook young Phaeton from the sky
>   No reins it needed but a guiding law.

The wretch, not monarch of his own desires,
    Say, can he rule another? But the hand
That quenches first the rage of mental fires,
    Can to whole worlds dispense supreme command.

Wouldst thou the tumults of the mind repress?
    Thyself by Virtue's rigid laws control:
Thus shall sage Wisdom all thy dictates bless,
    And tributary songs breathe incense to thy soul.

G.

From: *The Gentleman's Magazine*, December 1795.

Casimir, Epigram XIV.
Draw me, we will run after thee. **Cant. I.4.**

[Epig. 14]

Through dreary wilds, a trackless maze,
    Absent from thee I roam;
How can I bear these long delays!
    Jesus, my Saviour, come.

Mary, thrice happy, round thy feet
    Twists her dishevelled hair;
Bound to thy love a captive sweet,
    A captive thou to her.

May I, like her, thy captive be,
    From love I'll ne'er be free;
Dear Saviour, come, dwell here with me,
    Or draw me up to thee!*

U.U.

From: *The Gentleman's Magazine*, April 1796.

---

* 'Ergo trahas vel me, Sponse, vel ipse mane.' Casim. The same epigrammatic turn is used by Herbert: 'O shew thyself to me, / Or take me up to thee.' And frequently in Watts, in more varied and elegant language, 'Lord, I would tempt thy chariot down, / Or leap to thee on high.' [Note by U.U.]

Casimir's Address to the Dormant Rose.
(From the Latin.)

[Lyr. IV 18]

Child of the vernal sky, fair flow'r!
    No longer hide thy charming face;
Awake to hope! Awake to pow'r;
    And emulate the morn-star's grace!

Pale winter's fled on airy feet,
    And all his chilling frosts are o'er;
Haste, then, thy dew-distilling sweet,
    Haste to unfold thy balmy store.

Warm zephyr's gales, with am'rous haste,
    Wait to attend thee on thy way;
The honied florists long to taste
    Thy balmy kisses, as they play.

From: *The Weekly Entertainer*, May 1803.

Ad Memmium. Ode 7, Lib. II.

[Lyr. II. 7]

Since man, and all the works of man,
Are doom'd destruction's certain prey,
O might they end as they began –
With gradual change, and softly sink away!
But by a sudden overthrow
The highest, happiest, are undone;
And restless till they strike the blow,
The busy fates of men and nations run.
To bring the toil of ages down –
Does this a day – an hour – demand?
Alas! whole prostrate states have known,
When life and death hung in the moment's hand:
Forbear, dear dying Friend, to blame
— Impious – the cruelty of Heaven,
Though all around you it reclaim
From all you love, the being it had given.

Our death commences with our birth:
Life is laborious Virtue's prize:
And, full of days, he quits the earth,
Who has secured a life that never dies.

From: *Methodist Magazine*, March 1809.

Ad Pausilippium Ode 22 Lib. III.

[Lyr. III 22]

Let not, dear youth, your slippery age
In vain delights your heart engage.
Youth's is a short uncertain space;
And, eager to conclude the race,
The uncurb'd chariot leaves behind
The swiftest motion of the wind.
Beauty, that now secure appears,
Rais'd on a base of vigorous years,
As those deceitful sands retreat,
Beneath her unsuspecting feet
Shall see a hideous valley frown,
And fall precipitately down.
No words are equal to declare
The transiency of all that's fair!
The melting wax, the crystal frail,
The rose, that scents the morning gale,
And fades, e'er noon the region warms,
Are more secure than human charms.
 Whatever in her haste befall,
Her errors Fate can ne'er recall:
And, ceaseless flowing towards the ocean,
Life has no retrogressive motion.
 Thrice happy he, whose soaring mind
No momentary hopes can bind!
Who, young and fitted to receive
All joys a transient world can give,
The yoke of sense and folly spurns,
Still for his native country burns,

And claims, with undiverted sight,
His portion – in the Land of Light!

Note: Erroneously described as Lyr. III 23.

From: *Methodist Magazine*, March 1809.

Casimir, Lib. I. Ode 1.
On the Departure of the hostile Thracians from Pannonia.

[Lyr. I 1]

Now cease the menaces of War,
And Health and Peace, once driven far
    From our polluted land,
In milk-white chariots born along,
Revisit, midst the general throng,
    And in our cities stand.

Now Faith and Right, devoid of guile,
And Happiness, with gentle smile,
    Fly o'er the joyful fields;
While golden ages sweetly flow
In copious rivers soft and slow,
    And ample pleasures yield.

Now fairer suns, and days of yore,
Sprung from old veins of richer ore,
    Return in vigorous powers;
Bright gems descend like sounding hail,
And liquid gold with every gale
    Drops down in many a shower.

Me now the world permits to sing
Poetic lays on lyric string,
    On high and festive days;
To tell how Saturn's happy reign
Returns to bless the earth again,
    In pompous songs of praise.

New manners, primitive and white,
And honest Candour (charming sight!)
    Once banished from our coast,
Return, while Virtue fair descends, -
Bright goddess! from the skies she bends,
    And gains the seats she'd lost.

Rivers of milk and honey glide,
Warmed by the sun, the lands divide,
    Or rippling o'er the plains;
The banks are full, they swell, they rise –
'Tis nectar to the just and wise –
    The fields are blest again.

More gently waves the bearded grain,
Its close-set stems o'erload the plain,
    And make the valleys groan;
Delightful seasons spare the crop,
And crown the labourer's utmost hope,
    His utmost wishes crown.

The shepherd drives his flocks along,
Rivals the hoarse Cicada's song
    On his rude oaten straw;
Bellow the hills; and while the ground
Strong heifers till, the woods resound
    With every breath they draw.

Peace! the exulting mountains cry;
Peace! the wild shaggy rocks reply,
    Loud echoing with the noise;
Peace! o'er the scattered hills shall bound,
Sequestered valleys catch the sound,
    And burst in violent joys.

The rest of the Ode, consisting of high strains of compliments to Pope Urban VIII. does not seem to merit a translation.

U.U.

From: *The Gentleman's Magazine*, July 1816.

Ode of Casimir.
To His Lyre.

[Lyr. II 3]

Thou child of boxtree, that flexile combined
    Thy string'd frame sonorous, my lute! hang thou high
On the poplar that lofty upturns to the wind
    Its lightly twitch'd leaves, while all blue laughs the sky.
The shrill east's hissing gale shall but dally with thee,
    O'er thy quivering chords as it murm'ringly skims;
Let me lean back my neck at the root of the tree,
    And stretch on this bank's mossy verdure my limbs.

Ha! clouds – sudden clouds! how the heaven is o'ercast!
    How dreary the echo! the crashing of rains!
Up and hence! – human joys, thus ye come, thus are past,
    And only the print of your footstep remains!

                                      OLEN.

From: *The London Magazine*, January 1822.

23

Joshua Dinsdale

Joshua Dinsdale († c. 1750) was a Church of England divine, writer, and translator living in the first half of the eighteenth century. Very little is known of his life, while his published works include *Sermons* (1740) and *The Orations and Epistles of Isocrates. Translated from Greek by Joshua Dinsdale, and revised by the Rev. Mr Young* (1752). The following translations of Sarbiewski's odes were published in *The London Magazine* (and concurrently in *The Scots Magazine* in Edinburgh) between January and June 1741 along with several original poems by Dinsdale such as 'To a Friend'.

An Imitation of the Second Ode of the First Book of Casimire.

[Lyr. I 2]

Forbear, my friend, to knit your brow,
Or vex your breast with fruitless woe,
    And soul-distracting cares;
When heav'n, the wonted smile denies,
And fortune clouded, like the skies,
    Some dire event prepares.

Though storms disturb the sea today,
Loud thunders roar, and lightnings play,
    And wild confusion reigns;
The raging waves shall soon be still,
A gentle breeze the canvass fill,
    And sunshine gilds the plains.

Alternative joys, and grieves ascend
In life, as fortune's wav'ring hand
    Rolls round the various wheel;
Thus often, when the sprightly jest
Goes round, and laughter crowns the feast,
    The sudden tears distil.

Our life a chequered scene supplies,
In fullest joys our sorrows rise,
    Such is the fixed decree
Of fate; nor are we e'er secure;
This moment's bliss may not endure
    Till we another see.

Him, whom the setting sun beheld,
Tired with the labours of the field,
    Goading the steers to rest,
The dawning light, amazed, surveyed,
(His yoke o'er Rome's proud people laid)
    In regal purple dressed.

But should blind fortune's fickle reign
Take what she gave him back again,
    And load him with disgrace;
The emblems* of his pride behold
Piled up, to keep him from the cold,
    And crackling in the blaze.

Note: Published anonymously in January 1741 in *The London Magazine* and *The Scots Magazine*. The circumstances and time of publication indicate Dinsdale as the most probable translator – his translation of 'The Remedy' was published a month later also concurrently in the same two magazines, however, this time the London publication was signed.

From: *The London Magazine*, January 1741.

The Remedy. In Imitation of Casimire

[Lyr. IV 13]

If sighs, my friend, could banish grief,
    Or tears relieve the heart from pain,
I too would pour a briny flood,
    And of my adverse fate complain.

---

* The Fasces. [Note by Joshua Dinsdale.]

Joshua Dinsdale

I'd diamond quarries give for tears,
    And the rich miser's hidden store;
Nay, were both golden Indies mine,
    I'd part with all their shining ore.

But as thick flow'rs in vernal meads
    Luxuriant from soft dews arise,
So grief from grief incessant springs,
    And sorrow loves dim wat'ry eyes.

Then smile, my friend, erect your head,
    Whatever weight your mind oppress
To stoop beneath it will increase,
    But never make your burden less.

For should you to relentless fate
    Vow every day a sacrifice,
In vain would be your pompous woe,
    Did you with tears exhaust your eyes.

The tyrant pow'r with stern contempt
    Would ruthless hear your piteous moan,
But from the dauntless look will run,
    Though lord it o'er the humble groan.

How glad I see your op'ning face
    Again bright honest thoughts display!
No clouds should e'er prophane the mind,
    Where virtue beams immortal day.

From: *The London Magazine*, February 1741.

The Ecstasy

[Lyr. II 5]

What sacred raptures fire my breast,
    And snatch me to the skies,
While the low earth stretched out immense
    A spacious prospect lies!

Bright gilded palaces in view
    Their shining turrets rear,
And rivers in rich smiling vales
    With seats of bliss appear.

Lo! the wide shrinking orb no more
    Its florid beauty shows,
But wrapped in clouds its fading scene
    A group of figures grows.

What sparkling orbs, through the great void,
    Fill all the ambient skies!
While happy vales, and amber streams,
    Transport the ravished eyes.

Hail, glorious God! thy boundless pow'r
    Acts through all nature's sphere;
Where'er I look creation round,
    I see thy goodness there.

What rapid car thus whirls my soul
    Beyond the azure skies?
A burst of glory drowns my sight,
    And scenes ecstatic rise.

In bright effulgence here thy beams
    In all their splendour blaze,
And saints with angels emulate
    Each other's love and praise.

But one at Jesus' pow'rful hand
    Shines bright above the rest,
And love divine in dazzling rays
    Is writ upon her breast.

Methinks I hear th' harmonious strife,
    And thunder of the choir,
While to the height of gratitude
    The heavenly hosts aspire.

Joshua Dinsdale

Hark! How the floating anthems swell,
    And fill the realms above;
No wonder, when th' exalted theme
    Is God and endless love.

From: *The London Magazine*, July 1741.

24

Mary Masters

Mary Masters (c. 1694–1771) was a woman poet active in the literary circles of London of the mid-eighteenth century. According to Boswell, she knew and occasionally visited Dr Samuel Johnson who allegedly revised her volumes of poetry and 'illuminated them here and there with a ray of his own genius' yet still they are 'rendered ridiculous by ineptly handled elaborations' (Cummings 2005: 500). She published two volumes of poetry *Poems on Several Occasions* (1733) and *Familiar Letters and Poems on Several Occasions by Mary Masters* (1755). The latter volume includes several translations from Horace and Catullus as well as a selection of Psalms.

On a Fountain
Casimir, Lib. Epod. Ode 2

[Ep. 2]

Fair Fountain with unsully'd Stream,
That quivers in the Noon-day Beam;
Thy Face an equal Lustre shows,
To the Sun's glance on Scythian Snows.

When his plain Meal the Woodman takes,
With thy Pure Wave his Thirst he slakes;
Translucent Orb! that cheer'st the Ground,
Diffused in rich Embroid'ry round.

Harassed and spent with studious Toil,
O'er the dim Taper's midnight Oil,
To rural Pleasures I resign,
And on thy flow'ry Bank recline.

But o'er thy Mirror let me lave,
My lips in thy full brimming Wave,
Or from my Palm thy Crystal sup,
Or through the Reed imbibe it up.

So may the Cattle from thy Brink,
Dash the loose Earth, and as they drink
With miry Hoofs thy Course restrain,
And mar thy Beauties with a Stain.

Rent from the Willows neighb'ring Tree,
That sucks its verdant Life from thee;
So may no Bough presume to glide,
Along thine ever-honour'd Tide.

And while the checquered Shades, among
Thy silver waves and winds along;
And, thou, fresh-bubbling, still and still,
Pour'st from thy Urn a living Rill.

May Larks and Linnets cease to sing,
And Zephyrs check their wanton Wing,
To catch thy Gurgles as they rise,
Mixed with the Strains the Lyre supplies.

Nor count it a Disgrace that I,
Should join the warbling harmony;
For W*** approves my early Flame,
And W***'s Vote is endless Fame.

Casimir, Lib. I. Ode 2.

[Lyr. I 2]

My Friend forbear th'unmanly Cry,
Nor let the Bosom heave the Sigh,
  Nor cloud thy Looks with Woe,
If Phoebus' Rays should be restrained,
And Fortune from her fickle Hand,
  Some luckless Die should throw.

Today th' un-prisoned Whirlwinds sweep,
And rouse to Wrath the Boiling Deep,
  And warning Billows roar:
But ere th' approaching Morning comes,
Zephyr shall play his silken Plumes,
  And general Peace restore.

Casimir Britannicus

The Sun that sunk with Clouds opprest,
Tomorrow rising in the East;
    In his full Flame shall glow,
Grief and gay Smiles alternate rise:
Joy wipes the Dew-drop from your Eyes
    And transport treads on Woe.

The fullest Tides of Affluence,
And ev'ry Joy that springs from Sense;
    O'er Rocks of Danger roll:
Thus Heav'n decrees till the Great Day,
That sweeps these changing Scenes away,
    And rests the tossing Soul.

He* who last Night his Oxen drove,
Today to Rome makes his remove;
    An Orb supreme to fill,
The Yoke his Oxen wore he throws,
Resistless on his Country's Foes:
    The Vassals of his Will.

The evening Star the Man beheld,
A humble Tiller of the Field;
    But when the Morning came,
He by the Senate's suffrage raised,
In highest Rank of Glory blazed;
    And Realms revered his name.

Should Fortune, who delights to twine,
A Sable with a silver Line;
    But take a different Thread;
He a poor Swain hissed by the Throng,
That with his Triumph swelled his Song,
    Must seek his humble Shed.

His Axes that with Laurels crowned,
Once struck a trembling Terror round;

---

* Cincinatus. [Note by Mary Masters.]

>   His stubborn Billets rend,
> His Rods* which once the World controlled,
> To mend his Fire and chase the Cold,
>   Their last Assistance lend.

Note: The same translation with minor alterations was published by Thomas Gibbons first in 1769 in *The Universal Magazine* and republished in his collection of poems *The Christian Minister* in 1772. It is included in chapter 28.

From: *Familiar Letters and Poems on Several Occasions by Mary Masters*. London: Printed for the Author by D. Henry and R. Cave MDCCLV.

---

* An Axe and Rods were carried before the Consuls of Rome as the Marks of their Dignity. [Note by Mary Masters.]

25

Henry Price

Henry Price (c. 1702 – after 1741) was a graduate of Christ Church College, Oxford. Following a career in the Navy, from the early 1730s he was a landwaiter (custom officer) in the Port of Poole. His collection of *Poems on Several Subjects. By a Land-Waiter in the Port of Poole*, including several translations from and into Latin and French as well as original Latin compositions, was published in London in 1741. His translations from various Greek and Latin authors, however, had appeared for some years prior to that in various magazines starting with a translation of *Batrachomyomachia* attributed to Homer (two parts in December 1733 and January 1734) published in *Bee Revived* as *Battle of the Frogs and the Mice*.

To William Okeden Esq.
Imitated from Casimir.

[Lyr. II 2]

The snowy treasures of the sky,
That on the glitt'ring Mountains lie,
Soon from their brows will melt away,
Struck by the sun's dissolving ray.

But when old Age begins to spread
Its rev'rend Emblems round thy head,
There, Okeden, shall they shine display'd
Till thou thyself in dust art laid.

Let fate but only spare thy youth,
And fate shall justify this truth,
When chang'd from what thou wert before,
She bids thee die, and be no more.

See! mighty Marlbro', once the boast
Of all th' embattled British host,

Beneath the dreadful stroke expires,
Unbrac'd his nerves, extinct his fires;

For strength is naught, and tears shall flow
In vain when heav'n designs the blow.
If thou canst wish to stretch thy days,
Let all thy actions merit praise.

That man is old whom, when he dies,
His country views with weeping eyes.
Fame is his due; and that shall save
His name from darkness and the grave.

Note: First published in *Bee Revived or The Universal Weekly Pamphlet*, February 1734.

The First Ode of the First Book of Casimir.
Written to Pope Urban VIIIth when the Thracian Forces Departed out of Pannonia.
Inscribed to William Milner Esq. by Mr. Price.

[Lyr. I 1]

Now war is ceas'd, and we no more
Tremble to hear the tyrant roar;
Now gentle peace, descending down,
Shall visit ev'ry mirthful town.

While plenty, justice, truth, and love
Along the fields, united, move;
And better ages are restor'd,
That men might reap what they afford.

Now purer suns begin to burn,
And happier years once more return;
A show'r of gold the clouds bestow,
And pearls that cover all below.

Now worlds approve of my faithful lays,
That give to thee deserved praise;

While pleas'd their joy they thus proclaim,
These times and Saturn's are the same.

    The rules our fathers once pursued
Are now in us again renewed:
Religion ceases to appear
In heav'n, but dwells contented here.

    Streams that with milk and honey flow,
Through flow'ry meadows murm'ring go:
Nectarean waves swell o'er their mound,
And spread a deluge all around.

    The yellow harvests nodding stand,
And court the reaper's wiling hand:
The waving fruits, uninjured, play,
Nor feel the sun's malignant ray.

    The shepherd, wand'ring with his goats,
Provokes the little insect's notes:
The wearied ox, returning, fills
With lowings all the neighb'ring hills.

    See! how the lofty mountains spring!
Hark! how the rocks attempt to sing
For joy that o'er the humble plains
Peace still uninterrupted reigns!

    Fair Ceres, dressed in all her pride,
And Summer, glitt'ring by her side,
To crown thy temples ready stand,
Thou great Protector of our land!

    A shade of myrtles thee afford;
The laurel owns thee for its lord;
For thee the tow'ring oak ascends;
The pine to do thee homage bends.

    May the dread ruler of the skies
Behold thy Rome with pitying eyes;

Give thee to sway the world in peace,
And make the strife of nations cease!

    My fair Apollo's deathless tree
Point out a good old age to thee!
May fate permit thy thread to roll
For many a year, untouched, and whole!

    May that bright* Virgin who on high
Shines with those fires that fill the sky;
Whose radiant garments stars compose,
Take some compassion on your woes!

    May she her wonted succour lend,
And to the gen'ral wish attend!
May she our chaste complaints receive,
And help our Nobles when they grieve!

Poole, June 18

First published in *The Gentleman's Magazine*, June 1737.

From: [Henry Price], *Poems on Several Subjects By a Land-Waiter in the Port of Poole*, London: Printed for T. Astley, at the Rose in St. Paul's Churchyard, 1741.

---

* The Virgin Mary. [Note by Henry Price.]

26

James Hervey

James Hervey (1714–1758) was a Church of England divine and religious writer. Educated at Lincoln College, Oxford, Hervey was ordained in 1737 and until his death he was first a curate and from 1752 a parish priest. His earliest and most popular work was *Meditations and Contemplations* in which the following translation was included. Nothing is known about any other translations by Hervey. The poem is the only English translation of Sarbiewski which has ever been set to music. The composer was the little known Italian, Filippo Palma.

Ode from Casimire
[Lyr. IV 18]

Child of the Summer, charming Rose,
    No longer in Confinement lie,
Arise to Light, thy Form disclose;
    Rival the Spangles of the Sky.

The Rains are gone; the Storms are o'er;
    Winter retires to make the way;
Come then, thou sweetly blushing Flow'r
    Come, lovely Stranger, come away.

The Sun is dressed in beaming Smiles,
    To give thy Beauties to the Day:
Young Zephyrs wait, with gentle Gales,
    To fan thy Bosom, as they play.

From: *Meditations and Contemplations in Two Volumes by James Hervey, A.B.*, London: Printed by T. Sabine for J. Whitaker and C. Wilkin, 1775. Published with the score in *The Gentleman's Magazine*, December 1748.

27

Anne Steele alias Theodosia

Anne Steele (1717-1778), known under her pen name Theodosia, was both a poet and one of the first female British hymn writers, certainly the first to rise to fame as such. In 1760, she published *Poems on Subjects Chiefly Devotional* (reissued posthumously in three volumes in 1780), a collection including metrical versions of forty-seven psalms, with religious poems and hymns. In her works she was heavily indebted to Isaac Watts (from whom she might have taken her interest in Sarbiewski), Alexander Pope, and Thomas Gray. Although often accused of lacking originality, some of her hymns remained in circulation until the early twentieth century.

The Elevation

[Lyr. II 5]

    While I survey the azure sky
        With wonder and delight,
    A thousand beauties meet my eye,
A thousand lambent glories deck the night..
    I do not ask to know their names,
    Nor their magnitude enquire;
    What avails it me to prove
    Which are fix'd and which remove?
    Let the sons of science rove
    Through the boundless fields of space,
    And amazing wonders trace;
    Bright worlds beyond those starry flames,
My nobler curiosity inspire.

    When o'er the shining plain,
    Thought ranges unconfin'd,
    Night with her sparkling train
    Awhile may entertain,
    But cannot fix the mind.

The restless mind insatiate still,
(Which all creation cannot fill,)
      Fain would arise
      Beyond the skies,
And leave their glittering wonders far behind.
  Beyond them brighter wonders dwell,
    By mortal eyes unseen;
   Not angel eloquence can tell
The endless glories of the blissful scene.
   Wonders, all to sense unknown!
   Glories, seen by faith alone!
Come, faith, with heaven-illumin'd ray,
Arise, and lead the shining way,
    And teach my longing mind
    The path of life to find;
  A path proud science never found
  In all her wide unwearied round;
A path by bold philosophy untried:
Nor will I ask the twinkling of the night:
The sacred word alone directs my flight:
Nor can I miss my way with this unerring guide.

From awful Calvary the flight begins;
    For there the burdened mind
    Divine relief can find;
  'Tis there she drops her load of sins;
 Accursed load, which held her from the skies!
    'Tis love, almighty love,
    Which bids the load remove,
And shows the heavenly way, and bids my soul arise:
  Jesus, the true, the living way
  To the blissful realms of day!
  Come, dearest Lord, my heart inspire
  With faith, and love, and warm desire;
And bear me, raptur'd, to the blest abode,
Thy glorious dwelling, O my Saviour God!

In those happy worlds are given
To the favourites of heaven,
    Mansions brighter far,
    Than the brightest star,
Which gilds the fair ethereal plains.
Stars must resign their temporary ray,
These shine resplendent with immortal day,
Nor cloud, nor shade, their spotless glory stains.
    Radiant mansions, all divine!
      They shall forever, ever shine
      With undecaying light;
When stars no more shall set and rise,
    And all these fair expanded skies
And roll'd away and lost in everlasting night.

    Adieu, ye shining fields of air,
      Ye spangled heavens, that look so fair,
        And smiling court the eye;
    Your fading beauties charm no more,
While contemplation lost in sweet amaze,
Dwells on the splendour of a brighter sky:
But, O my soul, at humble distance gaze,
      With trembling joy adore.
    There reigns the eternal source of light,
    Full-beaming from his awful throne
Dazzling glories — Oh, how bright!
        To thought unknown.
    Too strong th' insufferable day
    For the strongest angel's eye!
    Seraphs veil'd and prostrate lie
      Adoring at his feet:
    But love attempers every ray,
And mingles holy awe with bliss divinely sweet.

    Ecstatic joy! immense delight!
    Here fainting contemplation dies,
    The glory overwhelms her sight;
    Nor faith can look with steadfast eyes,
    No more, my soul, attempt no more
    Those awful glories to explore,

From frail mortality concealed.
 Yet in the sacred word,
 I may behold my Lord;
 In those celestial lines
 A ray of glory shines,
 Pointing upwards to the skies;
 Scenes of joy, though distant, rise,
To faith, and hope, and humble love revealed.

 Jesus, whom my soul adores,
 O let thy reviving ray,
 (Sweet dawn on everlasting day,)
With heavenly radiance cheer my fainting powers;
 And when I drop this mortal load,
 Free and joyful to the sky
 Let my raptured spirit fly,
With unknown swiftness wing the aerial road,
And find a mansion in thy bright abode.
 Transporting thought – and shall I see
 The heavenly friend who died for me?
 While seraphs tune the golden lyre,
 Jesus, to thy charming name,
 Let me join the blissful choir,
 Thy love the everlasting theme!
 But no the joy resounding lay,
 Harmonious o'er the worlds above,
 Through endless ages can display.
Dear Saviour, half the glories of thy love.

From: Anne Steele, *Poems on Subjects Chiefly Devotional In Two Volumes. A New Edition. To which is added, A Third Volume, consisting of Miscellaneous Pieces. By Theodosia*, Bristol: Printed by W. Pine. Sold by T. Caddell, T. Mills, and T. Evans; – and by J. Buckland, Paternoster-Row, and J. Johnson, St. Paul's Church Yard, London, 1780.

28

Thomas Gibbons

Thomas Gibbons (1720–1785) was an independent minister, diarist, poet, hymn-writer and translator. Educated at dissenting academies in Deptford and Moorfields, Gibbons followed the footsteps of his father (also Thomas, 1700–1757) and was ordained in 1743. A major part of his career was connected with the Independent Church in London, first at Haberdasher's Hall and the Mile End (later Homerton) dissenting academy where he was tutor in logic, metaphysics and rhetoric, a post to which he was elected in 1754 and which he held for the rest of his life. Gibbons raised funds for New Jersey College (forerunner of Princeton University) which awarded him the degree of MA in 1760. Four years later he received a DD from Aberdeen University. Gibbons was a well-known and respected figure among the dissenters, a close friend of Isaac Watts, but his manners and ease of conversation helped him make friends outside this circle who included even Dr Johnson. The most important of his published works is *The Memoirs of the Rev Isaac Watts DD* (1780) which he based on Watts's papers and correspondence. He published forty-five volumes of sermons, a popular textbook on *Rhetoric* (1767), and a number of hymns in which he showed such a strong influence of Watts that they attracted a measure of satirical criticism. Gibbons left also an impressive diary covering the last thirty-six years of his life which has been published in parts since. Gibbons' poetry appeared in various magazines from the early 1740s. Heavily revised for this publication, his early translations (except for the first poem in the present selection) were republished in the volume *The Christian Minister* in 1772.

To Mr Roffey. Commencing a Poet.
A Pindarick Ode Imitated from Casimire
Book II. Ode XV.

[Lyr. II 15]

The sun, poised high in his meridian height,
    Was harnessing the hours,
    To run his evening tours;
And noon, arrayed in flamy robes of light,
  Diffused along the damask rose,
    The lily's nodding head,
    And violets purple bed,
    Sunk down to soft repose:
    Bright clouds that roamed the sky
    Hung motionless on high;
    The zephyr ceased to breathe,
    Hushed in his cave beneath;
      And all was still,
      Except the rill
That trickled from the neighb'ring hill,
And the laborious bee, whose drowsy sound
Made but the gen'ral slumber more profound.

  'Twas then (thrice memorable day!)
    Upon the flow'ry side,
Where Thames devolves his fruitful tide,
That I forgot my wonted play,
    And took the lyre
    With strange desire;
I touched; and string resounded; touched again,
  And still more pleasing rose the strain;
    Echo from her woody seat
    Did the dying notes repeat,
    How unutterably sweet!
Thus I the Muses votary became,
Swept o'er the chords, and felt th' ecstatic flame.

  In bold heroic verse unskilled,
My Muse could never paint the field,
Where the loud trumpet's dire alarms
Incense the soldier into arms,

Or where the cannon's flaming war
Bellows along the boundless air,
Or where the steel wide-wasting mows,
Or where the crimson deluge flows:
     I am only fit to sing
     To a softly-speaking string,
     Golden harvests of the plains,
     Bleating flocks and sporting swains,
     Blushing roses, violets blue,
     Drinking in the morning dew,
     Or the zephyr's balmy wing,
     Gentle harbinger of spring,
     Or the stream whose milky maze
     O'er the thirsty meadow plays,
Impregnating the rising ground,
And shedding blooming life around.

Though sometimes, 'tis confessed, that I
  To nobler themes aspire;
And fain would sing in numbers high
  Of friendship's sacred fire;
Thus, Roffey, fain would I proclaim
How much I love thy honoured name,
And found thee in the trump of fame.
  But, oh! th' attempt how vain!
I cannot half my zeal express,
Nor shalt thou ever think it less
  By a debasing strain.

From: *The Gentleman's Magazine*, July 1745.

Vicissitude, or the Mutability of Human Things.
Casimir, B. I. Ode 2.
To a Friend.

[Lyr. I 2]

My Friend forbear the unmanly Cry,
Nor let thy Bosom heave the Sigh,
 Nor cloud thy Looks with Woe,
If Phoebus' Rays should be restrain'd,
Or Fortune from her fickle Hand
 Some luckless Die should throw.

Today th' unprison'd Whirlwinds sweep,
And into Tumult rouse the Deep,
 That in loud Billows roars,
But ere the Morn her Reign resumes,
The Zephyr plays its silken Plumes,
 And balmy Peace restores.

The Sun, that sunk with Clouds opprest,
Tomorrow rising in the East,
 In his full Flame shall glow:
Grief and gay Smiles alternate rise;
Joy wipes the Dew-drop from your Eyes,
 And Transport treads on Woe.

How vain the Splendors of the Great! –
Upon the slipp'ry Edge of Fate
 See their proud Triumphs roll!
Thus Heav'n decrees, till Time's last Day
That sweeps these changing Scenes away,
 And rests the tossing Soul.

He,* who last Night his Oxen drove,
Today to Rome makes his Remove
 An Sphere supreme to fill;

---

* Quinctius Cincinatus taken from the Plough, and made Dictator of Rome. [Note by Thomas Gibbons.]

The Yoke his Cattle wore he throws
Resistless on his Country's Foes,
    The Vassals of his Will.

The Ev'ning Star the Man beheld
An humble Ploughman in the Field,
    But, when the Morning came,
He, by the People's Suffrage rais'd,
In highest Rank of Glory blaz'd,
    And Realms rever'd his Name.

Should Fortune, who delights to twine
A sable with a silver Line,
    Assume a different Thread,
He, a poor Swain, hiss'd by the Throng,
That with his Honours swell'd their Song,
    Must seek his ancient Shed.

The Axes* that, with Laurels crown'd,
Once struck a trembling Terror round
    His stubborn Billets rend;
His Rods, which once the World control'd,
To feed the Fire, and chase the Cold
    Their last Assistance lend.

Note: First published anonymously (signed T.G.) in *The Universal Magazine* in June 1769 and then reprinted in the book in 1772. The poem differs only in minor details from an earlier translation by Mary Masters published in 1755. Gibbons went so far as to copy and expand Masters' footnotes.

---

* A Dictator of Rome had a bundle of rods, to the amount of 24, carried before him, with an axe bound in the middle of them, so as to appear at the top. [Note by Thomas Gibbons – included only in the *Universal Magazine* June 1769, p. 322.]

The Nocturnal Elevation.
Casimire, B. I. Ode 19.
Imitated.

[Lyr. I 19]

The Beauty of my native Land
    My gazing Sight admires:
I feel the warmest Wishes rise,
    Enkindled by its Fires.

The Moon, with mild Effulgence crown'd,
    Each Planet's twinkling Ray
Invite me from this foreign Ground,
    And bid me come away.

O ye gay Choirs! that ev'ry Night
    Renew your mystic Dance,
And gild with ever-burning Light
    The infinite Expanse;

Ye Centinels, that watch the Pole,
    Nor ever quit your Lines,
Ever proclaiming as you roll,
    That Heav'n still brighter shines;

(For if its Portals and its Floors
    Glow with such vivid Flame
Of Glory what exuberant Stores
    Emblaze th' interior Frame?)

O why should you so long look down
    On me to Earth exil'd?
Your radiant Regions are my own,
    For I'm your Maker's Child.

Angels, commission'd to attend
    The weary Pilgrim Home,
Swift from the cleaving Skies descend,
    And swift prepare my Tomb.

Then free me from these Bonds of Death,
    That I have drag'd so long,
And lay this Flesh devoid of Breath
    Its kindred Dust among.

I ask no Marble Pomp: a Sod
    Will serve to dress my Bed;
Or, if you please, over my Clod
    A Show'r of Roses shed.

Then, while my Soul its Freedom sings,
    Ye Sons of Light arise,
Mount me on your triumphant Wings,
    And bear me to the Skies.

The Ecstasy; or an Adieu to Earth, and an Ascent to Heaven. Casimir, B. II. Ode 5.

[Lyr. II 5]

I Scorn this worthless Globe: ye Clouds, ye Winds,
Your Pow'rs unite, and waft me to the Skies.
See how the Wood-maz'd Mountains swift retreat!
How Kingdoms with their People widely spread,
Obscur'd in Mists of Air, recede from Sight!
The radiant Temples of the Deity,
The royal Tow'rs, the Cities spurn'd behind,
Contract their Space, and fade upon the view
Down on the Nations, through the world dispers'd
I look, all grasp'd in my immense Survey.
Here fickle Fortune plays her tragic Games;
The origin of Empires, and their fall,
Alternatively diversify the Scene.
Here Towns from their Foundations rise, and lift
Their lofty Battlements; here ancient Walls,
And ancient Tow'rs moulder'd by Time descend
Precipitate in Ruin; scarcely more
Than Ashes mark the low dismantled Spots,
Where once majestic Citadels arose.
Here a fair Climate and propitious sky
With Fruits, and Flow'rs, and Fragrance crown the Soil,

But the Inhabitants perverse, ingrate,
Fir'd into Rage and Faction, rush to Arms.
Tranquility here spreads her balmy Wing
Unruffled, undisturb'd, but Pestilence,
First-born of Death, insatiably devours.
Behold that Country in the Blaze of War:
Th' embattled Legions Front to Front advanc'd,
Expect in Horror the suspended Blow,
While Fury, pausing in her hot Career,
A Moment wavers where to bend the Storm.
In yonder Province see the Battle join'd,
And hostile Troops mowing each other down
In mutual Havock: all the wide Champain
Runs purple, and is swell'd with Heaps of Dead.
Another Clime a diff'rent Scene presents:
There trading Ships, laden with precious Freights,
Securely sweep the Main: the peaceful Ports
With Thousands swarm, that all delighted ply
Their fervent Toils, and house the various Stores.
Num'rous the Springs of War, and num'rous too
Its Modes of Mischief. Now for Helen's Charms,
Brighter than ever grac'd a female Form,
From her Liege Lord's dishonour'd Bed transferr'd
To a young Paramour's impure Embrace,
What Myriads rise, what Countries gleam in Arms!
For some opprobrious Word, that stung his Pride,
Here a mad mighty Monarch draws his Sword
In Vengeance, and unbounded Murder spreads.
Here Tyranny insatiably devours
Freedom, and Peace, and Properties, and Lives,
As human Hearts into canine were chang'd;
Uproar and Carnage all their savage Joy.
Here Crimes, embolden'd by Example, grow
Into supreme Enormity of Guilt.
Thus, while a Flood of Mis'ry whelms our Race,
From various Springs that Flood of Mis'ry flows.
Yonder behold the Bosom of the Deep
With martial Fleets, oustretch'd in dire Array,
Wide cover'd o'er: the floating Citadels
Disgorge their brazen Storms, and sulph'rous Flames

Outrageous: Ocean far and wide resounds:
Th' astonish'd Cliffs to their Foundations shake,
And huger Billows lash th' afflicted Shores.
Barbarians, check your Fury! What, shall Death,
So dreadful in its simple Form, by you
With triple Terrors arm'd, Sword, Wreck, and Flame,
Destroy your Fellow-Men? Is not the Land
A Theatre sufficient for this Rage,
But must you spread his Empire o'er the Deep?
Here Kingdoms by the Earth's Convulsions rent
To Ruin rush, and in one common Grave
Bury themselves and People. Silent Dust
O'erspreads the Places, where their Glories stood,
On which some Trav'ller in some future Age,
May deeply-pensive write this Epitaph,
'Under these Ashes in one Sepulchre
'Princes, Realms, Subjects undistinguish'd lie.'
Why should the Muse, to swell the sad Detail
Of human Woes, tell what imperious Floods
Whole Cities with their Ports at once o'erwhelm
In boundless Inundation? Temples, Tow'rs
Imperial, and the Shepherds humble Cots
Are sapp'd, are bury'd in th' insulting Wave,
And Pride's vain Pomp floats on th' encumber'd Stream,
The Sport of Ocean. Thus the World is doom'd
To wage with ev'ry cruel Form of Death
Hard Conflict, till it sinks in Floods of Fire.
Inexorably Destiny o'erspreads
Terrestrial Scenes, till that last Day arrives,
Which all this lower Theatre consigns,
Tho' roof'd with Sapphire, and emblaz'd with Stars,
To Ruin, and to Darkness' endless Reign.
      But why should I delay my heav'nly Course,
My Journey to the blissful Realms on high
To gaze on Things terrene? Bear me, ye Clouds,
To the pure crystal Skies, where Sun and Moon
Wheel their perennial Rounds. Say, do I dream?
Or do I feel the Gales assist my Flight
Aerial? – See how fast the Lands recede!
How fast the spacious Empires die away!

How fast the Globe itself contracts! It shrinks
Into a Point; 'tis vanish'd from my Sight.
All hail thou Ocean of the Deity!
All hail ye glorious Regions! where no Change,
Nor Death can come. All hail, ye Seas of Life
Unfathom'd, unconfin'd! Into your Streams
Serene receive a Pilgrim there to bathe,
There to enjoy Eternity of Bliss.

Note: First published anonymously (as T.G.) with changes in *The Royal Magazine*, April 1769.

Fortitude.
Casimir. B. 3. Ode 4. Imitated and Enlarged.
To a Friend.

[Lyr. III 4]

My friend, should Fortune's fav'ring gales
Just undulate your peaceful Sails,
    Or should the Billows roll,
Tumultous though the roaring Deep,
Still in one even Tenor keep
    Your Dignity of Soul.

Should Fortune smile, be still serene,
Let no responsive smile be seen,
    Or should she pour the Tear,
Be sure to wipe the tear away,
And through Life's miscellaneous Day,
    Firm to yourself appear.

A Consul's, or a Caesar's hand,
Should o'er your Passions bear Command,
    Nor intermit its Pow'r.
Should Fate intend some desp'rate wound,
And Ills on Ills besiege you round,
    Stand like a moveless Tow'r.

Nor quit your Road, nor 'bate your Speed,
Whatever Thorn or baleful weed
      May choak or curse the Ground;
Often from Sorrow's Cloud of Night,
Joy, like an Angel, bursts to Sight,
      And gilds th' Horizon round.

Prosperity its evil brings,
Relaxing oft the mental String
      In her soft sultry Air:
Adversity her Blessings gives,
And ev'ry Stroke the Soul receives
      Enables it to bear.

A Grief, protracted far by Fate,
Diminishes its massy Weight,
      And weakens by its Length.
Bend thy rough Fortune to thy Will:
Patience and Use have sov'reign Skill,
      To vanquish all her Strength.

Enlargement.

Almighty God, whatever Ills
Thy all-disposing Wisdom wills
      For me Thy meanest Care,
Teach me, enliven'd with Thy Love,
And op'ning Views of Bliss above,
      Magnanimous to Bear.

Fortune and Fame are wild and vain,
The Figments of a Pagan Brain:
      A God, a God is all.
O'er Nature he extends his Sway,
O'er Realms of Night, and Realms of Day,
      And this terraqueous Ball.

Prosperity sent from above
To win our Gratitude and Love
      Spreads her inviting Charms;

Adversity receives from God
Its Scorpion-stings and smarting Rod
    To drive us to his Arms.

Note: First published anonymously (as T.G.) in a slightly different version (as 'Constancy' and without the 'Enlargement') in *The Royal Magazine*, April 1769.

To a Young Gentleman.
Partly imitated from Casimir. B. 3. Ode 22.

[Lyr. III 22]

Be not, my Friend, by Youth deceiv'd,
Nor let the Siren be believ'd,
    Though smooth and soft her Strain;
Away on whirling Wheels she flies,
Swift as the Gust that rides the Skies
    Without or Yoke or Rein.

Youth must resign its blooming Charms
To age, whose cold, whose frozen Arms
    Will wither ev'ry Joy;
'Tis brittle Glass, 'tis rapid Stream,
'Tis melting Wax, 'tis Air-dress'd Dream,
    That time will soon destroy.

So smiles at morn the dewy Rose,
And to the genial Breeze's blows,
    Evolving Odours round:
But, crush'd by Ev'ning's furious Rains,
It droops, it sinks upon the Plains,
    Down trodden on the Ground.

Hours, Days, Months, Years impetuous fly,
Like Meteors darting through the Sky,
    And must return no more.
Know, my young Friend, that Moments fled
Are moments ever, ever dead,
    And cancell'd from thy Score.

See how the Globes, that sail the heav'n,
Around in rapid Eddies driv'n,
    Are hast'ning to their Doom:
Time rushes to Eternity,
Eager in his Embrace to die
    His Parent and his Tomb.

Though we in those low Vale were born,
Yet this low Vale our Souls should scorn,
    And to the Heav'n should rise:
So the Larks hatch'd on Clods of Earth
Disdain their mean inglorious Birth,
    And warble to the Skies.

Note: First published signed T. G. in a slightly different version in *The Universal Magazine* April 1769 (and reprinted there in December 1770 without the signature). The same version was published in *The London Magazine* (also in April 1769), and later reprinted by *The Scots Magazine* in May 1769.

From: *The Christian Minister, in Three Poetic Epistles To Philander. To which are added, I. Poetical Versions of several Parts of the Scripture. II Translations of Poems from Greek and Latin Writers. And, III. Original Pieces, chiefly in Verse, on Various Occasions, By Thomas Gibbons, D.D.*, London: Printed for J. Buckland, in Paternoster Row; and E. and C. Dilly, in the Poultry, near the Mansion-House, 1772.

29

William Mason

William Mason (1725–1797) was a Church of England clergyman, poet, garden designer, and amateur musician. Highly fashionable in his time, Mason's poetry is often characterised by its piety and bombastic style, originally influenced by Milton and Spenser. The style was entirely rejected by the next century and Mason is variously seen by contemporary critics either as a vital transitional figure between the late Augustan age and Romanticism or a poetaster and dilettante. Mason combined two highly incompatible literary personalities: on the one hand he was the highly respected author of odes, elegies, epitaphs, dramatic poems, and epic blank verse; on the other hand, however, he was at the same time the subversive satirist under the pen name of Malcolm MacGreggor. His translations included a versified chapter from the Book of Job. After the death of Thomas Gray, Mason published *The Poems of Mr Gray, to which are Prefixed Memoirs of his Life and Writings* (1775), in an innovative form combining Gray's letters, biographical commentary, and poems, a form which was later copied, e.g. by James Boswell. His *magnum opus* is *The English Garden* (four books, 1772–1781), a didactic poem in blank verse based on Virgil's *Georgics* concerning landscape, art, and gardening. Mason himself designed several gardens for his aristocratic patrons, the most famous is Nuneham Courtenay which still survives. Mason was an accomplished amateur musician and he collaborated with the most famous composers of his age such as Thomas Arne who composed music to accompany his dramatic poems *Elfrida* (1772) and *Caractacus* (1776). Mason himself composed religious hymns, some still sung today. He was responsible for the introduction of the piano to Great Britain and was the inventor of the celestinette. It was probably his interest in music that attracted his attention to Sarbiewski's poem, as he explains in his short note.

Ode of Casimire Translated

[Lyr. II 3]

Sweet harp, of well-fram'd box the vocal child!
Here shalt thou hang on this tall poplar's spray,
    While ether smiles, and breezes mild
    Amid its pendant foliage play.
Eurus shall here, but borne on softest wing,
Whisper and pant thy warbling chords among,
    While pleas'd my careless limbs I fling
    On this green bank, and mark thy song —
But lo! what sudden clouds veil the blue skies!
What rushing sound of rain! Rise we with speed —
    Ah always thus, ye light-wing'd joys
    Ye fly, and ere posses'd are fled!

This elegant little Ode was attempted to be translated, not only on account of its lyrical excellence, but also because the instrument described in it seemed not to be merely a fancied Poetical Lyre, but the real harp of Eolus, invented by Athanasius Kircher. This conjecture, it is presumed, will not appear improbable, when it is added that Casimir and Kircher were Jesuits and contemporaries. The mention of Eurus rather than Zephyrus, as a wind more proper to produce the sound, and the other circumstance of hanging it on a high tree, all seem to favour this notion, which if admitted, gives an added and appropriate beauty to the delicate original.

From: *The Works of William Mason, M.A. Precentor of York, and Rector of Aston. In Four Volumes.* Vol. I, London: Bulmer & Co., 1811.

Note: Although quite intriguing, this can hardly be true as the German Jesuit, scholar, scientist, and inventor Athanasius Kircher (1601–1680) invented his aeolian harp about the year 1649 and described it for the first time in his *Musurgia Universalis* (1650) i.e. some three decades after the poem was written and a decade after Sarbiewski's demise. The two Jesuits, although contemporaries, could not have met as Sarbiewski left Rome in 1625, whereas Kircher only arrived there in 1633. The aeolian harp, however, became extremely popular in the latter half of the eighteenth and the early nineteenth century. Mason's note is a testimony to this revival of interest in Kirchner's invention. The instrument features prominently in numerous works of the English Romantic poets such as Wordsworth ('The Prelude'), Coleridge ('The Eolian Harp'), Shelley ('Ode to Apollo'), and Keats ('Endymion') (Ecker 1963). Mason himself wrote 'Ode IX. To an Aeolus Harp. Sent to Miss Shepheard'.

30

John Glasse

John Glasse (c. 1730 – after 1765) graduate of Trinity College, Cambridge, was a minor Augustan poet. The only known collection of his poems is *Poems on Several Occasions* published in 1763. The volume includes a small collection of original poems ranging from elegies to animal fables. The following translation was accompanied by 'On the Image of Cupid, tending to the Flock of Thyrsis, An Epigram translated from the Greek'. In March 1765 *Royal Magazine* published his paraphrase of Psalm 23, in April it was followed by 'The Shipwreck of Simonides, a Fable Imitated from Phaedrus' after which date his known publications cease.

Epigram XVI of Casimire
Translated by the same [J. Glasse]

[Epig. 16]

I thirst, I thirst! thou, Magdalen, dost cry,
And yet no friendly stream these rocks is near:
Does not a torrent issue from thine eye?
Then, Magdalena, drink the briny tear.

From: *The London Magazine, or, Gentleman's Monthly Intelligencer*, March 1760.

31

Μέλη Εφημέρια

Μέλη Εφημέρια (from Greek 'Ephemeral Songs') is a small anonymous volume of poetry 'printed for the author' in Oxford in 1783 which opens with two translations from Sarbiewski. The book includes a selection of original compositions and a few translations from and into Latin and Greek. Its author is unknown but the place of publication and an impressive list of almost one hundred subscribers, most of whom were students, graduates, or professors of various Oxford colleges, suggest he was an Oxonian don himself.

**Taken for the Most Part
From Casimire's Ode
In Auram.**

[Lyr. IV 26]

Gale, that like a Fay unseen,
Wantonst in the blue serene,
Thither let thy course be sped,
Where yon poplar lifts its head.
Sportive Zephyr, loose and gay,
Midst the scatterr'd foliage play,
Swiftly through its branches pass,
Then vex in playful mood the grass.
Where yon streams the rose-bed lave,
Gently falling wave on wave;
While the sleep-persuading sound
I catch, reclin'd upon the ground,
Lightly o'er my temples fly,
While my Lyre hangs silent by.
So may skies for ever smile,
Suns their blessings shed the while;
So may dews with liquid tread,
All for thee their moisture shed;
So for thee may every plain,
Yield the Sweets of swelling grain.

Sportive Zephyr, loose and gay,
Midst my curling tresses play;
When my Muse attempts to sing,
Coming on auspicious wing,
Softly breathe the strings among,
Glad companion of my song.

From Casimir's Ode
In Rosam

[Lyr. IV 18]

Where hast thou tarried beauteous Rose, that late
In ruddy hue the stars did imitate?
Rise gentle daughter of the fost'ring Sky,
Nor let unseen thy matchless beauty die.
Fled is each brooding cloud full charg'd with snow,
And in their stead indulgent zephyrs blow.
The Northern blast no more is heard to rave,
In rude uproar high-tossing many a wave;
For thee Favonius bids the tempest cease,
Hush'd are the waves, and calm'd the winds in peace.
Rise then – nor let thy blushing honours bind
The forehead of the rough unpolish'd hind,
The sacred altar courts thy hallow'd wreath,
In chaste Diana's honour fragrance breathe;
Or seek some Nymph, whose pure and spotless heart
With conscious virtue glows, unknown to art,
Where charms of Chastity and Honour meet,
And Beauty serves to make the whole complete.
Fly to Lucinda's breast, and settle there,
For know Lucinda is as chaste as fair.

From: *Μέλη Εφημέρια*. Oxford: Printed for the Author and Sold by Mess. Fletchers, Booksellers in the Turle; and by W. Jackson in Oxford, 1783.

32

Talbot Keene

Talbot Keene (c. 1737–1824) went to Westminster School and later graduated at Cambridge University (BA 1761, MA 1770). Keene took holy orders and became the vicar of Brigstock and Stanion, Northamptonshire, a post which he held for the rest of his life. He published anonymously in 1787 a collection of original poems supplemented by a bilingual selection of translations from and into Greek and Latin including the following translation from Sarbiewski.

The Ode of Casimire, To the Grass-Hopper. Translated

[Lyr. IV 23]

Insect of envied song, that sit'st
Upon the top-most poplar bough,
Drench'd in the heaven-distilled dew;
With thy enchanting self-taught note
Thyself thou cheerest and the grove that's mute.

Winter now past, while short-liv'd spring
Is posting on its destin'd way;
Catch, quick, O! catch the tepid fun
And hail him on the rapid wind,
With thy own blithly-warbling throat
And nature's artless lay.

As each day in its gilded car
Shoots from the radiant seat of Jove,
So each with hasty step full soon
Thither returns again.
Our joy is ever short: Our grief,
Alas! Alas! too long -----------

From: [Talbot Keene], *Miscellaneous pieces: original and collected; by a clergyman of Northamptonshire, late of Trinity College, Cambridge*, London: Printed for the Author, 1787.

33

John Pinkerton alias Robert Heron

John Pinkerton (1758-1826) a Scottish antiquarian and historian, poet, and editor of Scottish ballads and poems, also author of studies in medals, rocks, geography etc. His original poetry was largely thought of as of little merit, although his studies in the history of Scotland were widely read and commented on. Pinkerton propagated a rather eccentric theory that Scots were not Celts but a Germanic people, the race of ancient Goths, which he supported with literary forgeries and spurious linguistic research. Pinkerton expressed his views on literature in *Letters of Literature* (1785) published under the pen name 'Robert Heron esq.'[*] His original compositions were published in 1781 as *Rimes*.

To his Harp

[Lyr. II 3]

Sonorous daughter of the pliant boxen stem,
On the high poplar, O my harp, thou shalt depend:
    While laughs the sky, and the gale
    Softly revives the listless leaves.
The Western Wind will solicit with gentlest breath
The music of thy charming strings: I the mean while
    Lost in sweet ease, will recline
    Along the green of this fair bank
Alas! What sudden clouds invade the sunny sky?
What unexpected show'rs in sounding haste descend!
    Let us be gone. Ah how soon
    Will happiness still pass away!

Pinkerton added to this translation the following comments:

---

[*] John Pinkerton a.k.a. Robert Heron should not be mistaken for Robert Heron (1764-1807) also a Scottish poet, historian, and translator. Pinkerton later claimed that he had based his pen name on his mother's maiden name and did not know of the existence of any other Robert Heron.

'I shall beg leave to subjoin to it [the Latin text of Sarbievius's ode] a translation of my own, upon a new plan, syllable for syllable, a little in the manner of Milton's translation of *Quis te puer gracilis sub antro* save that Milton, and his followers in this stanza, have only adopted the mechanic form, not the syllabification, which I shall religiously preserve' (p. 293)

'In the original I do not like *testudinem shell*, when it appears from the first line, to be made of box; nor the epithet *sutilis*, which implies *patched* or *sewed together*, not *capable of being wrought into musical or other instruments*, which must have been the author's idea; and which, perhaps, I have not strongly expressed by pliant. *Sibilantis* is unhappy, so I think is *collum*. The last stanza is faultless.' (p. 295)

From: [John Pinkerton] *Letters of Literature by Robert Heron Esq.*, London: Printed for G.G.J. and J. Robinson, in Paternoster Row, 1785.

34

Robert Burns

Robert Burns (1759-1796) is the national poet of Scotland. Burns was a voracious reader and autodidact, yet his knowledge of Latin was extremely slim (if it existed at all). However, in 1773, not long before the following poem was composed (which was most probably in 1776), he allegedly learned some Latin from John Murdoch in Ayr. Nevertheless, his other poems seem to confirm that his knowledge of the language was at best limited (e.g. 'Epistle to J. Lapraik', 1785) and his works do not include any translations. It is certain that Burns himself considered this poem an original composition, as he later stated: 'These two stanzas I composed when I was seventeen: they are among the oldest of my printed pieces.' The similarity to Sarbiewski's poem 'Ad suam testudinem' (Lyr. II 3), first noticed in an article in *The Classical Journal* signed V.L. (1814), is hard to miss. It may be, however, explained in two possible ways – either Burns became acquainted with the Latin original during his classes and liked it or, which is far more probable, he read one of its numerous English translations available at that time which saw a surprisingly sudden increase of interest in this specific poem (at least seven different versions are known). A testimony to its popularity in Scotland is a translation by John Pinkerton, quoted in the previous chapter. On the other hand, James Mackay (1992: 71) indicates Alicia Cockburn's 'exquisite song "Flowers of the Forest", published in an anthology called *The Lark* in 1765' as a possible source and there is in fact a certain similarity between the texts.

I dream'd I lay

[Lyr. II 3]

I dream'd I lay where flowers were springing
    Gaily in the sunny beam;
List'ning to the wild birds singing,
    By a falling crystal stream:
Straight the sky grew black and daring;
    Thro' the woods the whirlwinds rave;
Trees with aged arms were warring,
    O'er the swelling drumlie wave.

Such was my life's deceitful morning,
    Such a pleasure I enjoyed;
But lang or noon, loud tempests storming,
    A' my flowery bliss destroy'd.
Tho' fickle fortune has deceiv'd me,
    She promis'd fair, and performed but ill;
Of mony a joy and hope bereav'd me,
    I bear a heart shall support me still.

Vocabulary:
Drumlie – muddy
Lang or – long before
Mony – many

From: *The Poetical Works of Robert Burns*, Glasgow: John S. Marr and Sons, [1877].

35

William Margetson Heald

William Margetson Heald (1767–1837), Church of England clergyman. Heald first trained to become a doctor in Leeds, Edinburgh, and London but having decided upon a new career went to study at St Catharine's College, Cambridge (admitted 1790, BA in 1794 and MA in 1798) and took holy orders in 1794. In 1798, he became curate at Birstal near Leeds and from 1801 to 1836 he was vicar of the parish which was then inherited by his son, also called William Margetson Heald (1801–1875). Heald wrote poetry as a student, he was the author of the mock-heroic poem *The Brunoniad* (1789). In 1798, Heald added a small selection of poems, two original elegies and the translations from Sarbiewski quoted below, to a volume of poetry published by Joseph Hucks, a younger friend from the college.

Casimir, Book 2. Ode 3.

[Lyr. II 3]

In the high towering poplar thus swinging
   My lyre, hang, suspended at ease:
Thy strings, at wild intervals, ringing,
   When swept by the breath of the breeze.

The blue vault its full beauty displaying,
   Not a cloud the pure aether o'ershades,
And in sighs his soft wishes betraying,
   The green foliage fond zephyr pervades.

Thus I leave thee to murmur and quiver,
   As whispers the slow-rising wind;
While here, stretch'd on the banks of the river,
   I repose, in light slumbers reclin'd.

Ha! Along yon horizon dark-scowling,
   What tempest-fed shadows appear!

Clouds! clouds! rise, incessantly rolling;
    Hark! the show'r whistles loud on mine ear.

O my harp, my companion, my treasure,
    Let us rise, let us hasten away:
'Tis thus flies the phantom of pleasure,
    With quick step ever hasting away.

To the Grasshopper
B. 4. O. 23.

[Lyr. IV 23]

Tipsy with tears heav'n's dewy concave sheds,
Melodious insect! who delight'st to rove
Where its high foliage yon tall poplar spreads,
And with thy music, lull the listening grove;

Now, past the storms of winter, drear and long;
Too swift retreating, while her downward wain,
Rolls the brief summer; come, commence thy song,
And softly to the speeding suns complain.

Soon as each prosperous morn its beam displays,
Swift, on our view its orient blushes fade,
How short the transitory pleasure stays!
How long the woes that life's drear paths pervade!

To the Rose
B. 4. O. 18.

[Lyr. IV 18]

  Thy Front in starry splendour fair,
Why lingering still, delicious rose?
Sweet infant of the fostering air,
Uprais'd from earth, thine odorous blooms disclose.

Driven by young zephyr's whitening car,
For thee the watery clouds retire:
Rough Boreas stills his windy war,
As gay Favonius sooths the tyrant's ire.

Awake, unfold thy blushing train,
Careless what bloom thy locks arrays,
Gay-glittering round no front prophane,
Pure child of chastity! thy pomp shall blaze.

Round no plebeian temples twine,
Thee let the sacred altars wear.
O wreath the virgin's locks divine
Which float dishevell'd on the sweeping air.

To Publius Memmius
B. 2. O. 2.

[Lyr. II 2]

The wintry robe that clothes yon hoary vale,
Stript by the sun, will shortly disappear,
Soon as his shafts the neighbouring hills assail,
But when, at length, chill age's wintry year,

Around thy brows, its scatter'd frost displays:
It clings perpetual, and departs no more,
The approaching spring, the summer's gaudy blaze,
The autumn's ruddy blush, will soon be o'er.

But life-benumbing cold, and hoary hair,
When once arriv'd continual sway assume;
Nor aught avail thy beauty to repair,
The flowery garland, and the sweet perfume.

One youth adorn'd thee with its rosy prime,
One age shall snatch thee from our wishful gaze,
But, through the eras of revolving time,
The fame, my Publius, may surviving blaze.

When, by his country mourn'd, the patriot dies,
He sinks adorn'd with life's sublimest boon,
Fame's open path to none impervious lies,
All else must vanish like the changeful moon.

From: Joseph Hucks, *Poems by J. Hucks, A.M. Fellow of Catherine Hall, Cambridge*, Cambridge: Printed by B. Flower [etc.], 1798.

36

Joseph Hucks

Joseph Hucks (1772–1800) was a graduate of Eton, a student and from 1794 a fellow of Catherine Hall, Cambridge. In the summer of 1794 Hucks and Samuel Taylor Coleridge made a walking tour of North Wales during which Hucks wrote letters published in 1795 as *A Pedestrian Tour through North Wales in a Series of Letters*. In 1798 Hucks published quite a large collection of poems, both original compositions and translations such as this quoted below.

To a Stream[*]

[Epig. 21]

As late I wander'd from life's busy throng,
Where Tyber's waves complain'd the rocks among:
Flow on, O shipwreck'd stream! I cried, and mourn
My love, for tears have fail'd these eyes forlorn:
Unnumber'd are thy tears; and Ah! might mine,
Unceasing fall as prodigal as thine;
For ever would I flow through each lone vale,
And murmur as I flow'd my plaintive tale.
Sudden I ceas'd, for lo, the listening flood,
Stopp'd midway, where in sorrow's garb I stood;
Silent it slumber'd on the pebbled shore,
And like me mute and sad was heard no more:
Press'd by the heavier hand of wintry fate,
Haply it sigh'd for my more envied state.

From: Joseph Hucks, *Poems, by J. Hucks, A.M. Fellow of Catherine Hall, Cambridge*, Cambridge: Printed by B. Flower [etc.], 1798.

---

[*] Translated from Cassimer. Epigram 21. [Note by Joseph Hucks.]

37

Samuel Taylor Coleridge

Samuel Taylor Coleridge (1772–1834) poet, playwright, and literary critic (and Wordsworth's friend and collaborator) was fascinated with Sarbiewski's poetry. In his note preceding his translation of 'Ad suam testudinem' (he changed the title to 'Ad Lyram', replacing a learned word with a more common one), Coleridge wrote: 'If we except Lucretius and Statius, I know not of any Latin poet, ancient or modern, who has equalled Casimir in boldness of conception, opulence of fancy, or beauty of versification' (1912: 60). He intended to publish his translations of Sarbiewski in a collection of translations which he advertised in 1794 as *Imitations from the Modern Latin Poets*. Finally, however, 'Ad suam testudinem' appeared in 1795 in *The Watchman* as 'Song. Imitated from Casimir' while 'To a Friend in Answer to a Melancholy Letter' (a translation of Lyr. I 2) was published in the volume of *Poems* in 1796. The noble plan of publishing a collection of translations from Latin, like many other major plans of Coleridge, was never completed. Coleridge wrote these translations not long before January 1793, and the latter poem especially reflects the political atmosphere of the day, as well as the poet's personal attitude towards the French Revolution, leaving little of the original setting and the Neo-Stoic message of the original composition. It seems that Coleridge himself was not fully satisfied with the result. In a copy of *Poetic Works* from 1828 (now in the Fitzwilliam Museum, Cambridge) he wrote 'Very like one of Horace's Odes, starched.' Editors of his works suggest that the commentary was directed against his own work not against Horace whom Coleridge greatly respected (1912: 62).

Ad Lyram

[Lyr. II 3]

The solemn-breathing air is ended –
    Cease, O Lyre! thy kindred lay!
From the poplar-branch suspended
    Glitter to the eye of Day!

On thy wires hov'ring, dying,
    Softly sighs the summer wind:
I will slumber, careless lying,
    By yon waterfall reclin'd.

In the forest hollow-roaring
    Hark! I hear a deepening sound –
Clouds rise thick with heavy low'ring!
    See! th' horizon blackens round!

Parent of the soothing measure,
    Let me seize thy wetted string!
Swiftly flies the flatterer, Pleasure,
    Headlong, ever on the wing.

Lines
To a Friend in Answer to a Melancholy Letter

[Lyr. I 2]

Away, those cloudy looks, that labouring sigh,
The peevish offspring of a sickly hour!
Nor meanly thus complain of Fortune's power,
When the blind Gamester throws a luckless die.

Yon setting Sun flashes a mournful gleam
Behind those broken clouds, his stormy train:
Tomorrow shall the many-colour'd main
In brightness roll beneath his orient beam!

Wild, as the autumnal gust, the hand of Time
Flies o'er his mystic lyre: in shadowy dance
The alternate groups of Joy and Grief advance
Responsive to his varying strains sublime!

Bears on its wing each hour a load of Fate;
The swain, who, lull'd by Seine's mild murmurs, led
His weary oxen to the nightly shed,
Today may rule a tempest-troubled State.

Nor shall not Fortune with a vengeful smile
Survey the sanguinary Despot's might,
And happy hurl the Pageant from his height
Unwept to wander in some savage isle.

There shiv'ring sad beneath the tempest's frown
Round his tir'd limbs to wrap the purple vest;
And mix'd with nails and beads, an equal jest!
Barter for food, the jewels of his crown.

From: Samuel Taylor Coleridge, *The Complete Poetical Works*, ed. by Ernest Hartley Coleridge. 2 vols, Oxford: Clarendon Press, 1912.

38

William Herbert

William Herbert (1778-1847) was a scholar, Church of England clergyman, politician, poet, translator, botanist, and amateur painter. From an early age Herbert showed literary talent, he was a classical scholar and also a Neo-Classicist poet. On leaving Eton he obtained a prize for a Latin poem entitled *Rhenus*, followed in 1801 by *Ossiani darthula*, a volume of Greek and Latin poetry. During his studies at Oxford Herbert developed an interest in ancient Scandinavian literature, excerpts of which he translated and published as *Select Icelandic Poetry, Translated from the Originals with Notes* (1804-1806). His translations from other European languages were published in 1804 as *Translations from the German, Danish etc* from which volume the following translation was taken. The publications gained general acclaim, for the first time introducing the English reading public to early Medieval Scandinavian literature. Byron mentions Herbert's Icelandic translations in his *English Bards and Scotch Reviewers* (1809). An active politician, MP from 1807 to 1812, and clergyman (ordained in 1814) Herbert did not neglect his literary pursuits. He was the author of several narrative poems such as *Helga* (1815); *Pia della pietra* (1820); and *The Wizard Wanderer of Jutland* (1820-1822). *Attila, or, The Triumph of Christianity*, an epic poem in twelve books with a historical preface, was published in 1838, followed by a final volume of poems, *The Christian*, in 1846. Herbert was also a naturalist, an acquaintance of Charles Darwin, a specialist in bulbous plants (his *History of the Species of Crocus* was published posthumously in 1847) - his interest and research have been commemorated in the name of the genus *Herbertia*.

From Casimir Sarbievius. Book 2. Ode 2

[Lyr. II 2]

The snow, that crowns each mountain's brow,
    And whitens every spray,
From each high rock and loaded bough
    Will quickly melt away;

Soon, as the sun's reviving ray
    Shall warm the northern gale,
And Zephyrs mild their wings display
    To wanton in the vale.

When Time upon thine aged brow
    Shall shed the fatal show'r,
The hoary frost, the chilling snow,
    Will melt from thence no more.

Quick summer flies, and autumn's suns,
    And winter's cheerless gloom;
In changeful turn each season runs,
    And spring breathes new perfume.

Unchanged o'er us the tempest low'rs,
    Till death's last hour arrives;
Nor robe, nor garland deck'd with flow'rs,
    The bloom of live revives.

What youth on us but once bestows,
    Age once will snatch away;
But Fame can stop the fatal blows,
    And double life's short day.

Long shall he live, whose bright career
    Deserved a patriot's sigh;
All else flies with the fleeting year,
    But Fame can never die.

From: William Herbert, *Translations from the German, Danish etc to Which is Added Miscellaneous Poetry*, London: Printed for T. Reynolds, Oxford-Street; by I. Gold, Shoe Lane, 1804.

39

John Bowring

It is impossible to sum up the life of Sir John Bowring (1792-1872) in a short biographical note. He was a politician, merchant, businessman investing in railways, social reformer, supporter of Jeremy Bentham (the editor of *The Collected Works of Jeremy Bentham* in eleven volumes, 1838-1843), diplomat active in Europe and the Far East, British Consul at Canton, China, and finally governor of Hong Kong in the 1850s, to mention but a few of his numerous occupations. In literary history he is remembered for over thirty volumes of writings showing a great variety of interests from poetry to scholarly studies such as his most famous work, *The Kingdom and People of Siam* (1857). In the early 1820s, following his voyages to Central and Eastern Europe, Bowring published a number of volumes of translations from various European literatures. The first of these was *Specimens of the Russian Poets* (1820) for which he received a diamond ring from the Tsar Alexander I. The success of his Russian anthology inspired Bowring, who had an impressive command of foreign languages, to produce similar volumes of verse translations of Dutch (1824), Spanish (1824), Polish (1827), Serbian (1827), Hungarian (1830), and Czech (1832) poetry. The translations were the results of collaboration with various experts, a fact which Bowring often failed to acknowledge. In *The Westminster Review*, *The Foreign Quarterly Review*, and *The London Magazine* he published translations from an even greater variety of languages. The translations were initially received with enthusiasm but that soon declined. The importance of his verse translations, however, remains, as they introduced to the English-speaking world literatures which had been otherwise virtually unknown.

Sapphics
To a Rose
Intended to be used in the garlands for decorating the head of the Virgin Mary

Siderum sacros imitata vultus. Lib. IV ode 18

[Lyr. IV 18]

Rose of the morning, in thy glowing beauty
Bright as the stars, and delicate and lovely,
Lift up thy head above thy earthly dwelling,
   Daughter of heaven!

Wake! for the watery clouds are all dispersing;
Zephyr invites thee, – frosts and snows of winter
All are departed, and Favonian breezes
   Welcome thee smiling.

Rise in thy beauty, – Wilt thou form a garland
Round the fair brow of some beloved maiden?
Pure though she be, unhallow'd temple never,
   Flow'ret! shall wear thee.

Thou shouldst be wreath'd in coronal immortal,–
Thou shouldst be flung upon a shrine eternal,–
Thou shouldst be twined among the golden ringlets
   Of the pure Virgin.

Sapphics
To the Polish and Lithuanian knights

Exteros mores prohibete pulchra. Lib. IV ode 36

[Lyr. IV 36]

"Thebans! O let no foreign customs throw their
Scandal among you. Teach religious duties,
Laws of your country, virtues of your fathers,
   Teach to your children.

"Sacred your temples, – your tribunals, justice;
Peace, truth, and love dwell midst you, omnipresent;
All that is vile and all that is unholy
   Drive from your city!

"Walls screen not crime; and punishment will force its
Way through the tower, and through the thrice-bound portal,
Smiting the vicious. Thunderbolts but wait to
                Burst on the vile one.

"Painted deceit, tyrannical ambition,
Wealth-seeking lust, and luxury's excesses,–
Chase them far from you; let them never hold a
                Throne in your bosoms.

"Poverty gives to man unwonted vigour,
Teaches him patience 'neath the weight of suffering,
Arms him with courage; – but the stolen armour
                Wearies, though golden.

"Whether your lot be war or peace, ye Thebans!
Still be united; – for united brothers
Stand like a temple on a hundred pillars
                Firmly supported.

"So midst the rocks the sailor in his prudence
Looks to the stars; and so the friendly anchor
Steadies the vessel on the heaving ocean,–
                Steadies it surely.

"So doth the bond that binds the social fabric
Strengthen; while strife and mighty fraud and rancour
Overthrow cities, threatening desolation
                E'en to the mightiest."

Thus from his lyre in tones of wonted sweetness
Breathed out Amphion, – while in silent pleasure
Dirce stood listening, and the glad Cithaeron
                Waved its green branches.

So o'er the fields the rocks and cliffs delighted
Danced in their joy, and from the lofty mountain
Bow'd the tall trees, – and all the hills of granite
                Shouted accordant.

Then the bard ceased; – and stones to stones united,
Form'd in firm walls around the steadfast city,
And her seven brazen portals on their hinges
    Stood in their firmness.

Sapphics
To Publius
Quae tegit canas modo bruma valleis. Lib. 2 ode 2
                                           [Lyr. II 2]

Veil'd are the valleys with their hoary whiteness,
Which they shall banish when the sun awaking
Looks o'er the mountains. Snowy age, whose winter
    Throws on thy forehead

Hoar-frost, will sweep that hoar-frost from thee never,
Never. Its spring, its summer, and its autumn
Hasten and fly, – they crowd on one another,
    Swiftly they hasten.

But the cold winter and thy snowy hairs will
Cleave to thee ever. Nor will fragrant spikenard,
Nor the choice flowers of spring create the tinges
    Of thy young beauty.

One whom we love had youth conferr'd upon us, –
One whom we love age snatcheth from our bosom; –
Publius! enjoy the years of life twice over,
    Glory pursuing.

He hath lived long and well, whose death enforces
Tears from his neighbours, – who has made his glory
Heir to himself; – rapacious time will plunder
    All, all besides it.

Choriambics
To the Cicada
O quae populea sedens coma. Lib. IV ode 23

[Lyr. IV 23]

Thou, whose voice in the grove's silence is heard aloft,
While thou drinkest the tear-drops of the heavenly dews,
      Thy sweet music, Cicada,
      In thine ecstasy, pouring forth.

Come, come, Summer on light wheels is advancing fast,
While the hastening suns move, be they hail'd but chid
      For their tarrying too long,
      When the frosts of the winter flee.

As days dawn in their joy, so they depart in haste,–
So flee, speedily flee; speedily speeds our bliss,
      Too short are its abidings,–
      But grief lingeringly dwells with man.

Alcaic
To his lyre
Sonora buxi filia sutilis. Lib. II ode 3

[Lyr. II 3]

Sonorous harp! Hang high on the poplar tree,
Thou chorded shell, thou daughter of harmony!
      While zephyr-smiles, and breezes courting,
      Play round the tops of the tallest branches.

Soft round thy string blows Eurus, and whispering
Breathes gentle tones. – I throw me down carelessly,
      Pleased throw my head on verdant margin; –
      Rapidly mantles the arch of heaven

Clouds, darksome clouds. Ah! List to the clattering
Rain-drops. Arise! Our pleasures they rapidly
      Glide, wing'd by speed, their steps – how hurried
      Fleetingly ever they hasten onward.

To Liberty
Free translation
Nam quae revisas limina dulcius. Lib. IV ode 38

[Lyr. IV 38]

Queen of brave nations, – Liberty!
What land thy favourite seat shall be?
What land more suited to thy reign,
Than Poland's or Batavia's plain?
Daughter of counsel, and of bliss
The mother, and the nurse of peace;
Thou, sought midst many dangers round,
Midst more than many dangers found, –
Higher than thrones thy throne we see,
Majestic more then majesty;*
Thou mistress of our country's fame,
Now stop thy course, – thy smile we claim;
Arrest thy cloud-encircled car,
And linger where thy votaries are!

   O see upon thy Vistula
Lithuania's sons in long array,
The Lechan and Littavian ranks,
Like sea-waves gathering on its banks;
No servile crowds we bring to thee,
But heirs of ancient bravery, –
Sons of the North, whose blood remains
As pure as in their father's veins;
Untaught from faith and truth to swerve,
Train'd by the laws their king to serve,–
They spurn a stranger's stern commands,
And love their land o'er other lands.

   And is there aught so purely bright,
As when in truth and virtue's light
Impartial freedom deigns to shed
Her joys on prince and people's head!

---

* — Regibus altior, / Ipsaque Majestate major. [Note by John Bowring.]

Then the unfetter'd man disdains
Sloth's soul-debilitating chains,
And Genius, like a conqueror, flies
On to the goal, and claims the prize.

    No foreign calls our ranks can move;
We but obey the chief we love,
And follow where his footsteps lead,
To freedom's goal and victory's meed:
As o'er Carpathia's hoary height
Our sires achiev'd the glorious fight;
As on the wide-spread field of Thrace
Our fathers found their triumph-place;
As when our flags waved smiling o'er
The Bosphorus and the Baltic shore,–
And proud Teutonia, bearing all
Her Asian spoils, was forced to fall
Before those iron columns we
Had rear'd to mark our sovereignty;
Those mighty trophies of the brave,
The unconquerable Boleslaw;
And by the Borysthenes' side,
And by the Volga's current wide,
And past the Alexandrian shrines,
And to those dark Lapponian mines
Where the fierce North-wind has its birth: –
We trod the far Danubian earth,
Saw old Boötes freeze his waves,
And dug for the Maeotians, graves.

    Are we degenerate? – shall the fame
Of our own fathers blast our name?
Smile on our prayers, O Liberty!
And let the world thy dwelling be.

Urban* and Ferdinand combine,
O Wladislaw, their powers with thine,
And the world calls thee to confer
Her laurels on the conqueror,–
Thou, Sigismund's illustrious son,
Thou, of the blood of Jagellon!
O what can darken, what delay
The glory of our future day?
Hail, Wladislaw! thou hope of man, –
Fav'rite of God, – our Poland's van:
All hail! our warrior-senate cries,
All hail! a people's voice replies;
A thousand lances shine around,
And hills and vales and woods resound
The song of joy. And raised above
His watery throne, his praise and love
Old Vistula shouts forth; – their brow
Proudly the Crapack mountains bow
In homage.

     Say what project vast
Struggling in thy great soul thou hast?
For such a soul unceasing teems
With mighty thoughts and glorious dreams;
And still springs forward to the praise
Of distant deeds and future days:
Nor sloth nor luxury shall impede
That opening fame, that dawning deed;
Or quiet wisdom to o'erthrow
The dark designings of the foe,
Or splendid daring – swift and bold,
Sweeping like surges uncontroll'd,
The heir-loom of thy sires of old.

---

* Urban VIII. who distinguished Sarbiewski by very marked attentions; and when they parted, hung round his neck a golden chain, to which a miniature of His Holiness was attached. [Note by John Bowring.]

Thus did the Jagellons, – they spread
Their praise, their glory, and their dread –
Envied, admired, and fear'd: – the son
Soon made the father's fame his own:
And envy's wing could not pursue
A flight so high and glorious too;
The ambitious son outshone the sire,
As glory's mark ascended higher,
Till to our thought no hopes remain
Till fame and glory to maintain.
This is our noble heritage, –
A name, bequeath'd from age to age.
For thee, from centuries afar
A mingled wreath of peace and war,
Have generations waited, – now,
Wear the proud trophy on thy brow:
Make all thy father's victories thine,
With these thy gentle virtues twine;
Success shall show thee fairer, – woe
Shall bid thy roots yet deeper grow.
Such are Sarmatia's prayers. – Her prayers
Up to the heavens an angel bears;
On vows no chance shall e'er repeal
Eternity hath set his seal.

From: John Bowring, *Specimens of Polish Poets: with Notes and Observations on the Literature of Poland*, London: Priv. print., 1827.

40

Jesse Kitchener

Jesse Kitchener († 1829) was a graduate of Clare College, Cambridge, receiving his BA in 1819 and MA in 1822. The only known edition of his poems *Translations from Casimir etc.* appeared in 1821 when he was still a student. The volume includes, apart from translations from Sarbiewski quoted below, a number of others from Greek (Aeschylus, Sophocles, Aristophanes) and Latin (Horace), as well as original compositions by Kitchener.

Book 1 Ode 2
To Aurelius Lycus
Admonishing him not to complain of Adversity

[Lyr. I 2]

Scorn, Lycus, scorn th' unmanly tear,
From rough'ning clouds thy forehead clear,
    Nor heave the sad complaining sigh:
Smile, – tho' thy smiling hours be past,
And Fortune's fickle hand have cast
    An unpropitious die.

Tomorrow shall th' Etesian breeze
Sweep gaily over yonder seas
    Which southern gusts embroil today:
Today the sun has veil'd his head
In grief, – tomorrow he shall shed
    A cheerful morning ray.

The laugh, – the groan, – the joke, – the tear, –
In quick vicissitude appear;
    Joy rises from the midst of woe:
Thus will the fates – the fates who seem
To mark with danger and extreme
    The course in which they flow.

See Rome's intrepid sons obey
A ruler, who but yesterday
    His tiring ox to labour broke:
From oxen now the warrior clown
To Cures and the Gabian town,
    Transfers his lordly yoke.

Bright Hesper saw the low degree
Of him whom Phosphor smiles to see
    Exalted, – but perhaps in vain;
For chance, whene'er to sport inclin'd,
Shall bid her palace-keeping hind
    Be cottager again.

No common joke is he who now
Is forc'd to cleave an osier bough
    With the same axe that aw'd the state:
Or, should no osier be at hand,
To make his fasces of command
    A fagot for his grate.

Book 1 Ode 6
To the Sovereigns of Europe,
on The Recovery of the Eastern Empire

[Lyr. I 6]

Stern as the lords of Pontus are,
Those fierce Geloni train'd to war,
High as they lift their tyrant hand,
Where Bosphorus divides the land;
Yet still his wave is heard to roar,
As proud as ever on the shore,
And Neptune in that roaring wave,
Declares he will not be a slave.

  Pelasgia blushes to be broke
Beneath a Turk's barbarian yoke,
And Aemathy in restive mood,
Champs hard the bit of servitude.
The islands of the Aegean main,

Groan underneath the galling chain;
Tethys laments her urn's disgrace,
And down Achaea's furrow'd face,
Furrow'd with hills and dales of woe,
Lets all the tears of Hebrus flow.
Shall tall Abydos, or the towns
Of Aethiopia's sable sons,
Or those which rear their towery pride
Where Ganges rolls his swelling tide,
For ever dare to claim of thee
A suppliant bow, O Artace?
Must Bosphorus behold with pain
Th' Arabian and Ionian main
With each inferior sea concur
To keep him still their prisoner?

  In vain may dreams of future joy,
Plenty and peace our minds employ,
Unless we rouse each martial band
And to each warrior's faithful hand
Cause spear and shield to be restor'd,
And from its scabbard wake the sword.
Th' unbiass'd fates will nothing care
For courage which can nothing bear –
For words which do no action yield –
For cabinets without a field.

In vain beside our winter blaze
We sit and boast of former days
When Romans chas'd their hardy foes
Through Alpine and through Scythian snows.
Tho' often told, the pompous tale
On northern minds will nought prevail
Unless ourselves can make them feel
The temper of their Noric steel.
For we must fight those savage hordes,
With other than our modern swords.
A golden hilt empurpled o'er
With Tyrian die instead of gore,
And belts and trappings made for show,

Jingling and clatt'ring as we go,
And set with many a brilliant gem –
Such weapons will not vanquish them;
But, rather then be spoiled or broke,
Will make us fly to shun their stroke.
Romans, the man who by your leave,
Puts on a golden helm or greave,
Will doff th' Italian when he can,
And cease to be your countryman.
The wretch who knows no other care
Than tricking out his flowing hair,
And glittering helm, and gaudy plume,
Oh! Deem him not a man of Rome.
He could not work the Syrian's* fall;
He could not conquer Hannibal.
He could not urge the flying foe,
Thro' avalanches of Alpine snow,
Nor with a Caesar's flag unfurl'd,
Burst thro' the barriers of a world.

   Thus providence, who cannot err,
Gives ev'ry age its character,
Assigning its peculiar span
To each peculiar trait in man,
Nor lets e'en virtue's self proceed,
Beyond the mark he has decreed.

   One age delights itself in war,
Another wrangles at the bar.
That rears the veteran of the north,
This brings the soft Cilician forth.
Us has the world in sloth grown old,
Cast idly in a feeble mould,
A changeling brood – a puny race –
Decaying nature's last disgrace.
Whate'er of pure unsullied worth,
May happen to be found on earth,

---

* Antiochus. [Note by Jesse Kitchener.]

Instead of gain, is counted loss,
And turn'd to more congenial dross.
Freebooters of a lofty mind,
In craft and cruelty refin'd,
Our own oppression we applaud,
And praise the piety of fraud,
Laugh when the good man's blush we see,
And make a crime of honesty.

   Gold is our every god: for gold,
Our heads – our hands – our hearts are sold.
`Tis gold that makes the great man proud;
`Tis gold that animates the crowd,
Its lustre charms their dazzled eye,
Its chinking is their harmony.
It is the signal which invites
The guests of fortune's favourites;
But sound that signal in their ears
And they will be your worshippers,
And deal you out a thousand lies,
In compliments and flatteries.
But when your purse contains no more
And fortune's fickle smile is o'er,
Then will each faithless sycophant,
With cruel taunts deride your want –
Rejoice to see your greatness end,
And turn you off without a friend.

Book 1 Ode 7
To Telephus Lycus
On the instability of human Affairs

[Lyr. I 7]

Alas! my Telephus, 'tis all a cheat,
  We are but fortune's playthings after all:
There's nought immortal in this mortal state,
  Nor stands there aught which is not doom'd to fall.

To fall and rise – to rise and fall again,
  Toss'd like a shuttle, thro' his little span –

To have what ne'er was hop'd – and hope in vain,
　Is all the wit and providence of man.

Sun after sun its setting glory shrouds,
　This wears a brighter, that a blacker form:
The years ride past us in the winds and clouds,
　And ages in the darkness of the storm.

This very hour which I would fain beguile,
　With some short trial of my minstrelsy,
Of nought ambitious but to see it smile,
Alas! how swiftly does its chariot fly.

Nor harp nor lute can charm its thankless ear,
　Nor tempt it to compose its hasty wing,
But heedless of the muse's farewell tear
　It soars away upon the lightening.

And while it soars, it hurries to their fate
　Cities and kingdoms with their mighty crowd,
Robs many a monarch of his gorgeous state,
　And in their falling pride entombs the proud.

With dying princes and with nations slain
　It jokes awhile – then hastens to be gone;
And, letting loose the wildfire of its rein,
　Rolls round the stars and spurs the ages on.

Thus, Telephus, while day succeeds to day,
　And o'er our heads the silent moments steal,
Fortune does nought but cheat our lives away.
　And mock us with the swiftness of her wheel.

Say! is not life a long delusive dream?
　Is there no speck or jaundice in our eye?
See we or see we not the things which seem?
　Is there, or is there not – reality?

Book 1 Ode 8
An invective against Slothfulness and Effeminacy of the Age

[Lyr. I 8]

Or we have banish'd to the pole
The greatness of the Roman soul,
  Or barter'd it away to Tyre.
We dare not climb the steep of fame,
Nor lay a dying conqu'ror's claim,
  To Argos or Epire.

We love the fair and fruitful shore
Of Tigris and Meander, more
  Than our own Veii's rugged soil.
Our tender youth, afraid to feel
The pinching of a coat of steel,
  Refuse the warrior's toil.

They cannot urge the restive steed,
Nor bridle in his fiery speed;
  Nor breast old Tiber's foaming flood;
When, swell'd by winter's melting snows
Our careful mounds he overflows
  In wild and threat'ning mood.

But should the proud high-mettled horse,
Or start or stumble in his course,
  The cowards tremble heart and knee:
Not so unskilful are they found
In dancing to the timbrel's sound,
  On days of public glee.

Away, my countrymen, away
With all this womanish array
  Of lute, and harp, and plaintive strain;
For hark! The trumpet's clarion
Has sounded! and whole towns are gone
  To yon embattled plain!

Jesse Kitchener

And shall we hence? – or is the wine
Of our Campania too divine
      To let us from the banquet rise?
Ling'ring and lolling at the board
Which many a griping tax has stor'd
      With borrow'd luxuries.

There Hesper leaves us at the feast:
And there, arising in the east,
      Phosphor astonish'd, sees us stay.
The moon looks down with jocund beam,
And from the goblet's sparkling stream
      Reflects a purple ray.

And, while the bowl is push'd about,
We spill our wine, to measure out
      Trenches, and mounds, and fortresses;
And show how battles should be won,
And set a monarch on his throne,
      With most surprising ease.

Rise! for Aurora in the east,
Gives to the wind her saffron vest,
      And spurs her coursers from the main:
Rise! but alas the breezy call
Of early morn, which speaks to all,
      Has spoken to us in vain.

The sun to us is not a sun.
'Tis day: but day has not begun
      To wait on sleeping Italy.
She loves to turn that day to night,
Awaking only when the light
      Forsakes the western sky.

What! shall the sun to Romans leave,
His mere old age – while Turks receive
      The freshness of his youthful dawn?

Rise! and, upborne on victory's wing,
Add to the realms of evening
      The regions of the morn.*

Book 1 Ode 13
To Tarquinius Lavinius

[Lyr. I 13]

Aequam memento rebus in arduis
Servare mentem non secus ac bonis.
      Horatius [Carm. II 3, 1-2]

Tho' the sun for a season has fled,
  He soon will revisit the sky;
And the tear which the ev'ning has shed,
  The hand of the morning will dry.

Tho' fortune may cast thee quite down,
  And insult o'er thy sorrows awhile;
She is not so fond of her frown,
  As never to think of a smile.

Tho' stretch'd at her feet on the ground,
  Thou art licking the dust of her train;
Yet soon as her wheel is gone round,
  She will clothe thee in purple again.

Nor, when humbled, indulge in despair;
  Nor, exalted, be proud of thy place;
For remember – when fortune is player,
  Her card is not always an ace.

---

* Casimir here alludes to the subject of this 6th Ode. [Note by Jesse Kitchener.]

Jesse Kitchener

Book 1 Ode 17
On Royal Lenity

[Lyr. I 17]

Nor sumptuous courts nor splendid halls,
Glitt'ring with crystal gates and walls,
Nor doorposts of divinest mould,
Inlaid with ivory and gold,
Can fasten fame's immortal gem,
Upon a prince's diadem;
Nor bribe a single wreath to bloom,
Unmerited, upon his tomb.

The gold of mildness and of grace –
The crystal of a smiling face –
A countenance that cancels fear,
Kind, – condescending, – calm and clear,
Sweet as the rainbow's colours are –
Serene as evening's rising star –
Can fasten fame's immortal gem,
Upon a prince's diadem;
And make the wreath of glory bloom,
For ever fresh upon his tomb.

Your people, princes, are a book:
Where you may read your every look.
With smiles be present to their view,
And you will see them smiling too:
But, having met them with a frown,
Retire, and tremble for your crown.

A sov'reign, slow to punishment,
And ever ready to relent;
Has pow'r, sufficient to assuage
This rising mob's tumultuous rage;
To pacify and reconcile
Contending nobles with his smile;
And, with the calm his presence brings,
To check the menaces of kings.

Let vulgar spirits feel a charm,
In war's confusion and alarm;
'Tis not for you, in martial mood,
To make a sport of human blood;
And with the din of sword and spear,
To turn your people pale with fear.

Behold the Ram! Sweet peerless star!
Whose tresses twinkle from afar –
Whose antlers of refulgent gold,
The door of early spring unfold.
To him for pasturage are giv'n,
The meadows of the spangled heav'n.
With gentle rule he governs there
The Wolf, the Lion, and the Bear:
He nods his horns and they obey,
Nor dare beyond their bounds to stray;
But, by his watchful care control'd,
Are kept within Creation's fold.

The vulture spares th' unwarlike swan.
His horse obeys Bellerophon.
Th' Aemonian centaur scorns to aim
His jav'lin at th' unguarded game.
The Lion, soon as night begins,
Is seen to gamble with the Twins,
And, of complacent humour full,
To fawn upon the fearless Bull.

No sounds of discord stun our ears,
While night is moving on the spheres;
But all the world lied hush'd in sleep,
While they their peaceful vigils keep,
And round the still and tranquil pole,
Their chariot-wheels in silence roll.

First of the Zone's resplendent Signs,
The Ram, with placid luster shines;
Sweet fleecy messenger of peace –
His bleatings bid the winter cease.

And, while beneath his vernal beam
Creation's womb begins to teem,
The stars that glitter in the sky
With amorous fires each other eye.
With amorous step the planets move,
And all the universe is love.

Book 2 Ode 3
To his Harp

[Lyr. II 3]

Sweet daughter of harmony – source of my glee,
I'll hang thee, my harp, on the high poplar tree;
While the sky that looks on thee, is smiling and clear,
And the light gales are wooing the leaves that are near.

Thy Eurus shall pass thee on jovial wing,
And fan with a whisper thy delicate string;
And I, on the river's green bank will recline,
Restraining my music to listen to thine.

But alas! in an instant the sunshine is gone!
How swiftly the showers come pattering on!
How chang'd is the prospect! arise, – let us go,
How fleeting is pleasure! – how sudden is woe!

From: Jesse Kitchener, *Translations from Casimir etc. with Poems, Odes, and Specimens of Latin Prose. By J. Kitchener, B.A. Late of Clare College, Cambridge,* London: Published by Priestley, Holborn; Hatchard, Piccadilly; and J. & A. Arch. Cornhill; sold also by Webb, Redford; and Nicholson, Cambridge, 1821.

41

Caroline de Crespigny

Caroline de Crespigny (1795-1864) was a descendant of the literary family of Bathursts (her father was Henry Bathurst, Bishop of Norwich), yet there is little that is known about her beyond what can be found in her volume of poems *My Souvenir or Poems by Caroline de Crespigny with Translations etc.* published in 1844. The volume includes a large selection of translations from Latin, Spanish, Portuguese, French, and German poets. However, according to the accompanying notes, most of them (except translations from German: since de Crespigny lived in Germany for a large part of her life) were not translated directly from the originals. Her two translations from Sarbiewski (whom she insists on calling Sobieski, apparently mistaking for another famous Pole of the 17th century, King John III Sobieski) have very little in common with the original poems. De Crespigny published also *The Enchanted Rose: a Romant in Three Cantos. Translated from the German of Ernst Schulze* (1844) and *A Vision of Great Men with Other Poems as Translated from the Poetesses of Germany etc.* (1848).

To My Lyre
From the Latin of Casimir Sobieski

[Lyr. II 3]

O my treasure – thou child of the bleak Appenine!
Lightly sway on a branch of this tall towering pine!
And as everything basks in the smiles of the spring,
To the leaves, as they whisper delight, sweetly sing.

Bid those quivering strings, as they vibrate on high,
In the breath of the breeze faint and faintlier sigh;
And while all here below slumbers moveless and still,
Let me dream away life on this green sloping hill.

Ha! what clouds on the clear face of Heaven darkly lour!
Whistles loud in my ear the on-gathering shower!
Come my lyre! let us fly, ere to night turn the day,
Thus like shadows, our joys ever hasten away.

To a Rose
From the Latin of Casimir Sobieski

[Lyr. IV 18]

Born of the bright and Summer skies,
Gem of the world why lowly lies
Thy lovely head – Uplift thyself! Arise,
  Fair Child of Heaven!

To welcome thee, when thou goest forth
In all thy beauty; far from earth,
Into all regions of the biting North
  Dark clouds are driven.

Her heart should be like unsunned snow,
Her tresses dyed in sunset's glow,
Emblem of all that's pure, who thee should show
  Twined round her brows.

What hand could dare that wreath entwine?
What hand? no other hand but thine!
The flowing locks of but one Maid divine,
  Become the Rose.*

From: *My Souvenir or Poems by Caroline de Crespigny with Translations etc.*, London: Longman, Brown, Green and Longmans. Heidelberg: Hoffmeister, 1844.

---

* In Poland the Rose is 'The Virgin's' flower. [Note by Caroline de Crespigny.]

42

John Docwra Parry

John Docwra Parry (c. 1800 – c. 1845) a topographer and Church of England divine from Bedford. Graduate of Peterhouse, Cambridge (admitted 1818, BA 1824, MA 1827) in 1827 he became the curate of Aspley, Bedfordshire. The author of a number of moderately successful compilations such as *Sellected Illustrations, Historical and Topographical, of Bedfordshire* (1827), *The Legendary Cabinet: a Collection of British National Ballads* (1829), or *A Historical and Descriptive Account of the Coast of Sussex* (1833), the publication of which finally bankrupted him. Probably defrocked before 1831, Parry attempted to run a conservative newspaper, the *Portsmouth Herald* (1833) but without success due to lack of sufficient funds. The following translation from Sarbievius' *Silviludia* seems the only known poetic experiment of Parry.

Silviludium[*] III
Supposed to be spoken during a hunting expedition of Vladislaus King of Poland

Poet
Who rests upon this shady rock
No vulgar empty strains may shock;
To sooth his day-dreams light, alone
The Zephyr lends its whispering tone.

Courtier
O! what a pure and tranquil joy
                The life of rustics brings.

---

[*] No single English word will express this Latin term of Casimir's, which signifies a *sylvan* Eclogue or Idyll. [Note by John Docwra Parry.]

Poet
This gently murmuring silver stream
As in a precious vase doth seem;
And, whilst by emerald sides it flows,
An unpolluted cup bestows.

Courtier
Ah! thorns of direst point annoy
               The purple robe of Kings!

Poet
Whilst through the meads the Poet wends
Sweet Flora all his steps attends;
And flowery robes presents, which bear
The colours of the opening year.

Courtier
O what a pure and tranquil joy
               The life of rustics brings!

Poet
Oft, as beneath the embowering tree,
He lists the birds' sweet symphony,
With smiles serene, he gives to scorn
The phantoms that in Courts are born.

Courtier
Ah! thorns of direst point annoy
               The purple robe of Kings;
But pure and tranquil is the joy
               The life of rustics brings.

From: *The Gentleman's Magazine*, June 1831.

43

Richard Coxe

Richard Charles Coxe (1800-1865) a poet, Church of England divine, vicar of Newcastle (1841-1853) and canon of Durham. He was praised for his talents as a preacher and published his sermons in numerous volumes such as *Faithfulness and Charity* (1842); *The Pleasures of Taste Incentives to Devotion* (1842), and *Hold Fast the Form of Sound Words* (1862). In 1848 Coxe published a volume entitled *Wood-Notes: The Silviludia Poetica of M. Casimir Sarbievius with a Translation into English Verse. Musings at Cynemouth: Ten Sonnets. North & South: Ten Sonnets* which included a complete translation of Sarbiewski's *Silviludia* as well as two sequences of ten original sonnets each. It should be noted here that Coxe was apparently convinced that *Silviludia* was an original work of Sarbiewski while, actually, the text was largely 'borrowed' from the work of another Jesuit, Mario Bettini, a pastoral drama *Ludovicus, Tragicum Silviludium* (1612, publ. 1622). John Sparrow discovered that out of 440 lines of Sarbiewski's text 420 were taken from Bettini's work which is 1400 lines long. As Sarbiewski freely adapted the borrowings to his purposes, and as separating his original work from that of Bettini is hardly possible, we include the entire text of Coxe's translation.

Wood-Notes; the Silviludia Poetica

Preface
[fragments]

Casimir has always stood high in the estimation of scholars and men of taste. Grotius says of him 'Non solum aequitavit, sed interdum superavit Flaccus.' Coleridge, the poet and philosopher, writes – 'After Lucretius and Statius, I know no Latin poet who can be compared for sublimity of ideas to Casimir Sarbievius. His language, too, is worthy of any poet of the Augustan age.' And the author of an article in a recent number of the *Christian Remembrance* marks him as chief of the modern writers of Latin lyrics.

It is very certain however, that many will be disposed to agree in the opinion passed upon our author by that eminent critic Dr Jos. Warton, and charge him with a redundancy of glittering conceits. And I fear that the portion of his works now in the reader's hands in more liable to this charge that any other. Some excuse for them however may be found or felt, as I conceive, in the buoyant playfulness of spirit from which they appear to spring. The poet's enjoyment of the pure and simple things of nature is so fresh, so hearty, that ordinary tropes and figures would seem incapable of giving utterance to it. His style therefore flows with the gushing fervour of his feelings, and sparkles like the flowers, dews, and fountains that inspire it.

In this, I believe the first attempt at a translation of the Silviludia, my object has been to give the English reader as vivid an idea as I could of the author's spirit and manner. I have endeavoured at the same time to omit nothing that is characteristic, to add nothing that is not in keeping. The reader's ear will discover, I trust, that I have attempted also to convey to him some notion of the varied music of our author's metrical construction. If he fails to perceive this, I shall have enhanced the difficulties of my task to no purpose.

Silviludium I
When Ladislaus IV King of Poland, came to hunt in the woods at Bersti

Ye verdant groves, ye silent shades,
    Silence gend'ring sacred awe!
Balmy breezes, all your aids,
    Gentler spirits hither draw!
        The lab'ring mind
    By storms of state opress'd,
        With aspect kind
    Receive, and charm to rest.
All, O King, thine eye can see.

Eager homage offer thee! –
>> Thee to greet
Bashful nymphs whose full breasts yield
To each flowret of the field
>> Crystal nurture sweet,
>> Hie with silver feet.
Thee the winged minstrelsy,
Heart and throat expanding, vie
To welcome with full harmony.
Trembling throughout each tiny shoot and spray,
>> The struggling tree,
>> Rejoicingly.
Flutters her feathery leaves to meet thee on the way.
>> With suppliant bow the lordly pine
>> Owns the loyal forest thine!
>> Aided by the ushering
>> Of the Zephyr's herald wing,
Bright bands of flowers will thy path o'erspread,
And kiss with stealthy lip the welcome tread!

Silviludium II
To the Dew
Dance of shepherds when Ladislaus went out in the morning to hunt at Soleczniki

Gentile dews of early morning,
> Who descending, heavens own lending,
Are with sparkling eyes adorning,
> Flowers, all beauteous colours blending.
Ye who gleam in budding shells,
> Where the flowing meadow swells!

Wakeful, ye from eastern bowers
> Flora tend, her herbs to send her,
> While from silver urns your showers
Do the parch'd mead thankful render:
Silent rain, by bright dawn given!
> Fattening drops from teeming heaven!

Glistening milk of yellow morn!
> From the nipple straggling tipple
Little pets in perfume born,
> While with ruby lips where ripple
Wreathed smiles the roses press,
> Courting mother's fond caress.

Little stars of night retiring,
> Heaven's distilling each drop spilling,
Bright stars ye! the swains' admiring!
> Tears! the flowrets meek eyes filling
As with dewy cheeks they mourn
Night's departure, day's return.

Friendly dews! with faithful guiding
> Show where roving, feeding, loving,
Sought the stag at last his hiding,
> Cautious thro' the covert moving!
Show your King the cloven horn
> Gentle dews of early morn!

Silviludium III
Dialogue between a Poet and Courtier sitting together in the shade, while Ladislaus is hunting at Kotra

Poet
Happy the man who thoughtfully lying
> In the rocks quiet shade
> By the breeze vocal made.
Lists the trees tattle, the false world defying!

Courtier
Oh! the country's happy life!
Free from care and free from strife.

Poet
Murmuring soft the neighbouring river
> Bright draughts of silver sheen

> In cups of Emerald green
Gives, from all treachery pure as the giver.

Courtier
> Oh! the robe doth king's adorn
> Purple rent by many a thorn!

Poet
O'er the soft mead as the bard doth disport him,
> Flora with ready care
> Doth a sweet couch prepare
Heap'd with all flowers of beauty to court him.

Courtier
> Oh! the country's happy life,
> Free from care and free from strife.

Poet
Oft in the green shade carelessly straying,
> Him the glad birds beguile,
> Thinking with placid smile,
Of the vain shadows the worldly betraying.

Courtier
Oh! the robe doth king's adorn,
Purple rent by many a thorn!
Oh! the country's happy life,
Free from care and free from strife!

Silviludium IV
To the Breeze – that it would assuage the toil and heat for Ladislaus while hunting in the Merecian plains of noontide

Exulting now in mid-day glow
Apollo from his golden bow
> The vivid volley throws,
Fierce rages Sirius' rabid face;
More ardent still the royal chase,

Richard Coxe

Nor rest nor respite knows.
Such the love, so prized the fame
Of him who views the lurking game!

By furious zeal impell'd, the pack
Impetuous crowd the tained track,
    And thick the arrows fly:
A double fervour fires the throng,
Without, the sky, – within, the Song
    That honours victory.
Heaving flank and glazing eye
Tell the toils intensity.

Ye breezes gentle – breezes mild!
Then Zephyr, the Wind's fairest child,
    And verdure's fost'ring friend,
The last sigh thou of dying Day
As fades his fainting soul away,
    While Night his couch doth tend,
Prompt to close with savage care,
Eyes that late so beaming were: –

Ye flick'ring breezes summoning
By vocal reeds the coming Spring,
    And mingling in mad fight,
The scented hosts the meadows bear,
Then, conquer'd by night's languid tear,
    As dawns the morning light
Cooling with a breath the fray
And fickle hurrying for away;

O ye fly with hunters' speed
Now serve the weary hunter's need.
    Assuage the Delian flame,
Be nigh to wipe with cooling hand
The dews on labour's brow that stand,
    And wing the arrow's aim, –
Bear along each flagging hound
On your own light pinions bound.

An should ye find as o'er ye pass
That they upon the springing grass
    Their weary limbs have spread,
Then bid the breeze from every flower
Collecting sweets, to come and shower
    Its fragrance o'er each head.
Bid the laughing lilies kiss
Each drowsy dreamer into bliss.

So you o'er many a sea serene
May azure Tethys, Ocean's Queen,
    In silver car attend!
So as ye flit o'er vale and hill
May frolic flow'rs your bosoms fill,
    And each its light kiss lend!

Silviludium V
Song
**The poet wanders through the meads and woods,
while the court employs its leisure in hunting,
or
the sweetnes of celestial love**

Tender herbs! with flowers teeming,
    Flowers! the meadows bright stars beaming,
    Roses! ye the purest gems
    In Flora's fairest diadems,
Bosky vales, and bubbling springs,
While you love my spirit wings,
And I roam your sweets among,
Fill with Love divine my song!

With your beauties I combine
Image of the Form Divine,
In his delicate working see
Impress of the Deity,
Impress character'd on things
Colour'd by love's lustrous wings. –
You, ye sweet ones, having heard

Thankful the creative word,
With your Lord do seem to try
Vain tho' grateful rivalry.
Thou too, Lord! wilt stoop from Heaven
Reaping peace Thyself hast given,
Thou wilt come, my soul's repose
Whether ne'er mine eyelids close
Till the chasten'd pupils trace
All the glories of thy face!

Or whether touch'd by fire on high
Ashes into ashes die,
Still from Earth's funeral pyre
Shall my soul to thee aspire,
Wing its way to thee for rest,
In thy bosom find its nest.

Lo! the beauteous flowers to prove
Lord! to thee their mindful love,
Open to heav'n their leafy wings —
While each petal upward flings
Sigh, that fragrant incense bears,
Or soothes the earth with dewy tears.
See! the rose from yonder bed
With pouting lip all ruby red
Tells its tale of glowing love -
And what would that pallor prove
On the ivy's clasping arms,
But trusting timid love's alarms,
Upward ever upward stealing,
Tho' some pale doubt aye revealing!

While such raptures kindling spread
Shall I alone be cold and dead?
Ingrate vile! shall I alone
Cumber earth a senseless stone!
No! blest Father! let me show
O'er them all my glad heart's glow.
Shine with myriad leaves the tree,
Smile with countless flowers the lea,

Let innumerous stars distil
Dewy drops each flower to fill,
Still shall all my love confess
More intense and measureless!

Lo! the flowrets tiny lips —
Many colour'd, for the sips
From the rainbow's blended hue,
Silent, render homage due. —
Heaven accordant praise doth sing
The brooklet from its gurgling spring —
And air with her soft whispering.

Ingrate! 'mid the swelling sound
Shall I alone be speechless found?
Lord! my feeble powers raise,
Make then meet to hymn thy praise!
Honey culleth many a bee —
Chanteth birds from many a tree —
Many a nymph and many a fawn
Sing to thee from breezy lawn —
Make my voice O Lord! then all
More eloquent, more musical.

Silviludium VI
To the Moon,
when Ladislaus was hunting on a Monday

Since our chase the field hath ta'en
    Under gentle Dian's reign,
    Courting Dian's grace and pleasure
    Lead we crescent-wise the measure. —
Dian! the soft air sailing serenely,
    Hunt'st thou the stars with thy flaming horn!
Seek'st thou the twin bears hotly and keenly,
    Swift thro' the azure ethereal borne,
Plying the bright bow so warlike and queenly?

Richard Coxe

Hark! from nights silence rings a deep baying,
      Note of the hound, glad to forward thy chase.
So! the red dogstar after thee straying,
      Leaveth his hot lair thine hunting to grace,
Flakes of gold foam his presence betraying.

From the curv'd cradle sportively peeping
      Shone thy first light like a beautiful smile!
Now in full splendour onward thou'rt sweeping;
      Presently bending in weakness anile
Sadness and gloom thy glories are steeping.

Thee thine own orb in darkness enfolding
      Hides from the ken of inquisitive gaze;
Thou thine own tomb --- the sacred urn holding
      Cherish'd and treasured the relics of days
Kindling ere long to glad all beholding.

Heritress thou of splendour diurnal,
      Soon as Apollo doth sink in the west,
'Stead of the fading planet fraternal
      Jewel-like riseth thy glittering crest,
Pure as a gleam from Glory Eternal.

Fiercely thy form now falchion-like glanceth;
      Now on the mountain top peacefully strays;
Now on the wave like pinnacle it danceth;
      Now o'er the ocean celestial plays,
Taking each form that the gazer entranceth.

Beings that roam the billows of ocean,
      All the rich offspring of earth's happy womb,
Render to thee a duteous devotion;
      Prompt at thy bidding the wild waters come
To rise or to fall in orderly motion.

Blandly regarding, favour our hunting!
      Thine then the grimly curv'd tusk of the boar

Savagely stern our phalanx confronting:
        Thine be the antlers the gallant stag wore
Antlers the fork'd oak proudly surmounting.

Sees't thou amid the doubtful shades glancing
        Forms that would lovingly copy thine own!
All to thine honour we figure our dancing,
        Thou in the ring, in the crescent art shown —
Favour our hunting thy fame thus advancing!

Strength for the swift course do thou supply us!
        Scent to our sensitive beagles impart,
Weapon to hurl, and quarry to try us
        Grant, with a spell that shall prosper the dart,
And when our arm fails, Oh be thou nigh us!

But pause we — for golden Eos upsailing
        Comes as a huntress with roseate bow,
Nights fleeing legions triumphantly quailing.
        And see our bright Delia languisheth low
Sacred by the splendour her milder light paling!

Silviludium VII
To the Shadows,
**that, while Ladislaus was hunting at Merecina,
they would protect the sportsmen from the heat**

Enough, enough of sweltering toil!
    Tho' well the wild hunt's fierce turmoil
      A royal youth beseems:
    Nobly the heart hath stood the test,
So yield the weary limbs to rest,
    The minds to soothing dreams.

As now the aged God of Day
Declinging languisheth away
      Gigantic shadows come
His funeral obsequies to grace

And cast o'er nature's form and face
        Decorous garb of gloom.

Sworm foemen they of fleeing light,
Direct ye to their camp your flight
        Sol's myrmidons no more,
Then by some hospitable Shade
In cool tent shall your couch be laid,
        By darkness curtain'd o'er.

Lo! from the far horizon's verge
Silent their swelling forms emerge
        To meet you on the way;
Shedding no genial ray they rove,
But grimly dark each hill and grove
        In phantom forms display.

Here cool Merecian meads among
While we, a simple shepherd throng,
        In a mazy dance are twining,
By ye, our honour'd Monarch's court,
Spectators of the rustic sport
        On yonder bank reclining.

Silviludium VIII
To the lake Motela
Dance and songs of Fishermen

Song
Laud and thanks we render thee!
        By thy bounty sped this way,
Tethys, Queen of azure sea,
        Feels our net the welcome prey. —
Gift from ocean's choicest hoard,
Gift to grace a regal board.

Dance
When Aurora, genial power,
Wakes to quit her eastern bower,

Deftly she, to tire each grace,
Makes a mirror of thy face;
There her golden hair arrays,
And lights her cheek with saffron blaze.

Song
When her form in colours bright
        She would deck, thy little shells
Lend her brow their purple light,
        And from caves where coral dwells
Radiant wreaths her neck adorn,
And pearls as pure as tears of morn.

Dance
While clouds of roses she lets fall
From garden plots ethereal,
And below thy laughing seas
Redden in the morning breeze,
We a buoyant pleasure have
Dancing on the dancing wave.

Song
Thee thy furious wrath declaring
        Loud from many a mouth of foam,
Thee when angry storms are tearing
        As thou wer't theirs battle-home,
While winds the wild waves maddening
Stride as a steed, let others sing. —

Dance
Thee rather soft in tranquil light
Pillow'd on sand with gold bedight
        We hail with votive lay!
Only bid thou that fav'ring smile
The hardy fisher's toil beguile,
        And with full net repay!

Song
As with a mother's care caress'd
        Thine arms the huge earth hold,

And while upon thy swelling breast
                Thou dost the charge enfold.
That breast from fountains never dry
Doth limpid streams of life supply.

Dance
From thy deep abysses now
Phoebus lifts him beaming brow,
And as o'er the surface bright
Glows his globe of fervid light.
He a golden gem is seeming,
On a shell of silver gleaming.

Song
Apollo, thou at early morn
                And thou at dewy eve,
Rising in pride — in glory shorn,
                Descending dost receive;
Glad he seeks thy pillowing wave,
Then his cradle, now his grave!

Dance
Inclining o'er thy golden stream
To temper for our need his beam
                Thou paint'st the God of Day,
And playful dek'st with cheering smile —
Thus cheering thou our toil beguile,
              And with full net repay!

Song
While the Royal Hunter deigns
Thus to range the neighbour plains,
Bid thy waves with loud acclaim,
Each to other sound his name
Ladislaus! word of fame!
— Yet speed thou still the fisher's way
And with full net his toil repay!

Silviludium IX
Dance and Song of Harvestmen, when Ladislaus was hunting shortly before his marriage

Song
Does Fame but spread the whisper'd lie?
Or is it that tomorrow's sky
        Shall regal glory spread?
Is't here shall beam that ray so pure
Here in our shades the Sun endure
        To veil his lordly head?

Dance
Come thou propitious! and so prove
O Prince to thee the powers above,
        Pleased to thine espousals press,
    And bid their constant favour bless
Our homes with peace, your hearts with love!

Song
With thee may gentle Doris come,
And make our shores her quiet home!
        Here on the golden sands at rest,
Unite reflected earth and heaven,
And bid by each to each be given
        The tender pledge of love confess'd.

Dance
Round the darts of Mars entwining
May Minerva's bough be shining,
And the rude sword self-inclining
        Bend into the bill.
May to gentle dove the shield
Now nobly lost a refuge yield,
And foeman's helm on battle field,
        The bee with nectar fill!

Richard Coxe

Silviludium X
Song of the Zephyr
To Ladislaus arriving at Leypuni at Eventide

The starry eyes of dying light,
Are closing fast, and soon the bright
Aurora for her kindling pyre
Our fanning breezes will require:
      But first the day
Must turn like Phoenix to his nest,
And fain upon my wings would rest,
      To float him on the way.
Rise then and be our wonted succour near,
To day a cradle, but to night a bier.
      May our wet wings as we pass,
      Star with dewy rain the grass!
      The Monarch comes! Lepune fair
      Bids her meadows deck their hair.
Hyblaean splendour dons the wood,
      Sabaean sweets exhale,
And diamond tears with myrrh imbued
      Spread fragrance on the gale!
While by my pinions fann'd appear
The cloudless heav'ns serenely clear.
      Our king to greet with honour due
Shine the tranquil deep, — the air
Be calm and still — and earth prepare
      Her vernal garb of varied hue!
Only come thou! and all shall thee receive
Brights as the peaceful flash of Summer's Eve.
      Here as moves my gentle breeze
      Comes music from the whisp'ring trees,
      Here my fost'ring favour dresses
      Nature in her floral tresses,
      Smiling now in verdure bright,
      Now in many a hue bedight.
      Here where glad the vale appears
      Freshen'd by the fountain's tears,
      And the bank, those vales among,
      Rolls its flood of joy along,

May th' adoring woods proclaim,
With vocal leaves thy mighty name!
    I who now in sportive glee
    Roam the quiet glades with thee,
Shall rouse ere long thy spirit's might
A comrade in the bloody fight.
Phoebus' silver trumpet taking,
And the thrilling tube awaking,
    Thy triumphant might to sing,
Where the rolling Sun is leading
Thither shall thy fame be spreading
    Wafted on my heralds wing!

From: Richard Coxe, *Wood-Notes: The Silviludia Poetica of M. Casimir Sarbievius with a Translation into English Verse. Musings at Cynemouth: Ten Sonnets. North & South: Ten Sonnets. By R. C. Coxe, M.A. Hon. Canon of Durham, and Vicar of Newcastle upon Tyne,* **Newcastle**: M.A. Richardson, London: F. and A. Ribington, and John Russel Smith, Oxford: T.M. Parker, 1848.

44

Francis Sylvester Mahony as Father Prout

Francis Sylvester Mahony (1804-1866), Irish satirical poet and journalist, best known for his works published as Father Prout. He was a graduate of the Jesuits' College at Clongowes Wood. As he decided to become a Jesuit himself, he continued his education at Jesuits' colleges in Amiens and Rome, but ultimately failed to gain admission to the order. In the early 1830s he studied theology in Rome and finally was ordained in 1832 at Lucca, but his career as a priest was very short. In 1834, Mahony invented the character of Father Prout, whom he later described as the child of Jonathan Swift and Stella. In the years 1834 to 1836 Mahony regularly published in *Fraser's Magazine* 'Reliques of Father Prout', allegedly resurrected from the posthumous papers of a provincial cleric but actually witty commentaries mostly on current state of English literature. They were first collected in 1836 as *The Reliques of Father Prout Late PP. of Watergrashill, in the County of Cork, Ireland.*, a more complete editon, in which the following poems were included, appeared in 1862. Mahony's original poems were less admired, 'The Shandon Bells' is the only one of his poem which is still remembered. From 1837 on, Mahony wrote for *Bentley's Miscellany* edited by Charles Dickens. His most favourite trick was translating contemporary poems into Latin, French or Greek, and charging their authors, such as Moore and Wolfe, with plagiarism. From 1837 on Mahony lived on the continent, first in Italy (as Don Jeremy Savonarola he collected and published his contributions from the period in *Facts and Figures from Italy*) enjoying the company of the English visitors and expatriates there, including the Brownings. After 1850 Mahony settled down in Paris, through most of his stay abroad regularly contributing to various London magazines and newspapers such as *Bentley's Miscellany*, *Daily News*, *The Globe*, *Cornhill Magazine* and others.

Odarum Lib. 3 Ode XV
To the Bees (armorial bearings of the Barberini family), on Urban the Eight's elevation to the Pontificate.

Citizens of the Mount Hymettus,
    Attic labourers who toil,
Never ceasing till ye get us
    Winter store of honeyed spoil!

Nectar ye with sweets and odours,
    Hebes of the hive, compose,
Flora's privileged marauders,
    Chartered pirates of the rose!

Gipsey tribe, gay, wild, and vagrant,
    Winged poachers of the dawn,
Sporting o'er each meadow fragrant,
    Thieving it on every lawn!

Every plant and flower ye touch on,
    Wears, I ween, a fresher grace;
For ye form the proud escutcheon
    Of the Barberini race.

Emblem bright, which to embroider,
    While her knight was far away,
Many a maiden hath employed her
    Fairy fingers night and day!

Bees, though pleased your flight I gaze on,
    In the garden or the field,
Brighter hues your wings emblazon
    On the Barberini shield.

Of that race a pontiff reigneth,
    Sovereign of imperial Rome;
Lo! th' armorial bee obtaineth
    For its hive St. Peter's dome!

Hitherto a rose'a chalice
  Held thee, winged artisan!
But thou fillest now the palace
  Of the gorgeous Vatican.

And an era now commences,
  By a friendly genius planned:
Princely bee, URBAN dispenses
  Honeyed days throughout the land.

Seek no more with tuneful humming
  Where the juicy floweret grows,
Halcyon days for you are coming –
  Days of plenty and repose!

Rest ye, workmen blithe and bonnie;
  Be no more the cowslip suck'd;
Honeyed flows the Tiber, honey
  Fills each Roman aqueduct.

Myrtle groves are fast distilling
  Honey; honeyed falls the dew,
Ancient prophesies fulfilling
  A millennium for you!

Ode IV Book 4
Ode on the signal Defeat of the Sultan Osman, by the Army of Poland and her Allies. September 1621.

As slow the plough the oxen plied,
Close by the Danube's rolling tide,
With old Galeski for their guide –
  The Dacian farmer –
His eye amid the furrows spied
  Men's bones and armour.

The air was calm, the sun was low,
Calm was the mighty river's flow,
And silently, with footsteps slow,
  Laboured the yoke;

Casimir Britannicus

When fervently, with patriot glow,
    The veteran spoke.

"Halt ye, my oxen! Pause we here
Where valour's vestiges appear,
And Islaam's relics far and near
    Lurk in the soil;
While Poland on victorious spear
    Rests from her toil.

Aye! well she may triumphant rest,
Adorn with glory's plume her crest,
And wear of victory the vest,
    Elate and flushed:
Oft was the Paynim's pride repressed –
    HERE IT WAS CRUSHED!

Here the tremendous deed was done,
Here the transcendant trophy won,
Where fragments lie of sword and gun,
    And lance and shield,
And Turkey's giant skeleton
    Cumbers the field.

Heavens! I remember well that day,
Of warrior men the proud display,
Of brass and steel the dread array –
    Van, flank, and rear;
How my young heart the charger's neigh
    Throbbed high to hear!

How gallantly our lancers stood,
Of bristling spears an iron wood,
Fraught with a desperate hardihood
    That naught could daunt,
And burning for the bloody feud,
    Fierce, grim, and gaunt!

Then rose the deadly din of fight;
Then shouting charged, with all his might,
Of Wilna each Teutonic knight,
    And of St. John's,
While flashing out from yonder height
    Thundered the bronze

Dire was the struggle in the van,
Fiercely we grappled man with man,
Till soon the Paynim chiels began
    For breath to gasp;
When Warsaw folded Ispahan
    In deadly grasp.

So might a tempest grasp a pine,
Tall giant of the Apennine,
Whose rankling roots deep undermine
    The mountain's base:
Fitting antagonists to twine
    In stern embrace.

Loud rung on helm, and coat of mail,
Of musketry the rattling hail;
Of wounded men loud rose the wail
    In dismal rout;
And now alternate would prevail
    The victor's shout.

Long time amid the vapours dense
The fire of the battle raged intense,
While VICTORY held in suspense
    The scales on high:
But Poland in her FAITH's defence
    Maun do or die!

Rash was the hope, and poor the chance,
Of blunting that victorious lance;
Though Turkey from her broad expanse
    Brought all her sons,

Swelling with tenfold arrogance,
    Hell's myrmidons!

Stout was the Cossack heart and hand,
Brave was our Lithuanian band,
But Gallantry's own native land
    Sent forth the Poles;
And Valour's flame shone nobly fanned
    In patriot souls.

Large be our allies' meed of fame!
Rude Russia to the rescue came,
From land of frost, with brand of flame –
    A glorious horde:
Huge havoc here these bones proclaim,
    Done by her sword.

Pale and aghast the crescent fled,
Joyful we clove each turbanned head,
Heaping with holocausts of dead
    The foeman's camp:
Loud echoed o'er their gory bed
    Our horsemen's tramp.

A hundred trees one hatchet hews;
A hundred doves one hawk pursues;
One Polish gauntlet so can bruise
    Their miscreant clay:
As well the kaliph kens who rues
    That fatal day.

What though, to meet the tug of war,
Osman had gathered from afar
Arab, and Sheik, and Hospodar,
    And Copt, and Guebre,
Quick yielded Pagan scimitar
    To Christian sabre.

Here could the Turkman turn and trace
The slaughter-tracks, here slowly pace
The field of downfall and disgrace,
    Where men and horse,
Thick strewn, encumbered all the place
    With frequent corse.

Well might his haughty soul repent
That rash and guilty armament;
Weep for the blood of nations spent,
    His ruined host;
His empty arrogance lament,
    And bitter boast.

Sorrow, derision, scorn, and hate,
Upon the proud one's footsteps wait;
Both in the field and in the gate
    Accursed, abhorred;
And be his halls made desolate
    With fire and sword!"

Such was the tale Galeski told,
Calm as the might Danube rolled;
And well I ween the farmer old,
    Who held a plough,
Had fought that day a warrior bold
    With helmed brow.

But now upon the glorious stream
The sun flung out his parting beam,
The soldier-swain unyoked his team,
    Yet still he chaunted
The live-long eve: – and glory's dream
    His pillow haunted.

Note: Only 'Chapter I' of the article was included in the first edition of *Prout Papers* in 1836, 'Chapter II' with the translations from Sarbiewski was added (slightly corrected) to the second edition entitled *The Reliques of Father Prout Late PP. of Watergrashill*, *in the County of Cork, Ireland. Collected and arranged by Oliver Yorke, Esq. (Rev. Francis Mahony.) New Edition Revised and Largely Augmented*, London: H. G. Bohn, York Street, Covent Garden, 1862.

From: 'Modern Latin Poets. (From the Prout Papers. – No. XVI.) Chap. II. – Casimir Sarbiewski, S. [sic] Sannazar, Jerome Fracastor.' *Fraser's Magazine for Town and Country*, September 1835.

45

John Sheehan

John Sheehan (1809–1882), Irish journalist and poet. Sheehan started his education at Clongowes Wood College, where he was a student of Francis Sylvester Mahony. He entered Trinity College Dublin in 1829 but did not graduate. Neither did he complete his studies at Trinity College, Cambridge (admitted 1839), although he succeeded in his studies of law, he was called to the Irish bar in 1835 and to the English bar in 1846. It seems, however, that Sheehan never practiced law as his professional life concentrated on journalism. He started his career in Dublin as sub-editor of the satirical weekly *The Comet* (1831–1833). He was representative of *The Constitutional* in Paris and Madrid, parliamentary reporter of the *Morning Herald*, while his poems and sketches appeared in *Bentley's Miscellany*. In 1852 he became the proprietor and editor of *The Independent*. Having married a rich widow, Sheehan retired to the continent after 1868 and spent several years travelling. Sheehan is believed to be the original of Captain Shandon in *Pendennis* by William Makepeace Thackeray, whom he got to know well in the 1830s in Paris.

Floral Gems

**To The Violet,
With which the Poet is about to crown the Head of
the Infant Saviour,
On the Feast of Corpus Christi.**

[Lyr. IV 17]

Aurora of the young Spring-dawn!
    Queen of the flowers that now
Bud forth upon the blushing lawn,
    Come deck my Boy-God's brow!
Should pond'rous gems and golden crown
Opress the Infant Holy One?

In glaring robe of purple sheen
    Should He be decked by me,
To whom I've consecrated been
    By plighted poverty?
A garland wreath of leaf and stem –
Wreathe for my King a diadem!

Light favours make the coronal
    That God will ne'er despise
Whene'er the free heart yields its all,
    The poor man's sacrifice!
The humblest gifts, when greatly given,
Are pleasing in the sight of Heaven.

To The Rose,
With which the Poet is about to crown the Head of the Madonna,
On Lady Day in Spring.

[IV 18]

Oh, thou whose brightness only
    With Heaven's pure lights may vie,
So long, and all so lonely,
    Meek Rose, why dost thy lie?
    From earth's low bed
    Thy tender head
Upraise, fair nursling of the glowing sky!

For thee Heaven's rack is clearing;
    The clouds fly every one;
On milkwhite steeds careening,
    The zephyrs chase them on.
    And the sweet South,
    With laughing mouth,
For thee bids blustering Boreas to begone.

Arise. No more reclining,
    Ask not in doubt and fear
Whose locks with thee entwining
    Thy newborn wreaths may bear.

John Sheehan

>   No brow profane
>   Thy stem shall stain –
> That stem of heavenly purity severe!
>
>   The meaner duty scorning
>   A mortal's brows to bind,
>   Be thine the wreaths adorning
>   The altar where enshrined
>   Our blest Ladye
>   Waits but for thee
> Her locks to rescue from the wanton wind!

Note: Sheehan supplemented the two translations with a lengthy footnote in which he discussed the meaning and tradition of floral offerings and decorations.

From: *Temple Bar, a London magazine for town and country readers,* February 1872.

46

William Crosse

The only thing we know about William Crosse is that in No. III. Vol. I. of *The Museum of Entertainment*, published in London in the mid-nineteenth century without a date, he included (in the collection of 'A Glance at the Authors of the Middle Ages') a short paper on Casimir which was illustrated with the following selection of 'original translations'.

Ode VII. Book I.
[Lyr. I 7]

Alas! we're but a plaything still!
Of Fortune's swiftly changing will
    The plaything still we are;
For nought eternal is there found
Within the wide material round
    Of this mortality.

On slippery chance we stand; whate'er
Now soars, may falling soon appear
    Again to rise and fall;
As when rebounding from the stroke
With hollow hand the youth provoke
    The sportive winged ball:

Now soaring high it cleaves the wind,
Now bounding, leaves the earth behind
    In rapid flight again.
Eve yields to eve, but varying still
Now bright with joy, now dark with ill,
    They form a mingled train.

High on the restless clouds their seat
The years obtain, and coursing fleet
    On changeful zephyrs glide;

Along the dark and troubled sky
Sweeping upon a whirlwind by,
 The shadow ages ride.

The hour that even now from care
To our Pierian lyre we spare,
 Alas! how fast it flees!
Yoked to lightning's fiery steeds,
On, on the reckless wanderer speeds,
 And wearies every breeze.

In vain the lyre its festive lay,
In vain the mournful lute doth play,
 Nought heeds the fleeting sprite;
Nay though itself the subject be,
From its own praises doth it flee,
 And envious speeds its flight.

Meantime before it cities fall,
And in one gloomy funeral
 Are nations swept away;
Kings and their sceptres in one fate
It overwhelms, nor can their state
 Resist its mournful sway.

To earth it hurls the sceptre's pride,
And levels smiling kingdoms wide
 Low in their rulers' dust;
The gilded roof, the altar stone,
The subject cot, the monarch's throne,
 In one wide ruin crush'd.

And on a gorgeous cloud upborne,
Far, far above the wreck forlorn,
 Of slaughtered realms it flies;
O'er shattered towers, and hoary piles,
Along whose consecrated aisles
 In death each chieftain lies.

Then seizes in its swift career
Long ages, and the glowing sphere,
    Where rolls each distant star.
Alas! as days roll on we feel
Still mocked by Fate's revolving wheel,
    A plaything still we are.

O are we, Telephus, deceived?
Or have the forms of things perceived
    An image just and true?
Or does our false and darkling sight
Offered with an uncertain light?
    Or do we dream we view?

Ode XV. Book I.
When Ladislaus, king of Poland, led his army into winter-quarters, after defeating Osman, the Turkish emperor

[Lyr. I 15]

Will ye believe? Ye future race,
Doubt not the glorious theme is true;
Lo! Where the recreant bands of Thrace
Their lawless way no more pursue;
But, bought with heaps of kindred slain,
A base, ill-omened peace obtain.

With rapid wing, what mighty fear
Urged the Odrysians' headlong flight,
When Ladislaus with lightning spear
Impetuous broke the ranks of fight,
And, as before him swept they fled,
Withered their hearts with unknown dread!

How toiled the savage Scythian clan,
What heat the Euxine hordes oppressed,
When red with blood the Danube ran,
When, shamed, the Bosphorus confessed
A captive wave, and blushed to see
Its sons before their victors flee!

William Crosse

When, as they urged their backward way,
Their shields with quivering spears were set;
While sounding to the hollow bay,
Byzantium's towers the war-cry met,
And Artacen with loud alarms
Echoed the din of vanquished arms.

And have we now achieved in vain
A glory ransomed with our blood
For future years? Or yet again,
High as their great forefathers stood
Shall our descendants raise their name,
And emulate their ancient fame?

Shame! Shame for this degenerate age!
How far beneath its injured sires!
How sunk below their generous rage
The boldest thought our breast inspires!
Long wintry years their blights have shed,
And half our once fair strength is dead.

The records of our glories gone,
The swords and chariots of the slain,
And, late from hostile temples won,
The trophies of the Oemonian plain,
Let us consume, – and view no more
The proofs of what we were before.

Let us, unmoved with shame, destroy
The marbles, in whose sacred face
Our sires we view. With shameless joy
The brazen statues of our race,
The effigies of other days,
The annals mindful of their praise,

Let us now whelm beneath the wave
Of the deep Vistula; or swear, –
If we would emulate the brave,
And sloth no more supinely bear, –

Swear to redeem our fathers' meed,
And iterate each warlike deed.

O thou who, on the fervid wing
Of glory borne, in flight sublime
O'er the wide world dost ride, a king
Renowned in every city, clime, –
At once the upholder and the grace
Of a degenerate, falling race, –

O snatch from Polish walls once more
The lance, that late too long hath lain
Unsated with the Scythians' gore;
Unsheath the conquering sword again,
That checked the Thracian's fierce career,
And taught their bannered ranks to fear!

Ode I. Book I.
When the hostile forces of the Thracians had quitted the country

[Lyr. I 1]

No more on our polluted plain
Are heard the fierce alarms of war;
Now banished Safety comes again,
And Peace, through all the land to reign,
    Conducts her radiant car.

Now Faith with Plenty joined, and Right,
O'er the glad land delighted flies;
The ages, ere they sink in night,
With generous streams glow on more bright
    To all beneath the skies.

Unclouded suns and purer years
Return, such years as were of old;
All heav'n milder aspect wears,
In glittering pearls the hail appears,
    And rain descends in gold.

William Crosse

And while among the choral train,
That autumn's festive rights renew,
I sing of ancient Saturn's reign,
And hail his happy days again, –
    The world approves it true.

The golden thought, the purpose fair,
Our fathers knew, to Thule's shore
Far exiled hence, again appear;
And Candour now and Virtue dare
    Descend from heav'n once more.

The streamlets, babbling as they go,
O'er sunny plains delighted stray:
Honey and milk their banks o'erflow,
And round the fruitful fields below
    Rich floods of nectar play.

In the glad stalk of rustling grain
Waves with a more than wonted joy;
Rich fruits oppress the reeling plains,
The sun a generous warmth sustains,
    Nor envious heats destroy.

While near his flock the shepherd sings,
The hoarse cicada's notes reply:
From all the hills loud bellowings
Are heard, the painting forest rings
    With the steer's homeward cry.

The hills in joy of peace rebound,
In peace the rugged mountains smile:
Light ease now loves some distant bound
To seek, where tranquil joys are found
    To soothe the peasant's toil.

For thee, whose ever-watchful care
Hath hushed the angry world in peace, –
Ceres for thee entwines her hair

With yellow corn; the boisterous year
    Delights thy reign to bless.

The myrtle, with its humble shade,
To serve thee waits – the laurel too;
For thee the tall oak lifts its head,
And high o'er the sequester'd glade
    The trembling pine-tops bow.

May He who rules the land and skies,
From heav'n high towers regarding Rome,
Calm the wide earth, and bid thee rise
A parent to their longing eyes,
    A guardian to their home!

Emblem of lengthened life, to thee
The laurel be; to twine thy thread
Let fates and destinies agree,
Unhurt, unbroken may it be,
    Till thy full years are fled.

And she who 'mid yon beauteous fires
An everlasting seat hath found,
For thy sake pitying our desires,
The Virgin whom the circling choirs
    Of glowing stars surround, –

Oh may she Latium's cares relieve,
Her youths' and virgins' suppliant lay
With favour hear, forbid them grieve,
And with indulgent ear receive
    The vows her nobles pay!

Ode XIX. Book I.
He aspires to the celestial abodes

[Lyr. I 19]

The glory of that spirit-land,
    My native country, fires my soul,
And glowing in the ethereal strand,

William Crosse

    The watchful stars that ceaseless roll,
The moon's soft light, the lamps nights sets
    Around heav'n's golden minarets.

Inflame my soul. O sacred choirs
    That wait on night! – O torches sworn
To follow with your holy fires
    The sceptre by your mistress borne! –
O beauteous aspect of my home,
And guardians sweet of heav'n's bright dome!

O wherefore do ye still behold
    Me exiled from your star-lit clime?
O why, alas! Must I grow old,
    Shut out from heaven too long a time,
And born of that bright clime a guest,
Still, still to earth be downward pressed?

O strew me here a grassy bed,
    Ye inmates of the shining sky!
O here your spotless lilies shed
    To deck the tomb where I would lie!
Here am I from death's fetters loosed,
Freed from my dross, though still but dust.

Of this lingering body, here,
    O here, the wretched spoil dispose,
The sad remains of me, whate'er
    Survives the parted spirit's loss.
Away, away to boundless skies
The rest of me impatient flies.

Ode III. Book II.
To his Lyre

[Lyr. II 3]

Daughter of the box-wood tree,*
Child of sweetest melody,
On the poplar's lofty height
Thou shalt hang while heaven is bright,
And the sportive air doth play
With the idle leaves so gay;
Softer still the breeze will be
As it murmurs over thee.
Meanwhile, I'll delight to lean
On the grassy border green;
There a careless hour to lie,
Listening as the stream flows by.
Ah! what sudden darkness lours!
O'er the sky what tempest pours!
Up, away! Alas, how soon
All our dearest joys are done!

From: *The Museum of Entertainment: or Repository of Philosophy, Science, Literature, Music, and the Drama...* No. III. Vol. I. London: C. Mitchell, Red Lion Court, Fleet Street. No date of publication.

---

* Alluding to the box-wood tree that formed the body of the lute. [Note by William Crosse.]

Bibliography

Primary sources

1. Manuscripts

MS DD/HU/1 Hutchinson Manuscripts, Nottinghamshire Record Office. Translation by Lucy Hutchinson.

MS Lt 40. Leeds University Library, Brotherton Collection. Translations by Sir Philip Wodehouse.

MS Rawl. poet 94, Bodleian Library, University of Oxford. Translations by John Chatwin.

2. Printed sources

[Anonymous], Μέλη Εφημέρια, Oxford: Printed for the Author; and sold by Mess. Fletchers, Booksellers, in the Turle; and by W. Jackson, in Oxford, 1783.

[Anonymous], *Miscellany Poems and Translations by Oxford Hands*, London: Printed for Anthony Stephens, 1685.

Bowring, John, *Specimens of the Polish Poets; with Notes and Observations on the Literature of Poland*, London: Priv. print., 1827.

B[rome], R[ichard], ed., *Lachrymae Musarum: The Tears of the Muses; Exprest in Elegies; Written By divers persons of Nobility and Worth, Upon the death of the most hopefull Henry Lord Hastings ... Collected and set forth by R. B.*, London: Printed by T. N. and are to be sold at the blue Anchor in the New Exchange, 1650.

Burns, Robert, *The Poetical Works of Robert Burns; with Memoir, Prefatory Notes, and A Complete Marginal Glossary*, Glasgow: John S. Marr and Sons, [1877].

Chudleigh, Mary, *Poems on Several Occasions. Together with the Song of Three Children Paraphras'd by Lady Mary Chudleigh*, London: Printed by W. B. for Bernard Lincott, 1703.

Coleridge, Samuel Taylor, *The Complete Poetical Works of Samuel Taylor Coleridge*, ed. by Ernest Hartley Coleridge. 2 vols, Oxford: Clarendon Press, 1912.

Cowley, Abraham, *The Works of Mr. Abraham Cowley. Consisting of Those which were formerly Printed: And Those which he Design'd for the Press, Now Published out of the Authors Original Copies*, London: Printed by J. M. for Henry Herringman, at the Sign of the Blew Anchor in the Lower Walk of the New Exchange, 1668.

Coxe, R[ichard] C., *Wood-Notes: The Silviludia Poetica of M. Casimir Sarbievius with a Translation into English Verce. Musings at Cynemouth: Ten Sonnets. North & South: Ten Sonnets. By R. C. Coxe, M.A. Hon. Canon of Durham, and Vicar of Newcastle upon Tyne*, Newcastle: M. A. Richardson, 1848.

Crespigny, Caroline de, *My Souvenir, or, Poems by Caroline de Crespigny with Translations etc.*, London: Longman, Brown, Green &. Longmans. Heidelberg: Hoffmeister, 1844.

Crosse, William, 'A Glance at the Authors of the Middle Ages: Matthias Casimir Sarbievius', in *The Museum of Entertainment: or, Repository of Philosophy, Science, Literature, Music, and the Drama*, London: C. Mitchell, no publication date given.

Gibbons, Thomas, *The Christian Minister, in Three Poetic Epistles to Philander. To which are added, I. Poetical Versions of several Parts of Scripture. II. Translations of Poems from Greek and Latin Writers, And, III. Original Pieces, chiefly in Verse, on various Occasions, By Thomas Gibbons, D.D.*, London: Printed for J. Buckland in Paternoster-Row; and E. and C. Dilly, in the Poultry, near the Mansion-House, 1772.

Herbert, William, *Translations from the German, Danish etc to Which is Added Miscellaneous Poetry*, London: I Gold Shoe Lane, 1804.

Hervey, James, *Meditations and Contemplations in Two Volumes by James Hervey, A.B.*, London: Printed by T. Sabine for J. Whitaker and C. Wilkin, 1775.

Hill, Aaron, *The Works of the Late Aaron Hill, Esq; in Four Volumes. Consisting of Letters on Various Subjects, and of Original Poems, Moral and Facetious. With an Essay on the Art of Acting*, London: Printed for the Benefit of the Family, 1753.

Hucks, Joseph, *Poems by J. Hucks, A.M. Fellow of Catherine Hall, Cambridge*, Cambridge: Printed by B. Flower, 1798.

Hughes, John, *The Ecstasy. An Ode*, London: Printed and Sold by J. Roberts in Warwick Lane, 1720.

—, *Poems on Several Occasions. With some Select Essays in Prose*, London: Printed for J. Tonson and J. Watts, 1735.

Jeffreys, George, *Miscellanies in Verse and Prose*, London: Printed for the Author, 1754.

[Keene, Talbot], *Miscellanous Pieces: Original and Collected; By a Clergyman of Northamptonshire, Late of Trinity College Cambridge*, London: Printed for the Author, And sold by Ginger, College-Street, Westminster; Nicolls, St. Paul's Church-Yard, Merrill, Cambridge; and Lacy, Northampton, 1787.

Kitchener, Jesse, *Translations from Casimir etc. with Poems, Odes, and Specimens of Latin Prose*, London: Priestley, Holborn; Hatchard, Piccadilly; and J. & A. Arch, Cornhill, 1821.

Lovelace, Richard, *Lucasta: Epodes, Odes, Sonnets, Songs etc. to Which is Added a Aramantha, A Pastoral*, London: Printed by Tho[mas] Harper, and are to be sold by Tho[mas] Ewster, at the Gun, Ivie Lane, 1649.

[Mahony, Francis], *The Reliques of Father Prout Late PP. of Watergrashill, in the County of Cork, Ireland. Collected and arranged by Oliver Yorke, Esq. (Rev. Francis Mahony.) New Edition Revised and Largely Augmented*, London: H. G. Bohn, York Street, Covent Garden, 1862.

Mason, William, *The Works of William Mason, M.A. Precentor of York, and Rector of Aston. In Four Volumes*, Vol. I, London: Bulmer & Co., 1811.

Masters, Mary, *Familiar Letters and Poems on Several Occasions by Mary Masters*, London: Printed for the Author by D. Henry and R. Cave, 1755.

Norris, John, *A Collection of Miscellanies: Consisting of Poems, Essays, Discourses and Letters Occasionally Written. By John Norris, M.A. and Fellow of All-Souls College in Oxford*, Oxford: Printed at the Theater for John Crosley Bookseller, 1687.

[Pinkerton, John], *Letters of Literature by Robert Heron Esq.*, London: Printed for G. G. J. and J. Robinson, in Pater-noster Row, 1785.

[Price, Henry], *Poems on Several Subjects. By a Land-Waiter in the Port of Poole*, London: Printed for T. Astley, at the Rose in St. Paul's Church-yard, 1741.

[Sarbiewski, Maciej Kazimierz], *The Odes of Casimire. Translated by G[eorge] H[ils].*, London: Printed by T. W. for Humphrey Moseley, 1646.

Say, Samuel, *Poems on Several Occasions: and Two Critical Essays, viz. The First, On the Harmony, Variety, and Power of Numbers, whether in Prose or Verse. The Second On the Numbers of Paradise Lost*, London: Printed by John Hughs, near Lincoln's-Inn-Fields, 1745.

Sherburne, Edward, *Poems and Translations. Amorous, Lusory, Morall, Divine: By Edward Sherburne Esq.*, London: Printed by W. Hunt, for Thomas Dring, at the Sign of the George, near Cliffords-Inn in Fleetstreet, 1651.

[Steele, Anne], *Poems on Subjects Chiefly Devotional. In Two Volumes. A New Edition. To which is added A Third Volume, consisting of Miscellaneous Pieces. By Theodosia*, Bristol: Printed by W. Pine. Sold by T. Cadell, T. Mills and T. Evans; - and by J. Buckland, Paternoster Row, and J. Johnson, St. Paul's Church Yard, London, 1780.

Vaughan, Henry, *Olor Iscanus. A Collection of Some Select Poems and Translations, Formerly written by Mr. Henry Vaughan Siluris*, London: Printed by T. W. for Humphrey Moseley, and are to be sold at his shop, at the Signe of the Prince's Arms in St. Paul's Churchyard, 1651.

Watts, Isaac, *The Works of The Late Reverend and Learned Isaac Watts, D.D. Published by himself and now collected in Six Volumes ... Now* first published from his manuscripts, and, by the Direction of his Will, revised and Corrected by D. Jennings, D.D. and the late P. Doodridge, D.D., Vol. 4, London: Printed for T. and T. Longman at the Ship, and J. Buckland at the Buck, in Paternoster Row; J. Oswald at the Rose and Crown in the Poultry; J. Waugh at the Turks's Head in Lombard Street; and J. Ward at the King's Arms in Cornhill, 1753.

Watts, Isaac – Thomas Yalden, *The British Poets. Including Translations. In One Hundred Volumes. XLVI. Watts, Vol. II. Yalden*, Chiswick: Printed by C. Whittingham, College House, 1822.

Yalden, Thomas, *The Poetical Works of Thomas Yalden*, London: William Mark Clark, 1833.

Different translations are taken from:

Bee Revived or The Universal Weekly Pamphlet
The European Magazine, and London Review
Frazer's Magazine for town and country
The Gentleman's Magazine
The London Magazine, or, Gentleman's Monthly Intelligencer
Methodist Magazine
The Museum of Entertainment: or Repository of Philosophy, Science, Literature, Music, and the Drama
The Mirror of Literature, Amusement and Instruction
Poetical Courant
Royal Magazine
The Scots Magazine
Temple Bar, a London magazine for town and country readers
The Universal Magazine of Knowledge and Pleasure
The Weekly Entertainer or, Agreeable and instructive repository

Secondary sources

[Anonymous], 'Bowring's Poetry and Literature of Poland. Review of Specimens of Polish Poets; with Notes and Observations on the Literature of Poland. By John Bowring. London. 1827', *North American Review*, 26 (1828), 146-157.

Arens, J. C., 'Sarbiewski's Ode Against Tears Imitated by Lovelace, Yalden and Watts', *Neophilologus*, 47 (1963), 236-239.

Baldwin, Barry, The Latin & Greek Poems of Samuel Johnson: Text, Translation and Commentary, London: Duckworth, 1995.

Birrell, T. A., 'Sarbiewski, Watts and the Later Metaphysical Tradition', *English Studies* (Amsterdam), 37 (1956), 125-132.

Borowski, Andrzej, 'Obecność Sarbiewskiego w literaturze europejskiej', in *Nauka z poezji Macieja Kazimierza Sarbiewskiego SJ*, ed. by Jacek Bolewski, Jakub Z. Lichański and Piotr Urbański, Warszawa: Bobolanum, 1995, 189-204.

Bradner, Leicester, *Musae Anglicanae: A History of Anglo-Latin Poetry, 1525-1925*, Modern Language Association of America, London: Oxford University Press, 1940.

Brown, Marshall, 'Toward an Archaeology of English Romanticism: Coleridge and Sarbiewski', in *Turning Points: Essays in the History of Cultural Expression*, Stanford: Stanford University Press, 1997.

Buszewicz, Elwira, *Sarmacki Horacy i jego liryka. Imitacja – gatunek – styl. Rzecz o poezji Macieja Kazimierza Sarbiewskiego*, Kraków: Księgarnia Akademicka, 2006.

Clarke, Martin Lowther, *Classical Education in Britain 1500-1900*, Cambridge: Cambridge University Press 1959.

Clarke, Susan A., 'Royalists Write the Death of Lord Hastings: Post-Regicide Funerary Propaganda', *Parergon*, 22:2 (2005), 113-130.

Cummings, Robert, 'Post-Classical Latin Literature', in *The Oxford History of Literary Translation in English. Vol. 3 1660-1790*, ed. by Stuart Gillespie and David Hopkins, Oxford: Oxford University Press, 2005, 479-505.

Dictionary of National Biography, accessed online at <www.oxforddnb.com>.

Ecker, Ronald L., 'The Aeolian Harp', accessed online at <http://www.ronaldlecker.com/harp.htm 1963>.

Ezell, Margaret J. M., *Social Autorship and the Advent of Print*, Baltimore and London: The Johns Hopkins University Press, 1999.

Foster, Joseph, *Alumni Oxonienses. The Members of the University of Oxford 1500-1714. Their Parentage, Birthplace and Year of Birth with Record of their Degrees*, Oxford: Parker and Co., 1891-1892.

Foster, Joseph, *Alumni Oxonienses. The Members of the University of Oxford 1714-1886. Their Parentage, Birthplace and Year of Birth with Record of their Degrees*, Oxford: Parker and Co., 1891.

Giles, Peter, 'An Unknown Emmanuel Poet', *Emmanuel College Magazine*, 9 (1897), 2.

Groot, Jerome de, 'John Denham and Lucy Hutchinson's Commonplace Book', *Studies in English Literature, 1500-1900*, 48:1 (2008), 148-163.

Hammond, Paul, 'Sir Philip Wodehouse's Pantheon of Renaissance Poets', *The Seventeenth Century*, 18 (April 2003), 54–60.

Hucks, J[oseph], *A Pedestrian Tour through Northern Wales, in a Series of Letters by J. Hucks, B.A.*, ed. by Alun R. Jones and William Tydeman, Cardiff: University of Wales Press, 1979.

Johnson, Samuel, *Prefaces Biographical and Critical to the Works of the English Poets*, London: Printed by J. Nichols for C. Bathurst [et al.], 1779.

Kaiser, Leo M., 'The First American Translations from Sarbiewski by Robert Proud', *The Classical Bulletin*, 58 (November 1981), 6-11.

Kraszewski, Charles S., 'Maciej Kazimierz Sarbiewski – The Christian Horace in England', *The Polish Review*, 51:1 (2006), 14-40.

Mackay, James A., *Burns. A Biography of Robert Burns*, Edinburgh: Mainstream Publishing, 1992.

Madison, Carol, *Apollo and the Nine: A History of the Ode*, London: Routledge and Kegan Paul, 1960.

Mannin, Ethel, Two Studies in Integrity. Gerald Griffin and the Rev. Francis Mahony ('Father Prout'), London: Jarrolds, 1954.

Mertz, James J., 'Sarbiewski – The Sarmatian Horace', *Classical Bulletin*, 24 (1947/1948), 43-47.

Mikołajczak, Aleksander Wojciech, *Antyk w poezji Macieja Kazimierza Sarbiewskiego*, Poznań: Wydawnictwo Polinfo, 1994.

—, *Studia Sarbieviana*, Gniezno: Tum Gnieźnieńska Firma Wydawnicza, 1998.

Money, David K., *The English Horace: Anthony Alsop and the Tradition of British Latin Verse*, Oxford: Oxford University Press, 1998.

—, 'Aspects of the Reception of Sarbiewski in England: From Hils, Vaughan, and Watts to Coleridge, Bowring, Walker, and Coxe', in *Pietas Humanistica: Neo-Latin Religious Poetry in Poland in*

European Context, ed. by Piotr Urbański, Frankfurt am Main: Peter Lang, 2006, 157-187.

Pollak, Roman, 'Coleridge o Sarbiewskim', *Pamiętnik Literacki,* 53:2 (1962), 475-476.

Praz, Mario, 'Stanley, Sherburne and Ayres as Translators and Imitators of Italian, Spanish and French Poets', *Modern Language Review,* 20 (1925), 280-294.

Röstvig, Maren-Sofie, 'Benlowes, Marvell, and the Divine Casimire,' *The Huntington Library Quarterly,* 18 (1954-1955), 13-35.

—, 'Casimire Sarbiewski and the English Ode', *Studies in Philology,* 59 (1954), 443-460.

—, *The Happy Man. Studies in the Metamorphoses of a Classical Ideal,* 2nd ed., 2 vols, Oslo: Akademisk Forlag, 1962, vol. I.

Sova, Milos, 'Sir John Bowring (1792-1872) and the Slavs', *Slavonic and East European Review,* 21:2 (November 1943), 128-144.

Sparrow, John, 'A Horatian Ode and its Descendants', *Journal of the Warburg and Courtauld Institute,* 7 (1954), 359-365.

—, 'Sarbiewski's *Silviludia* and their Italian Source', *Oxford Slavonic Papers,* 8 (1958), 1-48.

—, 'Sarbiewski's *Silviludia*: a Rejoinder', *Oxford Slavonic Papers,* 12 (1965), 80-93.

Starnawski, Jerzy, 'O Sarbiewskim na łamach *Classical Journal* (1814-1822)', in *Nauka z poezji Macieja Kazimierza Sarbiewskiego SJ.,* ed. by Jacek Bolewski, Jakub Z. Lichański and Piotr Urbański, Warszawa: Bobolanum, 1995, 211-216.

—, 'Ze studiów nad Sarbiewskim', in *W świecie barokowym,* Łódz: Wydawnictwo Uniwersytetu Łódzkiego, 1992, 24-61.

Stawecka, Krystyna, *Maciej Kazimierz Sarbiewski prozaik i poeta,* Lublin: Wydawnictwo Towarzystwa Naukowego Katolickiego Uniwersytetu Lubelskiego, 1989.

Ulčinaite, Eugenia, ed., *Mathias Casimirus Sarbievius in Cultura Lithuaniae, Poloniae, Europae,* Vilnius: Institutum Litterarum Etnographiaeque Lituaniae, 1998.

Urbański, Piotr, *Theologia Fabulosa. Commentationes Sarbievianae,* Szczecin: Wydawnictwo Naukowe Uniwersytetu Szczecińskiego, 2000.

V. L., 'Casimir and Burns', *Classical Journal,* 9 (1814), 169-170.

Venn, J. A., ed., *Alumni Cantabrigienses. A biographical list of all known students, graduates and holders of office at the university of Cambridge, from the earliest times to 1900. Part II From 1752 to 1900,* Cambridge: Cambridge University Press, 1951.

Venn, John – J. A. Venn, ed., *Alumni Cantabrigenses. A Biographical List of All Known Students, Graduates and Holders of Office at the University of Cambridge, from the Earliest Times to 1900*, Cambridge: Cambridge University Press, 1922.

Wedeck, Harry E., 'Casimir, the Polish Horace', *Philological Quarterly*, 16 (1937), 307-316.

Weintraub, Wiktor, 'Coleridge i Sarbiewski', *Pamiętnik Literacki*, 54:2 (1963), 535-539.

Index of Original Poems by Maciej Kazimierz Sarbiewski

Lyricorum lib. I
1
George Hils 36
U.U. 188
Henry Price 201
William Crosse 300
2
George Hils 38
X.Y. 181
Joshua Dinsdale 191
Mary Masters 197
Thomas Gibbons 212
Samuel Taylor Coleridge 239
Jesse Kitchener 252
4
Isaac Watts 140
6
Jesse Kitchener 253
7
Jesse Kitchener 256
William Crosse 296
8
Jesse Kitchener 258
13
George Hils 39
U.U. 180
Jesse Kitchener 260
15
"Oxford Hands" 121
William Crosse 298
17
Jesse Kitchener 261
19
Isaac Watts 127
Thomas Gibbons 214
William Crosse 302

Lyricorum lib. II
2
George Hils 39

Isaac Watts 130
John Duncombe 169
Henry Price 200
William Margetson Heald 235
William Herbert 242
John Bowring 246
3
Samuel Say 153
John Hughes 164
X.Y. 179
OLEN 190
William Mason 223
John Pinkerton 229
Robert Burns 232
William Margetson Heald 233
Samuel Taylor Coleridge 239
John Bowring 247
Jesse Kitchener 263
Caroline de Crespigny 264
William Crosse 304
5
George Hils 40
Abraham Cowley 86
Lady Mary Chudleigh 106, 107
John Norris 109
Isaac Watts 128
John Hughes 158
Aaron Hill 167
Anonymous 171
Joshua Dinsdale 193
Anne Steele alias Theodosia 205
Thomas Gibbons 215
7
George Hils 42
U.U. 178
Anonymous 186
8
George Hils 43
Henry Vaughan 96
10
Samuel Say 154
15
Isaac Watts 145
Thomas Gibbons 210

Index of Original Poems

19
George Hils 44
24
George Hils 44
25
George Hils 47
26
U.U. 183

Lyricorum lib. III
4
George Hils 48
Thomas Gibbons 218
6
George Hils 49
12
George Hils 49
15
Francis Sylvester Mahony 286
22
Henry Vaughan 97
U.U. 182
Anonymous 187
Thomas Gibbons 220
23
Henry Vaughan 97

Lyricorum lib. IV
3
George Hils 50
4
Isaac Watts 132
Francis Sylvester Mahony 287
7
Isaac Watts 145
10
George Hils 52
11
George Hils 53
12
George Hils 54
Isaac Watts 142

13
George Hils 55
John Denham 82
Richard Lovelace 83
Henry Vaughan 99
John Hall of Durham 104
Isaac Watts 131
Thomas Yalden 151
Samuel Philips 165
Joshua Dinsdale 192
14
George Hils 55
15
George Hils 56
Henry Vaughan 98
Isaac Watts 138
17
John Sheehan 293
18
John Chatwin 114
"Oxford Hands" 116
Anonymous 186
James Hervey 204
Μέλη Εφημέρια 227
William Margetson Heald 234
John Bowring 244
Caroline de Crespigny 265
John Sheehan 294
19
George Hils 57
21
George Hils 58
23
Thomas Brown 112
John Chatwin 115
Samuel Say 155
Anonymous 175
U.U. 180
Talbot Keene 228
William Margetson Heald 234
John Bowring 247
25
"Oxford Hands" 118

26
Anonymous 175
X.Y. 176
Μέλη Εφημέρια 226
28
Sir Edward Sherburne 91
Henry Vaughan 96
Isaac Watts 126
30
George Hils 59
31
G. 184
32
George Hils 61
34
George Hils 62
"Oxford Hands" 117
35
George Hils 63
36
Sir Edward Sherburne 90
John Bowring 244
38
John Bowring 248

Epodon liber
1
George Hils 65
2
George Hils 69
Mary Masters 196
3
George Hils 69
Henry Vaughan 100
Lady Mary Chudleigh 106
5
Isaac Watts 144

Epigrammatum liber unus
2
Sir Edward Sherburne 92
4
George Hils 72

5
Sir Philip Wodehouse 78
6
Sir Philip Wodehouse 78
8
Sir Philip Wodehouse 76
10
Sir Philip Wodehouse 77
11
Sir Philip Wodehouse 78
13
U.U. 177
14
Sir Philip Wodehouse 76
Sir Edward Sherburne 92
U.U. 185
15
Sir Philip Wodehouse 77
16
Sir Philip Wodehouse 79
Sir Edward Sherburne 92
John Glasse 225
18
Sir Edward Sherburne 93
21
Joseph Hucks 237
33
Sir Philip Wodehouse 76
34
Sir Philip Wodehouse 76
Lucy Hutchinson 94
37
George Hils 73
40
George Hils 73
48
George Hils 73
51
George Hils 73
54
Sir Philip Wodehouse 75
Sir Edward Sherburne 89
64
Sir Philip Wodehouse 79

Index of Original Poems

74
Sir Philip Wodehouse 79
100
Isaac Watts 128
110
George Hils 110

Silviludia
III
John Docwra Parry 266
I–X
Richard Coxe 268
   I 269
   II 270
   III 271
   IV 272
   V 274
   VI 276
   VII 278
   VIII 279
   IX 282
   X 283

MHRA Critical Texts

This series aims to provide affordable critical editions of lesser-known literary texts that are not in print or are difficult to obtain. The texts will be taken from the following languages: English, French, German, Italian, Portuguese, Russian, and Spanish. Titles will be selected by members of the distinguished Editorial Board and edited by leading academics. The aim is to produce scholarly editions rather than teaching texts, but the potential for crossover to undergraduate reading lists is recognized. The books will appeal both to academic libraries and individual scholars.

Malcolm Cook
Chairman, Editorial Board

Editorial Board
Professor Catherine Maxwell (English)
Professor Malcolm Cook (French) (*Chairman*)
Professor Ritchie Robertson (Germanic)
Professor Derek Flitter (Spanish)
Professor Brian Richardson (Italian)
Dr Stephen Parkinson (Portuguese)
Professor David Gillespie (Slavonic)

Published titles

1. *Odilon Redon, 'Écrits'* (edited by Claire Moran, 2005)
2. *Les Paraboles Maistre Aluin en Françoys* (edited by Tony Hunt, 2005)
3. *Letzte Chancen: Vier Einakter von Marie von Ebner-Eschenbach* (edited by Susanne Kord, 2005)
4. *Macht des Weibes: Zwei historische Tragödien von Marie von Ebner-Eschenbach* (edited by Susanne Kord, 2005)
5. *A Critical Edition of 'La tribu indienne; ou, Édouard et Stellina' by Lucien Bonaparte* (edited by Cecilia Feilla, 2006)
6. *Dante Alighieri, 'Four Political Letters'* (translated and with a commentary by Claire E. Honess, 2007)
7. *'La Disme de Penitanche' by Jehan de Journi* (edited by Glynn Hesketh, 2006)
8. *'François II, roi de France' by Charles-Jean-François Hénault* (edited by Thomas Wynn, 2006)
9. *Istoire de la Chastelaine du Vergier et de Tristan le Chevalier* (edited by Jean-François Kosta-Théfaine, 2009)
10. *La Peyrouse dans l'Isle de Tahiti, ou le Danger des Présomptions: drame politique* (edited by John Dunmore, 2006)

11. *Casimir Britannicus. English Translations, Paraphrases, and Emulations of the Poetry of Maciej Kazimierz Sarbiewski* (edited by Krzysztof Fordoński and Piotr Urbański, 2008)
12. *'La Devineresse ou les faux enchantements' by Jean Donneau de Visé and Thomas Corneille* (edited by Julia Prest, 2007)
13. *'Phosphorus Hollunder' und 'Der Posten der Frau' von Louise von François* (edited by Barbara Burns, 2008)
14. *Le Gouvernement present, ou éloge de son Eminence, satyre ou la Miliade* (edited by Paul Scott, 2010)
15. *Ovide du remede d'amours* (edited by Tony Hunt, 2008)
16. *Angelo Beolco (il Ruzante), 'La prima oratione'* (edited by Linda L. Carroll, 2009)
17. *Richard Robinson, 'The Rewarde of Wickednesse'* (edited by Allyna E. Ward, 2009)
20. *Evariste-Désiré de Parny, 'Le Paradis perdu'* (edited by Ritchie Robertson and Catriona Seth, 2009)
21. *Stéphanie de Genlis, 'Histoire de la duchesse de C***'* (edited and translated by Mary S. Trouille, 2010)
22. *Louis-Charles Fougeret de Monbron, Le Cosmopolite, ou le citoyen du monde (1750)* (edited by Édouard Langille, 2010)
24. *Narcisse Berchère, Le Désert de Suez: cinq mois dans l'Isthme* (edited by Barbara Wright)
25. *Casimir Britannicus. English Translations, Paraphrases, and Emulations of the Poetry of Maciej Kazimierz Sarbiewski. Revised and Expanded Edition* (edited by Krzysztof Fordoński and Piotr Urbański, 2010)

Forthcoming titles

18. *Henry Crabb Robinson, 'Essays on Kant, Schelling, and German Aesthetics'* (edited by James Vigus, 2010)
19. *A Sixteenth-Century Arthurian Romance: 'L'Hystoire de Giglan filz de messire Gauvain qui fut roy de Galles. Et de Geoffroi de Maience son compaignon'* (edited by Caroline A. Jewers, 2010)
23. *La Chastelaine du Vergier. Livre d'amours du Chevalier et de la Dame Chastellaine du Vergier* (edited by Jean-François Kosta-Théfaine, 2011)
26. *'Eugénie et Mathilde' by Madame de Souza* (edited by Kirsty Carpenter, 2011)

For details of how to order please visit our website at
www.criticaltexts.mhra.org.uk

www.ingramcontent.com/pod-product-compliance
Lightning Source LLC
Chambersburg PA
CBHW071316150426
43191CB00007B/639